THE GLORY AND FULLNESS
OF JESUS CHRIST

THE GLORY AND FULLNESS OF JESUS CHRIST

In the Most Remarkable Types, Figures, and Allegories of the Old Testament

William McEwen

Edited by Gordon J. Keddie

Reformation Heritage Books
Grand Rapids, Michigan

The Glory and Fullness of Jesus Christ
© 2022 by Reformation Heritage Books

All rights reserved. No part of this book may be used or reproduced in any manner whatsoever without written permission except in the case of brief quotations embodied in critical articles and reviews. Direct your requests to the publisher at the following addresses:

Reformation Heritage Books
3070 29th St. SE
Grand Rapids, MI 49512
616-977-0889
orders@heritagebooks.org
www.heritagebooks.org

Printed in the United States of America
22 23 24 25 26 27/10 9 8 7 6 5 4 3 2 1

First published as *Grace and Truth; Or, the Glory and Fulness of the Redeemer Displayed. In an Attempt to Explain, Illustrate, and Enforce the Most Remarkable of the Types, Figures, and Allegories of the Old Testament* (Edinburgh: printed by John Gray and Gavin Alston, 1763).

Library of Congress Cataloging-in-Publication Data

Names: McEwen, William, 1735-1762, author. | Keddie, Gordon J., 1944- editor.
Title: The glory and fullness of Jesus Christ : in the most remarkable types, figures, and allegories of the Old Testament / William McEwen ; edited by Gordon J. Keddie.
Other titles: Grace and truth
Description: Grand Rapids, Michigan : Reformation Heritage Books, [2022]
Identifiers: LCCN 2021059579 (print) | LCCN 2021059580 (ebook) | ISBN 9781601789396 (hardcover) | ISBN 9781601789402 (epub)
Subjects: LCSH: Typology (Theology) | BISAC: RELIGION / Christian Theology / Christology | RELIGION / Biblical Studies / Old Testament / General
Classification: LCC BS478 .M18 2022 (print) | LCC BS478 (ebook) | DDC 220.6/4—dc23/eng/20220126
LC record available at https://lccn.loc.gov/2021059579
LC ebook record available at https://lccn.loc.gov/2021059580

For additional Reformed literature, request a free book list from Reformation Heritage Books at the above regular or email address.

Contents

Preface ix
A Memoir of the Life and Character of the
  Reverend William McEwen xv
Preface (1763) xxi

Book 1
TYPICAL PERSONS

1. Christ and Adam Compared 3
2. Noah 9
3. Melchizedek 15
4. Isaac 21
5. Jacob 29
6. Joseph 37
7. Moses 43
8. The Priesthood 49
9. Joshua 57
10. Samson 63
11. David 69
12. Solomon 75
13. Jonah 81

Book 2
TYPICAL THINGS

1. Jacob's Ladder 89
2. The Burning Bush 93
3. The Pillar of Cloud and Fire 99
4. The Manna in the Wilderness 105
5. The Rock in the Wilderness 111
6. The Brazen Serpent 117
7. Thoughts on the Veil of Moses 123
8. The Sacrifices 129
9. The Ordinance of the Passover 139
10. The Ordinance of the Scapegoat 145
11. The Ordinance of the Red Heifer 151
12. The Ordinance of the Year of Jubilee 159
13. The Law of the Leper 165
14. The Law of the Near Kinsman 175
15. The Holy Nation of Israel 181
16. The Victory over the Nations of Canaan 187
17. The Allegory of Hagar and Sarah 191

Book 3
TYPICAL PLACES

1. The Cities of Refuge 199
2. The Tabernacle in the Wilderness 205
3. The Temple of Solomon 215
   3.1. The Ordinance of the Ark and Mercy Seat 219
   3.2. The Ordinance of the Golden Table 225
   3.3. The Ordinance of the Golden Candlestick 229
   3.4. The Ordinance of the Golden Altar 233
   3.5. The Ordinance of the Brazen Altar 237
   3.6. The Ordinance of the Brazen Laver 241
   3.7. The Ordinance of the Anointing Oil 245
4. The Land of Canaan 249

5. The Holy City of Jerusalem and the Holy Hill of Zion 253
   5.1. The Feast of Tabernacles 257
   5.2. The Fast of Anniversary Atonement 263
   5.3. The Feast of Firstfruits and of Pentecost 269
   5.4. The Feast of the New Moon........................ 275
   5.5. The Metaphorical Priesthood of All Christians 279

An Evangelical History of the Birth, Life, Death, Resurrection, and Ascension of Jesus Christ, the True Messiah, in Whom All the Types of the Old Testament Are Fulfilled.............. 283

The Great Matter and End of Gospel Preaching 301

Preface

William McEwen's book on the glory and fullness of Jesus Christ as foreshadowed in the Old Testament swam into my ken only toward the end of my preaching a series on the prophetic portraits of Christ in Scripture. It would have been so helpful had this discovery been made much earlier. Out of print for almost two centuries, this little gem turned out to be available in an unedited electronic text file from the Library of Congress in Washington, DC, and in facsimile paperback courtesy of the Expresso Book Machine at the Harvard Bookstore in Cambridge, Massachusetts.[1] The language and muddy print of the mid-eighteenth century melted away before the liveliness of the writer's style and his obvious love of the Scriptures and his Savior. Long before I finished the book, the conviction developed in my mind that it ought once more to see the light of day.

Several reasons suggest the usefulness of McEwen's work to Christians in the twenty-first century. First and foremost is the value of the subject matter. For nearly a century, "McEwen on the Types" was popular on both sides of the Atlantic.[2] But typology as a subject

---

1. Expresso Book Machines can print on demand any title available in electronic form—at one hundred pages per minute—and deliver a perfect bound volume (i.e., paperback) in five to ten minutes. These are found in a growing number of bookstores across the world.

2. Many editions rolled from the press between 1763 and 1841. Samuel Miller's personal copy from an American edition in 1796 is still in the library of Princeton

fell into increasing neglect in the middle of the nineteenth century. It is probably not a coincidence that the last of an eight-decade string of editions of McEwen's book—published in Edinburgh in 1841—appeared in the same decade in which Patrick Fairbairn in his landmark exposition of biblical typology noted a decreasing interest in the subject.[3] Peter Masters, in his foreword to the 1989 republication of Fairbairn's *Typology*, observes, "The recent drift toward a highly technical and less theological method of interpretation is chiefly a reaction against the whimsical and extravagant 'spiritualization' of biblical passages heard in so many pulpits. However, this reaction often goes too far, creating a hermeneutical strait-jacket that greatly reduces the pastoral scope of the text and inhibits the applied expository approach laid down by Paul [Rom. 4:23–24; 15:4; 1 Cor. 10:1–14; 1 Tim. 3:16–17]. Indeed the new drift seems to want to treat the Bible as a human rather than a divine book."[4] What would be regarded as merely literary flourishes in any human writing becomes in the Bible inescapably prophetic as to its content and accordingly supernatural in its scope. This argues for more exegetical care, and not summary dismissal, in the handling of typological and figurative allusions in the Word of God. In these respects, McEwen's treatment is restrained. He is careful not to read too much into the text and on occasion enters gentle cautions against such excesses. More recently, David Murray has expressed the need "to restore a sane, yet spiritually edifying typology to the Church to help Christians profit not just from Jesus' prophetic words, but from His prophetic pictures (typology)." He adds that "one problem is that there are so few good modern books on the subject."[5] Perhaps this "good [old] book" from

---

Theological Seminary, where he served as professor of ecclesiastical history and church government from 1813 to 1849.

    3. Patrick Fairbairn, *The Typology of Scripture* (1845–1847; repr., Grand Rapids: Baker, 1975), book 1, p. 1.

    4. Patrick Fairbairn, *Typology of Scripture: Two Volumes in One* (Grand Rapids: Kregel, 2000), ix.

    5. David Murray, *Jesus on Every Page* (Nashville: Thomas Nelson, 2013), 137.

William McEwen will rekindle an interest for some modern attention to the Bible's types and foreshadowing of Christ.

A second reason for a new edition is the infectious zest in the simplicity of the writer's style. Whereas most of the Puritans and their theological descendants developed their sermonic work into often massive, and not infrequently profound, theological disquisitions (which have stood the test of time), McEwen deliberately distilled and simplified his material from sermons on the various Scripture passages to provide concise, conversational, and user-friendly explanations of each subject under review. He cannot be accused of the sin of those who think they will be heard for their many words (see Matt. 6:7).

Third, William McEwen—like another youthful minister of Christ of an earlier generation, Andrew Gray (1633–1656)[6]—died in his twenties, leaving to posthumous publication the fragmentary harbingers of a fruitful ministry cut off almost before it had begun. Even so, Professor John Macleod, in his classic lectures on Scottish theology, reviews the literature of the Secession Church,[7] mentioning some better-known authors, such as William Arnot, John Swanston, Adam Gib, and John Brown of Haddington,[8] but writing of our author,

---

6. See Andrew Gray, *Loving Christ and Fleeing Temptation*, ed. Joel Beeke and Kelly Van Wyck (Grand Rapids: Reformation Heritage Books, 2007).

7. The Secession Church emerged from the 1733 secession from the Church of Scotland of those who maintained the rights of congregations to call their own pastors against the prevailing practice of patronage, whereby the heritors of the parish might impose a man of their choosing over the desires of the Lord's people. See John McKerrow, *History of the Secession Church*, revised and enlarged edition (Glasgow: A. Fullarton, 1841), for a full account of the Secession movement. The Secession lives on in the Associate Reformed Presbyterian Church in the United States, mainly in the southern states. The ARPs maintain Erskine College and Seminary in Due West, S.C., and the fine Bonclarken conference grounds in Flat Rock, N.C.

8. William Arnot (1732–1786), minister of the Associate Church in Kennoway, published *The Harmony of Law and Gospel* in Perth in 1785. See Robert Small, *History of the Congregations of the United Presbyterian Church* (Edinburgh: David Small, 1904), 2:373. John Swanston (1720–1767), minister of Kinross, was not published in his lifetime, but was remembered in a volume of sermons published after his

MacEwen of Dundee we name by himself. He was one of the brightest ornaments of the Secession movement. He died at the early age of 28. But he left a book that embalms his memory.... This work deals with the types of Scripture in a vein of fine Evangelical teaching and it is expressed in what was regarded as the classical English of the middle of the 18th century.... And such a high and dry Anglican Churchman as Dean Burgon makes the rather grudging admission that the best book he knew in English on the types was by a Scotsman and a Presbyterian.[9]

In the wisdom of God, however, it has been the very cutting short of useful lives full of potential that has drawn our attention to what the Lord can and will do with young men called to the gospel ministry. The fragrant godliness of an Andrew Gray—called home at twenty-two, after only a few months as an ordained minister—and the lively exposition of William McEwen, lifting up Christ from the Old Testament with simplicity and evident love for the Savior and the people of God, testify to the existence of old heads on young shoulders and call us all, in Paul's words, "Brethren, be not children in understanding: howbeit in malice be ye children, but in understanding be men" (1 Cor. 14:20).

A word is in order about the editorial amendments of the original work. The text itself has been amended very sparingly, with the removal of some of the excess commas common to eighteenth-century writers and modernizing of the occasional obsolete word

---

death. See McKerrow, *History of the Secession Church*, 850–52. Adam Gib (1714–1788), minister of the Associate Church, Edinburgh, was author of many polemical works. See McKerrow, *History of the Secession Church*, 848–49. John Brown of Haddington (1722–1787) was most famous for his *Self-Interpreting Bible* (1878) but was voluminously published on a vast array of topics theological and ecclesiastical. See McKerrow, *History of the Secession Church*, 858–59.

9. John Macleod, *Scottish Theology in Relation to Church History since the Reformation* (Edinburgh: Banner of Truth, 1974), 181. Note that "McEwen" is correctly spelled without the "a" and that the evidence is that he died in his twenty-eighth year—that is, age twenty-seven (see John Patison's *Memoir* below). See also McKerrow, *History of the Secession Church*, 868–71, for an account of McEwen's life and ministry.

and the division of a few excessively run-on sentences. The original title, *Grace and Truth*, seemed too general for the subject matter. A new title, drawn from the original subtitle, has been adopted for this edition: *The Glory and Fullness of Jesus Christ*, together with the subtitle, *In the Most Remarkable Types, Figures, and Allegories of the Old Testament*. The former is simply the purpose of the latter. In two respects, however, I have attempted to modify both the look and the scriptural cogency of the book.

As to the look of the book, I have divided the author's argument in each chapter and supplied headings to each section, often from his own language. Hopefully this will remove the impression of a volume of large chunks of words and help the reader get ahold of the gist and flow of the message.

As to the scriptural cogency of the book, I have sought to provide easier access to the Scriptures the author employs in one way or another to support his arguments but which he rarely references with formal citations. Like many of the "old" Reformed writers, McEwen positively breathes Scripture in his writing. Scripture pervades the text but is very rarely cited with explicit chapter and verse. Much of this will be missed by many a modern reader, so every effort has been made to identify these and cite the precise Bible references. We need to know not just what the author has to say but how it faithfully represents the teaching of the Word of God. So great is McEwen's grasp of Scripture that he quotes it, conflates this verse and that, and alters the language to flow into his assertions and applications. This he does, mostly it would seem, from memory, and only rarely with citation, but always with a sound grasp of the text and its theological and practical thrust. His comprehensive grasp of Scripture is astounding. His mind inhabits the Bible so that Scripture truth flows from his pen. Accordingly, the principal Bible passages from which each exposition flows have been supplied after each chapter heading, and hundreds of Scripture verses, whether quoted or merely alluded to by the author without citation, have been supplied. Where lapses in his precise recollections were discovered, the appropriate corrections were made. The Authorized Version of the Bible has been retained throughout. Editor's notes have been furnished where some particular explanations of context or content seemed helpful.

This edition of McEwen's book includes two additions to his treatment of the types. One is an essay found in the original book published in 1763 with the title "An Evangelical History of the Birth, Life, Death, Resurrection, and Ascension of Jesus Christ, the True Messiah, in Whom All the Types of the Old Testament Are Fulfilled." The essay was then included in McEwen's *A Select Set of Essays, Doctrinal and Practical* (1767) under the title "On the Manifestation of the Son of God in Human Flesh," while subsequent editions of his book on types dropped it. It seems that the original editor thought that McEwen's overview of the life of Christ would make a fitting capstone to a book on types of Christ, so the essay was adapted for the purpose. It is retained in this edition with the same purpose in mind.

Also included with this edition is the one piece published in McEwen's lifetime—his sermon at an ordination service in Aberdeen. The principal interest of this (apart from the solid content of the sermon) is the fact that the preacher was perhaps twenty-three years of age and yet was in his fourth year as a pastor, having been licensed to preach at age eighteen and ordained at age nineteen or twenty! As with the other material in this volume, McEwen's divisions have been highlighted with suitable headings that preserve the flow of the sermon but highlight the development of his argument and application. Editor's notes have been added to explain some contexts, sources, and expressions employed by the author. Notes not labeled as editor's notes belong to the original publication. May God bless young McEwen's ministry today: "by it he being dead yet speaketh" (Heb. 11:4).

—Gordon J. Keddie
Greenwood, Indiana

A Memoir of the Life and Character of the Reverend William McEwen

The worthy author of the following studies was descended from pious and respectable parents in the town of Perth, who spared neither pains nor expense to give him a truly Christian and liberal education. To this end, they were greatly encouraged by the early attachment which he himself showed both to piety and learning.

His constitution of body was rather delicate and weakly, though in common he was tolerably healthy, but his intellectual powers were sound and strong. He had a penetrating and comprehensive mind, a fine perception, and an elegant taste. These happy talents were attended with solidity of judgment and a sense of the truly beautiful and sublime, peculiar to himself, and still further heightened by an imagination and invention equally lively and a memory uncommonly capacious and retentive.

To cultivate and improve these admirable natural endowments, he employed the most assiduous care and unwearied industry. By his diligent study of the Roman and Greek classics, of logic and philosophy, of the best English poets and historians, and, above all, the Scriptures of truth in their originals, with the most judicious and evangelical books of our own and foreign divines, he collected a large stock of the best ideas and enriched his mind with a variety of select knowledge and suitable literature.

His studies in divinity were assisted for some years by the advice of the late celebrated Mr. Ebenezer Erskine of Stirling and finished under the tuition of the Reverend James Fisher of Glasgow.

He was in 1753 licensed to preach the gospel by the Associate Presbytery of Dunfermline, and in the beginning of the year 1754 he was ordained by the same presbytery the minister of the Associate congregation in the town of Dundee.

Having in a solemn and public manner devoted himself to the more immediate service of the blessed Jesus in the ministration of His gospel, and had committed to him the charge of a particular flock, he was earnestly desirous to have them grounded in the principles and actuated by the true spirit of Christ's gospel. Entirely satisfied that the scriptural plan of redemption by the blood of Christ is divinely calculated to draw men's affections from iniquity, attach them to the blessed God, sweeten their tempers, and form them to true happiness, it was his daily endeavor, by the most easy and engaging methods of instruction, to fill their minds with the knowledge of these heavenly doctrines. He longed particularly to have a lively sense of God Almighty's goodness, manifested in freely offering pardon and peace to rebellious sinners in the gospel, impressed on their souls, because from this source, and the influences of the sanctifying Spirit, he was persuaded that all of the noble qualities, the amiable graces, and the important duties, which constitute the dignity or the happiness of our nature, could only be derived.

Far from addressing his hearers in that flattering and dangerous strain, which supposes the powers of the human mind to be as perfect as ever, or but vitiated in a small degree, or that the soul of man is possessed of such principles of virtue as need only to be roused into action, he was solicitously concerned to have them thoroughly convinced that they were ignorant, guilty, impotent creatures. That from such convictions they might perceive their indispensable need of a Savior, of a Savior in all His mediatorial offices: as a prophet to instruct them and, by His Word and Spirit, make them wise unto salvation; as a priest to make an atonement and expiation for their sins and make their persons acceptable to that awful majesty, who dwelleth in light inaccessible; as a king to subdue their iniquities, to write His laws in their hearts, making them partakers of a divine nature, and enable them to deny ungodliness and worldly lusts and to live soberly, righteously and godly in this present world (Titus 2:12).

In fine, the point he chiefly labored was to beget in his people's minds a deep and abiding sense that God was their chief good, their only sufficient happiness and portion; that the blessed Jesus was the foundation of their pardon, acceptance, and salvation; that all their dependence for acquiring the beauties of holiness and tasting the consolations and pleasures of a religious life was to be placed in the Holy Spirit, the Comforter, whose office is to take the things of Christ and show them to sinful men (John 16:14) and to give them to "know the things that are freely given to [them] of God" (1 Cor. 2:12).

Our author's talent of preaching was much admired. The propositions he insisted on were few but always of very weighty and edifying import and naturally resulting from the passage of sacred writ under immediate consideration. His explanations were clear and accurate, his proofs plain and decisive, his illustrations beautiful and entertaining, and his applications close and searching. All the heads of the discourse were remarkably distinct yet connected in such regular order, and in such pleasing succession, as gave his instructions the greatest advantage, and every part contributed to the strength and beauty of the whole.

And, indeed, such was the depth of his thoughts—such the propriety of his words and such the variety, force, and fire of his style, so remarkable was the justness and solidity of his reasoning and so judicious the change of his method—that notwithstanding he invariably pursued the same end; yet proceeding by different paths and varying his address, according as he meant to alarm, to convince, or to comfort, he was so far from growing tedious that he never failed to please as well as to improve his audience.

In imitation of the great apostle of the Gentiles, that most amiable and accomplished preacher, he was peculiarly careful to cultivate a spirit of zeal and devotion in all his discourses. Accordingly, he was fervent in spirit as well as cogent in argument. When he argued, conviction flashed; when he exhorted, pathos glowed. And by distributing to each of his audience a portion suitable to their several states, he endeavored "rightly" to divide "the word of truth" [2 Tim. 2:15].

The same zeal and fervor which influenced and animated his public addresses from the pulpit appeared also in the discharge of the much neglected duties of catechizing, teaching from house to house, and visiting the sick as well as in the administration of the holy sacraments.

In December 1758 he published a sermon delivered at the ordination of the Reverend Alexander Dick, in Aberdeen, entitled *The Great Matter and End of Gospel Preaching*, from 2 Corinthians 4:5. This discourse was reprinted in 1764 and has been much esteemed by the best judges on account of the clear evangelical strain of doctrine, together with the vigorous and affecting manner of address, which runs through the whole of it. It has now undergone five impressions.[1]

In 1763 his meditations on the types and figures of the Old Testament were published in a neat volume. The favorable reception which this piece met with from the public shows in a much stronger light the distinguishing excellency of it than anything else that could be advanced. Five editions of this work have been already sold, and the demand for it still continues. It is hoped that the reader who peruses these studies with the humble, childlike spirit of a Christian, and seeks spiritual advantage in all he reads, will not lose his labor.

On Tuesday the 29th December 1761, he came from Dundee to Edinburgh and on January 3rd, the Sabbath following, preached (his last sermon) in Bristo meetinghouse from Isaiah 63:4: "For the

---

1. Editor's note: *The Dictionary of National Biography*, 35:72, records that "M'Ewen was an attractive preacher and writer. He was author of: 1. 'Grace and Truth; or the Glory and Fulness of the Redeemer displayed in an Attempt to explain… the Types, Figures, and Allegories of the Old Testament,' 12mo, Edinburgh, 1763 (numerous editions). 2. 'A select Set of Essays, doctrinal and practical, upon Subjects in Divinity,' 2 vols. 12mo, Edinburgh, 1767; 7th edit., 'enlarged, with fourteen new Essays on the Perfection of God,' 1799."

day of vengeance is in mine heart, and the year of my redeemed is come." On the Monday evening, January 4th, 1762, he was married at Dalkeith to the oldest daughter of Mr. John Wardlaw, late merchant of the same place. In this important period of his life, when a variety of temporary prospects engross the attention of the most part of mankind, it was observed that, in his social intercourse with his friends, he discovered a strong inclination to fix the conversation to that awful yet delightful subject, the eternal world, into which all must soon enter. Like one established in the faith, he seemed daily to be "looking for and hastening to the coming of the Lord Jesus."

On the Wednesday afternoon, attended by his friends, he went to Leith on his way home to Dundee, and that same night he was suddenly taken ill owing, as is supposed, to the cold and wet he had suffered in his crossing the Firth the preceding week. His disorder soon issued in a violent fever, which rendered him unfit for any conversation, and on Wednesday night the 13th of January 1762, put an end to all his labors in the twenty-eighth year of his age and the seventh of his ministry. Cut down in the prime of life and public usefulness, his death was universally lamented as a severe and afflicting loss to his wife of some ten days, his friends, his congregation, and the church of God. His body was interred in the churchyard of Dalkeith.[2]

In the most unaffected devotion toward God and in a diffusive love to all men; in modesty, humility, and candor; in a gravity of deportment, tempered with becoming cheerfulness; in purity of manners and integrity of conduct, Mr. McEwen was a pattern to all around him. His heart, his time, and his study were entirely devoted to the duties of his profession. His hearers had abundant reason afforded them to believe that he lived above this sordid world, even while he was in it; that he was no lover of filthy lucre, no hunter of

---

2. Editor's note: The entry for William McEwen in *The Dictionary of National Biography* records that he "died suddenly at Leith on 13 Jan. 1762, having been married two days before to the eldest daughter of John Wardlaw, merchant of Dalkeith." McEwen did indeed die in Leith on January 13, but he was married to Miss Wardlaw on January 4, some ten days—not two—prior to his death.

carnal pleasures but that his hopes, and all his views of happiness, were "hid with Christ in God"; that he directed all his aims to the glory of God and considered the honor of Jesus Christ as the final cause of his existence; that he carried on no base and sinister design; that he had no separate interest from the glory of his divine master and the welfare of his people but that the whole desire and delight of his soul was to set forward their salvation, that by their being "made meet to be partakers of the inheritance of the saints in light," his exalted Lord might "see of the travail of his soul and be satisfied."

—John Patison

Preface (1763)

The candid reader, who shall be pleased to peruse the following essay, is desired to take notice that as the discourse itself is not of the argumentative kind, it is taken for granted, as a preliminary maxim, that the grand doctrines of Christianity concerning the mediation of Christ, and the inestimable blessings of His purchase, were typically manifested to the church by a variety of ceremonies, persons, and events under the Old Testament dispensation. It is true, there are some who affect to call this truth in question and yet pretend to be the friends of a divine revelation, but with what sincerity it is not difficult to perceive. For to suppose that the gospel is a new invention and hatched in the age of the apostles, or that the religion of Jews and Christians are entirely different, is signally injurious to them both: for as a living creature, when cut in two, will seem at first to preserve some faint remains of life in both its parts, but in a short time will totally expire, so if the true religion is cut asunder and the faith of Jews and Christians be wholly severed and detached from one another, instead of having one religion of Jews and another of Christians, we shall in reality have no true religion at all surviving. But we do not propose so much as to enter on any dispute on this head, as the following treatise was not intended by the author either for the conviction of infidels or for the confutation of false opinions but for the edification of them who have obtained precious faith. Such persons it will not be difficult to persuade that in the law were exhibited the shadows of good things to come, but the body is of Christ.[1]

To exhibit a compendious view of the persons, events, ordinances, and things that the author apprehended were figurative of the person and mediation of the Son of God is the design of the first part of the following sheets. For though there are some books on this subject already published in our language, it must be owned they are far from being judiciously executed. The looseness of their method and inaccuracy of their style are perhaps the true reasons they are so much neglected and so little known. For the theme they treat of, if properly handled, might, one should think, recommend itself to a more universal perusal than they have hitherto obtained.

It cannot be refused that the doctrinal system the author has chosen to follow in this small work, though once reputed orthodox in the Protestant churches, is now fallen into great contempt with many who sustain themselves great judges of sentiment and composition. But if this little treatise is accepted with the saints, the censures of others need not excite either anxiety or surprise. For so long as the devil is suffered to deceive the nations, and so long as the heart is unconvinced of sin, we may assure ourselves the doctrine of complete justification and everlasting acceptance with God, by the righteousness of Immanuel, freely imputed to wretched sinners, and of sanctification of heart and newness of life through the power of the blessed Spirit will meet with opposition.

Some have conceived an invincible aversion to all allegories of every kind on account of the ridiculous and distorted fancies, the false, misshapen glosses of Scripture, of which, it must be confessed,

---

1. For the display and confirmation of this argument, that the gospel was emblematically preached, and Christ in a figure exhibited in these usages practiced by the ancient Jews, I do, with great pleasure, refer to that admirable and well-known book entitled *Theron and Aspasio*, Dialogue 3. [Editor's note: The author here refers to a then-popular work by the Anglican divine James Hervey (1714–1758), first published in 1755: *Theron and Aspasio, or a Series of Letters upon the Most Important and Interesting Subjects*. While a student at Oxford, Hervey was a member of the famous Holy Club with John and Charles Wesley, George Whitefield, Benjamin Ingham, and others. With the two last-named, he became a decided Calvinist.]

the humor of allegorizing, not properly restrained, has been exceeding fertile. To hunt for allegories everywhere and to labor at giving a mystical turn to these passages of holy writ that are the most plain and literal indicates a vitiated taste that nauseates wholesome food. Many of the ancient fathers have been guilty of this fault; and especially Origen, a man of an extraordinary genius, has been not unjustly blamed on this account. Yea, some men have carried the humor of allegorizing to such an exorbitant pitch as to rummage the heathen mythology itself for the sacred truths of religion and allegorize even that most empty book, the *Metamorphoses of Ovid*. But though some have transgressed all bounds of sobriety in their mystic interpretations, we must not immediately discard all figurative senses of the Scripture, however discreetly investigated. For at this rate we behoved not only to condemn the infallible apostle of the Gentiles but also Jesus Christ Himself, who compares Himself to the manna, to the brazen serpent, and to Jonah in the belly of the fish.

In order to settle the proper limits of allegorical interpretation, two things must be observable, to which our author, in the course of this work, appears to have steadfastly adhered. First, to make a proper divine allegory, type, or figure, it is necessarily required that there be a resemblance, less or more, betwixt the literal history, person, or thing and the spiritual doctrine, truth, or mystery which is supposed to be represented. Second, there must be some good reason to think that this resemblance is not merely casual, or the child of fancy, but is actually intended by the Holy Ghost. And where even both these requisites are found, due care should be taken not to strain the type or allegory beyond the bounds of a just and reasonable comparison, lest, instead of following the clue, we stretch it till it breaks.

In this age of disputes, it must doubtless be a considerable recommendation of a performance when the reader is informed that while the author discovers the most zealous attachments to the cause of truth and appears a devoted champion of the evangelical doctrines, he is careful not to lay a disproportionate stress upon anything by which one Christian may be distinguished from another. Professing Christians agreed in many things, agreed in laying Jesus Christ the one and only foundation of present holiness and future happiness, are not here taught or stirred up to bite and devour one another. No oil is here administered to increase the flame or keep awake the conflagration of animosity and dispute, which have so long and so sadly disturbed the peace and hindered the union of the professed friends of the truth as it is in Jesus; nor are any problematical questions here determined with authoritative airs that may be a new bone of contention in the church. These are employments, whoever are engaged in them and whatever be their motives and pretenses, our author was far from approving.

The conciseness, the propriety, the energy with which the several important and interesting subjects here taken into consideration are treated, will, I persuade myself, both entertain and edify the intelligent reader and delight his taste while his judgment is informed, his heart improved, and his practice directed.

In order to remove these suspicions which often arise concerning the authenticity of posthumous works, I think it incumbent on me to acquaint the public that the following sheets contain the substance of what the author originally composed and delivered from the pulpit in the form of sermons. To contract the force and spirit of a subject into a small compass, and exhibit it to the mind in one clear and easy view, was a branch of study he was remarkably fond of. Therefore, though his diligence and accuracy in preparing for his public appearances were rare and uncommon, he frequently employed his leisure moments in digesting his sermons, after they had been preached, into the form of little essays. This method he pursued, with particular application and assiduity, with regard to the whole of these discourses he made on the types, figures, and allegories of the Old Testament.

His design on this head being executed in the form and dress in which it now appears, he began to entertain serious thoughts of offering it to the public. This engaged him to review and examine the whole with a critical attention and to make such alterations and improvements as appeared necessary in the view of gratifying a further aim at public service.[2] Thus prepared and corrected, he was pleased, amid the familiarities of our long and intimate friendship, to indulge me with the perusal of the manuscript. I read it with eagerness and delight. Such instructive, animating, and evangelical compositions seemed to me finely calculated, under a divine blessing, to be productive of considerable good. I could not therefore forbear urging upon the author an immediate publication of such an excellent work. After further consideration and fresh application to the throne of grace for that wisdom which is profitable to direct, he became resolved.

In a short time, coming to Edinburgh on another account, he settled everything with the gentlemen who are now the publishers relative to the printing of it. The manuscript he left in my hands, except a few sheets that he proposed to carry home with him and take under a repeated perusal. At Leith, on his way home, he was suddenly taken ill. His disorder soon issued in a most violent fever, which put an end to his life and labors in the twenty-eighth year of his age and seventh of his ministry.

He was truly a most accomplished and amiable person, and if the Lord had been pleased to spare him, it is very likely he would have soon risen high in the public esteem on account of his growing worth and abilities. But as my present business is only to satisfy the public with regard to the progress the author himself had made toward the publication of this work before his death, in order to ascertain the authenticity of it and not to write an account of his life or delineate his character, I must beg leave to refer the reader to that public description given of him in a short paragraph, which

---

2. In December 1758, Mr. McEwen published an ordination sermon entitled *The Great Matter and End of Gospel Preaching*, from 2 Corinthians 4:5. A general satisfaction was expressed by all who were present at the delivery of this sermon. And it has been much esteemed by many who have read it, not only on account of the evangelical strain of doctrine that runs through it but also on account of the clear, nervous, and pathetic manner of address.

appeared in the Edinburgh newspapers immediately after his death and which may be seen at the bottom of the page.[3]

The publication hath been delayed so long after his death that it may perhaps seem necessary to make some apology for that delay. But it would be tedious to enumerate a variety of circumstances which have concurred to occasion it.

May the God of all grace follow the piece with His special blessing, give it an extensive spread, and make it subservient to the glorious cause of evangelical truth, real holiness, and Christian charity.

—John Patison
Bristo
September 26, 1763

---

3. "At Leith died of a sudden illness, on the 13th Jan. 1762, the Rev. Mr. William McEwen, minister of the gospel at Dundee. A good genius, a clear head, a lively fancy, cultivated by a liberal education, improven by close study, and enlarged by an early acquaintance with real and vital religion, laid the foundation of that amiable, important, and useful character he maintained throughout the whole course of his ministry. Courteous and condescending, meek and humble in his own eyes, far from affecting human applause, he aimed at an object infinitely more noble, the honour that cometh from God alone, which made him both faithful and diligent in his holy vocation. Conciseness of method, and perspicuity of style, added to solidity of judgment, rendered his preaching equally instructive to the wise, and intelligible to the ignorant. Warm with zeal for God, and compassion for men, his constant endeavour was, to display the amiable excellencies of the incarnate Redeemer to the needy souls of perishing sinners. Not neglecting in his own conduct what he recommended to the practice of others, his life was a fair and beautiful transcript of his doctrine. Cut down in the prime of life and public usefulness, his death is universally lamented as a severe and afflicting loss to his friends, his congregation, and the church of God."

BOOK 1

Typical Persons

1

Christ and Adam Compared
Genesis 3:1–24; Romans 5:12–21

The almighty Creator had now finished the universal frame of nature. He saw the heavens shining in all their glory; He beheld the earth smiling in all her beauty: the sea was stocked with fish, the air with fowls, and the field with beasts. But still the masterpiece of this inferior world was wanting—a creature endued with reason, of upright stature, and qualified at once to rule over the rest of the creation and correspond with his Creator. "And the LORD God formed man of the dust of the ground, and breathed into his nostrils the breath of life; and man became a living soul" (Gen. 2:7). Thus far we are told by the Hebrew lawgiver. And we are further informed by the great apostle of the Gentiles that this first man, whose name was Adam, was the type or figure of "him that was to come" (Rom. 5:14). For aught we know, it might not so much as enter into the heart of Adam to conceive of this divine mystery; and Moses himself, the inspired penman of that truly ancient and authentic history, might not perhaps advert to it. But since God hath revealed it to us by His Spirit, let us attend where the resemblance lies, of the first to the second Adam, which we shall obviously find, whether we view him as the first man, the first father, the first lord, the first husband, or the first covenant-head. And let us learn to contemplate the glory of that illustrious person who was so early typified, while we admire the depth of God's foreknowledge, in ordering matters so, that the history of the first man, who was of the earth and earthly, was a prophecy of the second man, who is the Lord from heaven.

Adam as a Son of God
To begin with the creation of our general ancestor: Adam was the first man in the world of nature, who being formed out of the dust of the ground, by the immediate hand of his Creator, was without father and without mother and, in a sense peculiar to himself, is called "the son of God" (Luke 3:38). He was also a creature perfectly new, to whom there was nothing like, and nothing equal, among all the visible works of God; for his person, consisting of a visible body and an invisible soul, was made after the image and in the likeness of God, which chiefly consists in knowledge, righteousness, and holiness.

Now, sure it is not difficult to perceive that all these characters exactly agree to the second man, who is the firstborn among many brethren in the world of grace—without father as man, without mother as God. His body was formed (not indeed of the dust of the ground but in a manner equally unexampled and miraculous) of the virgin's substance by the immediate power of God, and so soon as a reasonable soul was united to it in the womb of the virgin, both were, that very moment, assumed into the divine person of the Son, wherefore, in all propriety, that holy thing which was born of her was called "the Son of God" (Luke 1:35), or, to use the expression of an Old Testament prophet, was "created a new thing in the earth" (Jer. 31:22). In the man Christ Jesus is found more of the divine likeness than all the saints, than all the holy angels can dare to boast. For which of them have been called at any time the brightness of the Father's glory and the "express image of his person" (Heb. 1:3)? Or to which of them has He said, "Thou art my Son, this day have I begotten thee" (Heb. 1:5)? Adam, indeed, might resemble his Creator as the image on the coin resembles the king upon the throne; but Jesus Christ resembles God as the prince and heir to the crown resembles his royal father, being not only like him but of the same nature and substance with him. And though all similitudes must be infinitely defective in shadowing forth the constitution of Immanuel's person, yet the union of Adam's soul and body is perhaps the best natural emblem of it we can expect to find. Nor does it seem unlawful for us to assist our conception of this high mystery by this natural union, inasmuch as the Holy Spirit Himself, in the Scriptures of the New Testament, seems to allude unto it, when He calls His humanity the flesh and His divinity the spirit. In the former He was manifested; in the latter He was justified (1 Tim. 3:16). In the one He was put to death, and in the other He was quickened (1 Peter 3:18). If the constitution of the first Adam's person was a wonderful mystery in nature, the constitution of the second Adam's person is no less an incomprehensible mystery of grace.

Adam as the Father of Humanity
As Adam was the first man that God created, so he was the first father and progenitor of all other men, who are everyone born in his image as they come into the world of nature and breathe the vital air. Just so, from Jesus Christ, the everlasting Father, all who come into the world of grace derive their spiritual being; His image they bear (1 Cor. 15:49), and from Him "the whole family in heaven and earth is named" (Eph. 3:15). Though here also there is a considerable disparity betwixt the earthly man and the heavenly Adam. The first man is not the immediate, but the remote, father of our flesh; for "one generation passeth away, and another generation cometh" (Eccl. 1:4). But Jesus Christ is the immediate Father of all His saints, who in every age receive from Him the light of life, as the silver moon and all the sparkling stars draw light immediately from the sun, the fountain of the day. "The first Adam," as Moses relates, "was made a living soul," that he might convey a natural life to them who had not received it; but "the last Adam," as the apostle declares, "was made a quickening spirit" (1 Cor. 15:45) to impart a spiritual life to them who had lost it and were dead in trespasses and sins, and at the resurrection of the just to quicken also their mortal bodies. For "as in Adam all die, even so in Christ shall all be made alive" (1 Cor. 15:22).

Adam as Lord and King of the World

Once more, Adam was the first lord and king of the world. Being made a little lower than the angels, he was crowned with glory and honor. He had dominion over the works of God's hands, and all things were put under his feet: all sheep and oxen, the beast of the field, and whatsoever passeth through the paths of the seas (Ps. 8:3–5). But, alas! The dominion of this lord of the inferior creation was short-lived, for being in honor, he continued not (Ps. 99:12). Nevertheless, in the person of Jesus Christ, God-man, the primeval sovereignty of the human nature is most amply restored, for He is made "head over all things" unto His body the church, both in the heights and depths (Eph. 1:22). The jurisdiction of Adam, though wide, was not universal; but the kingdom of Jesus Christ rules over all (Ps. 103:19; Eph. 1:22). He can if He pleases extinguish the stars and the sun, which shine by His permission, and "of his government and peace there shall be no end" (Isa. 9:7).

Adam and His Bride

Now let us come to the marriage of our great progenitor. God saw it was not good for man to be "alone" (Gen. 2:18). He casts him into a deep sleep, opens his side, takes from him a rib, by His creative power He forms a woman out of it, closes the wound, and presents the newly formed creature to her husband, who being awaked knew what was done unto him and with wonder acknowledged this last and best gift of heaven to be "bone of his bone" and "flesh of his flesh." For this cause, says the sacred historian, "shall a man leave his father and his mother, and shall cleave unto his wife" (Gen. 2:24). Now, may we be allowed to allegorize this real history? Does not the apostle seem to say that this is spoken of Christ and the church (Eph. 5:32)?

Let us modestly pursue the allegory a little. The second Adam, that He might give life and being to His beloved spouse the church, the mother of all that are truly living, was content to sleep the sleep of death. This sleep of death was not the effect of nature, for He died not of old age or sickness, but He was voluntarily cast into it and was delivered by the determinate counsel and foreknowledge of God to be crucified and slain. His side was opened with a spear, and from the gaping wound came water and blood, that He might sanctify and cleanse and present to Him "a glorious church, not having spot, or wrinkle, or any such thing" (Eph. 5:27). By this sleep of death, into which He was cast, He becomes at once her husband and her Father, for she is a part of Himself, of His body, of His flesh, and of His bones (Eph. 5:29). When He awaked at His resurrection, His wounds were healed; He found Himself a glorious conqueror; He saw the travail of His soul and was satisfied. He acknowledges the relation and betroths her to Himself forever in loving-kindness, in mercies, and in faithfulness. A bloody spouse was the church to Thee, O dying Redeemer (see Ex. 4:25–26)? So matchless was His love, He left His Father and His mother to cleave to His unworthy bride—left His Father in heaven when He came from thence into this lower world and consented to be forsaken for a season, left His mother on earth when He ascended on high as the Captain of Salvation. He left the blessed virgin that bare Him to provide for herself; He left the church of the Jews, although it was His mother-church, that He might cleave unto the Gentile church gathered out of all nations.

Adam as Our First Covenant-Head and Representative
Lastly, Adam was the first covenant-head and public representative. It is true, the hints of this transaction are but sparingly given in the book of Genesis. However, the truth of it is clearly evinced from the tenor of divine revelation, and it is evident that before the law was given by Moses, a law was given to Adam, because "death reigned from Adam to Moses" and there behoved to be a law by which this death did reign (Rom. 5:14). For, as the inspired apostle argues with the greatest force of reason, "sin is not imputed when there is no law" (Rom. 5:13). Was there then a law before the covenant of Sinai? It was surely none other but the law of works, which God gave to the first man, in whom, as their covenant head, his posterity were either to stand or fall. Full well we know the doleful event: But "as by one man's disobedience many were made sinners, so by the obedience of one shall many be made righteous" (Rom. 5:19).

The first Adam through pride disobeyed the most easy precept, and the last Adam obeyed the most difficult commandment. The first Adam, being a man, affected to be as God; the second Adam, being God, was "found in fashion as a man" (Phil. 2:8). The first Adam was assaulted by the devil in paradise and was overcome; the second Adam was tempted in the wilderness by the same malicious spirit, but He was a conqueror (Luke 4:1–13). The first Adam, breaking the law in one point, was guilty of all; the last Adam, observing it in every point, did magnify and make it honorable (James 2:10; Heb. 4:15). The moment we become the children of Adam by natural generation, we die for a sin which we could not personally commit; the moment we become the children of Christ by regeneration, we are made alive by a righteousness which we could not actually work out. In Adam we are condemned for one sin, but in Christ we are justified from innumerable offenses (Rom. 5:18).

New Life in Christ, the Second Adam

In the first book of the Bible we have a melancholy relation, how the first Adam was so far from being able to transmit life and happiness to his posterity, or to give them to eat of the tree of life, that he himself was driven out from the terrestrial paradise and debarred from all access to that sacramental tree; but in the last book of the sacred oracles, we are presented with a view of the second Adam, in a far more glorious place than that happy garden, and hear Him declaring from His own mouth, "To him that overcometh will I give to eat of the tree of life, which is in the midst of the paradise of God" (Rev. 2:7).

Forever blessed be the glorious name of God, that what the first Adam could not keep, the second hath amply restored to us. For as in Adam "sin hath reigned unto death, even so might grace reign through righteousness unto eternal life by Jesus Christ our Lord" (Rom. 5:21), who is not only come that we "might have life, [but] that [we] might have it more abundantly" (John 10:10).

2

Noah
Genesis 8:20–9:17

That Noah was a figure of Jesus Christ seems not obscurely hinted in his very name given him by his religious father, not without prophetic instinct. It signifies rest, comfort, and, as some have observed, grace, when its letters are a little transposed. So Christ is our consolation, our rest, and by Him grace reigns unto eternal life. Of Him we may truly say with the strictest propriety, "This same shall comfort us concerning our work and toil of our hands" (Gen. 5:29). Noah "was a just man and perfect in his generations, and…walked with God" (Gen. 6:6). When the wickedness of men was grown to the most exorbitant height and all flesh had corrupted their way, he dared to be good when all were turned degenerate; and, fearless of reproach or violence, he admonished them of their wicked ways, preaching righteousness in their assemblies (2 Peter 2:5). So Christ preserved His integrity in every the smallest instance, in an evil and adulterous generation, preaching what He practiced, with not unlike success to Noah. For it is written of Him in the Psalms, "I have preached righteousness in the great congregation: lo, I have not refrained my lips, O Lord, thou knowest" (Ps. 40:9). In some seasons of the Almighty's vengeance, we are informed that the righteousness of Noah, Daniel, and Job could not deliver a sinning people, nor yet their nearest relations, from the lifted stroke (Ezek. 14:14). Truly Noah, though righteous, could not by his righteousness avert the waters of the flood. But the righteousness of our adorable Redeemer is of such infinite value and perfection as to deliver from death an innumerable multitude of transgressors.

The History of Noah

But let us chiefly consider that memorable history of Noah, his preparing an ark for the saving of his house, the antitype of which remarkable event we are informed by the apostle Peter is our being saved by baptism "(not the putting away of the filth of the flesh, but the answer of a good conscience toward God,) by the resurrection of Jesus Christ" (1 Peter 3:21–22). The long-suffering of God was now tired out, and His Spirit ceased to strive with rebellious men, whom all means had proved ineffectual to reclaim. The time was come when the threatened vengeance was to descend with resistless fury. Noah, being long before warned of God, had prepared an ark against the approaching deluge; for he believed God, and being moved with fear, he obeyed the commandment of the Lord. He despised the jeers of the unbelieving world and considered not the huge difficulties he behoved to surmount before he could get a vessel constructed of such bulk as would contain in its capacious hold all sorts of beasts and birds, together with their necessary provisions, for so long a time as he was to be a prisoner. That God who commanded him, that God in whom he believed and whom he feared, enabled him also both to begin and finish. The ship is built, the cargo is taken in, the flood comes, and the waters prevail above the tallest trees and loftiest mountains. The sinful race of man is buried in a watery grave. But the ark, the peculiar care of heaven, though without helm or mast, rides triumphant over the foaming billows, is preserved from dashing on the craggy rocks, or foundering in the mighty waters.

At length, a dove fetching in her mouth an olive leaf (Gen. 8:11) informs the inhabitants of the ark that the waters were abated. They are at last released from their tedious confinement. The venerable patriarch, overwhelmed with gratitude for such a wonderful preservation amid the howling waste, sacrifices unto the Lord, who smells a savor of rest (Gen. 8:21) and renews with him His gracious covenant, that He will no more curse the ground for man's sake. A glorious rainbow is seen over his head stamping the clouds (Gen. 9:13), which from that time became a peaceful sign that the waters shall never more cover the face of the earth, and though the waves shall toss themselves against the sandy shores, they shall never prevail.

Ark, Sacrifice, and Rainbow
Who sees not, in this whole transaction, a lively picture of the method of our salvation by Jesus Christ from a far more dreadful flood that shall, sooner or later, descend upon the head of every sinner? In Jesus Christ we have the antitype of Noah, both floating in the ark, standing at the altar, and compassed with the rainbow. Indeed, He is at once the ark that saves us from the floods of divine wrath, the sacrifice that atones the incensed justice of God, and the rainbow that makes our clouds of every sort to wear sweet smiles. Though Noah's ark and sacrifice and rainbow were things different from himself, and from one another, in Jesus Christ they are all conjoined.

What mortal wit would have contrived such an expedient as the ark of Noah to save from a universal deluge? There is no doubt but the whole scheme appeared very ridiculous to the generality of the world. Noah himself was not the contriver of this project. It was wholly planned by God. Even so, if men and angels had tortured their invention to save a guilty world, they could never have so much as suggested that method which the wisdom of God has fallen upon in the mediation of Jesus Christ. So far does it transcend the thoughts of men that naturally they cannot receive the mystery of God's will. For it is "unto the Jews a stumblingblock, and unto the Greeks foolishness" (1 Cor. 1:23).

In this wonderful vessel were found only eight souls (1 Peter 3:20), the little family of Noah; and how small was that number to the myriads that perished in the waves? Even so the flock of Christ is but a little flock, for though many are called, yet few are chosen (Matt. 20:16). O how unsearchable are His judgments! It was no doubt very strange to see the wildest beasts and birds dwelling peaceably together under the same roof in that time of common danger—but no more strange than what happens every time when sinners are converted unto God and enter into His sanctuary. For in Jesus Christ, the men of ravenous natures forget their natural ferocity and put on, as the elect of God, bowels of mercy, humbleness of mind, meekness, and long-suffering; and, to use the lofty style of the prophet, "the wolf also shall dwell with the lamb, and the leopard shall lie down with the kid; and the calf and the young lion and the fatling together;… They shall not hurt nor destroy in all my holy mountain" (Isa. 11:6, 9).

Dreadful, to be sure, were the buffetings of the rolling surges on the sides of the ark, when heaven and earth seemed to conspire its ruin; but being protected by a superior providence, the vessel, though heavy laden, weathered the storm, preserved alive all the creatures that were within her, and at last rested upon the mountains of Ararat. So did the waves and billows of the Father's wrath go over Thine head, O suffering Savior, and the floods of ungodly men made Thee afraid (Ps. 18:4); but Thou wast more than a conqueror and at last did find Thy rest on the mountains of eternal glory, having both saved Thyself and all that are found in Thee. Thou art our hiding place from the storm and a covert from the tempest. If it had not been the Lord who was on our side, the waters of God's wrath had swallowed us up quick: then the waters had overwhelmed us, the stream had gone over our soul; the proud waters had gone over our soul (Ps. 124:4).

When we are told in the sacred history that a dove alighted on the ark with an olive leaf, what should hinder us to think of the Holy Spirit of Jesus Christ, who alighted upon Him in the waters of Jordan in the likeness of that gentle bird? And who brings glad tidings of great joy to all the inhabitants of the ark when He assures them by the most incontestable proofs that the winter of wrath is past and the rain is over and gone (Song 2:11)? The holy fire is now gone forth at the appointed season, and beholding the dismal desolation he offers an atoning sacrifice of every clean bird and beast, and the Lord smelled a savor of the rest.

This naturally leads us to think of Him who gave Himself for us an offering and a sacrifice of a sweet-smelling savor (Eph. 5:2).

So well pleased is God with Jesus Christ that with Him He establishes His covenant, and with all His seed, that they shall never come into condemnation. Hear what He Himself declares by the mouth of the holy prophet Isaiah: "This is as the waters of Noah unto me: for as I have sworn that the waters of Noah should no more go over the earth; so have I sworn that I would not be wroth with thee, nor rebuke thee,… O thou afflicted, tossed with tempest, and not comforted" (Isa. 54:9, 11). See how the frowning clouds now smile with the glorious colors of the rainbow, the cheerful token of God's covenant. It is a bow, but it has no arrow, and the face of it is turned away from us in token of reconciliation.

Such is the glorious transformation of all your afflictions by Jesus Christ, O ye heirs of righteousness. They are clouds—indeed, dark clouds—but so far from drowning, nay, they shall even fructify your soul and make you revive as the corn. What before was an indication of wrath and a cause of fear is now a token of love and an encouragement of faith. A rainbow forever encompasses the throne of your God (Rev. 4:3), though from it should proceed lightning and thunders and voices. Though, like that mighty angel in the Revelation (Rev. 10:1), He should be clothed with a cloud in the dispensations of His providence, His sunny face will produce a rainbow round about His head. He is ever mindful of His covenant, and you need not fear the terrors of His glory.

3

Melchizedek
Genesis 14:18–24; Psalm 110; Hebrews 7:1–8:6

Now we shall come to the short but comprehensive history of Melchizedek, the figurative meaning of which is not only hinted to us in the sacred oracles but the Holy Spirit condescends to enter on a very particular explication of it (see Heb. 7). The narrative related by Moses is shortly this (see Gen. 14): The patriarch Abraham had, with his little army, surprised and defeated the forces of the confederate kings who had plundered Sodom and, among other prisoners, had carried away captive his kinsman Lot, who living in that wicked city was now a very singular blessing to his sinful fellow-citizens, being the occasion of their rescue from the invaders of their country. As he returned from the slaughter he was met by the king of Sodom, with another king of a very different character: his name was Melchizedek, which though a very fine one, for it signifies "king of righteousness," was not unsuitable to his real character and is a proper admonition to all other kings for what they should be distinguished. The name of this city was Salem: whether it was that Salem where Jehovah afterward had His tabernacle, or another place of the same name, is not precisely determined. However, we are assured that upon this occasion he brought forth bread and wine—not as a sacrifice to God, O ye papists, but to refresh the patriarch's men, fatigued with toil. But the most extraordinary circumstance of all is that, though living in that wicked country, he was priest of the Most High God and vested with regal dignity. When all around him was sunk in superstition and idolatry, this illustrious Gentile retained the knowledge of the true God and thought it no disparagement of his kingly honor to officiate in the solemn rites of His holy worship. The hospitable monarch was a no less religious priest. As in the former capacity he brought forth bread and wine, so in the latter he blessed the renowned patriarch and received from him tithes of all. Thus far the sacred story. But from what parents he descended, when he was born or when he died, who were his predecessors, or who succeeded him are questions we are not permitted to resolve. And even the silence of the Scripture is expressive: "For he was made like unto the Son of God," both in what Moses relates concerning him and in what he conceals from the curious inquirer. Let us carefully observe these two heads of resemblance, and we shall easily understand how David in spirit says of the Messiah, "Thou art a priest for ever after the order of Melchizedek" (Ps. 110:4).

King of Righteousness and King of Peace
We shall first begin with what Moses relates of this extraordinary man. To whom can his name Melchizedek so properly belong as to the King that reigns in righteousness, who, righteous Himself, has wrought for all His subjects a justifying righteousness by the merit of His blood and works in all His subjects a sanctifying righteousness by the power of His spirit? He, He is the king of Salem, which is by interpretation, "king of peace." Peace is the disposition for which He was renowned, who with His dying breath implored forgiveness to His bloody murderers: peace is the grand blessing He died to purchase and lives to confer. O glorious peace, of which righteousness is the foundation and joy in the Holy Spirit the inseparable attendant! Hail ye subjects of His auspicious government, who call the blessings of His purchase all your own! Lo, in your princely Savior the great Jehovah lays aside His vindictive wrath and becomes your loving Father; the angels no more stand aloof but commence your ministers and guardians; the inferior creatures are turned into your faithful friends and allies; the Jews and Gentiles, forgetting their former enmity, join in the most cordial friendship; and

conscience, no more an accuser, whispers peace in gentlest accents. Though "in the world you should have tribulation, yet in him you shall have peace." O Prince of Peace, extend the borders of Thy peaceful kingdom far and wide, and let the wished period come when the nations shall learn war no more! O let Thy peace rule in our hearts through these tumultuous scenes of life, and bring us at last to these calm regions of joy and felicity, where peace extends her dove-like wings forever and ever!

Priest of the Most High God
He "brought forth bread and wine" to refresh the hungry and thirsty soldiers when returning from the slaughter of the kings (Gen. 14:18). Such is the refreshment which the true Melchizedek affords and will afford to all that are truly engaged in the spiritual warfare. He "hast prepared of [His] goodness for the poor" (Ps. 68:10). O come unto Him, and you "shall never hunger"; believe on Him, and you "shall never thirst" (John 6:35). Eat of this bread, and drink of the wine which He has mingled (Prov. 9:5). Happy they who shall conquer in the holy warfare, for they shall "eat of the hidden manna" (Rev. 2:17), and "the Lamb which is in the midst of the throne shall feed them" (Rev. 7:17).

And Melchizedek was the "priest of the most high God" (Heb. 7:1)—an honor not usually appropriated to those that sit on thrones, for God Himself was pleased to provide against the blending of these offices in the commonwealth of Israel. Witness thy fate, Uzziah, who snatching at the censer, lost the scepter (2 Chron. 26:18). And shall the triple-crowned priest of Rome, who exalts himself above all that is called God, go always unpunished? But of Jesus Christ, a prophet testifies, He "shall sit and rule upon his throne; and he shall be a priest upon his throne" (Zech. 6:13), as once He was a king upon His cross.

And Melchizedek blessed Abram: "Blessed be Abram of the most high God, possessor of heaven and earth: and blessed be the most high God, which hath delivered thine enemies into thy hand" (Gen. 14:19–20). So Christ our royal priest was sent of God to bless the children of Abram, not with a verbal, but real, benediction, in turning every one of us from our iniquity; and men shall be blessed in Him.

Jesus Our Great High Priest
Consider, in the last place, how great this man was, to whom even the patriarch Abraham gave the tenth of the spoils; and, as we may say, even Levi, who received tithes from the people by the commandment of God, was tithed in the loins of his progenitor (Heb. 7:5, 10), a most convincing proof that this Melchizedek was both a greater man than Abram and a greater priest than Aaron. But we Christians have a Great High Priest in whose presence Abram must not glory and Levi has no preeminence. To our Melchizedek, the royal priesthood, the holy nation, the peculiar people do pay not only tithes but all they have and are when they present their bodies a living sacrifice, holy and acceptable unto God, which is their reasonable service (Rom. 12:1).

But the circumstances which Moses conceals are no less worthy of our notice than those he reveals. In vain you ask his genealogy, his birth, his death, or the ceremonies of his consecration, for those are buried in darkness, the Holy Spirit intending to signify that Jesus Christ is really and truly what this mysterious king is in the history. "Without father," not as He was God, but man. "Without mother," not as He was man, but God. "Without descent," for having no predecessors in office, He needed not to prove that He was sprung from the priestly tribe, which was an essential qualification in the Levitical priesthood. Having "neither beginning of days, nor end of life," for being set up from everlasting, He "abideth a priest continually" (Heb. 7:3); for though He died, yet even in death He was a priest, and now He "ever liveth to make intercession for them" (Heb. 7:25). What shall we say more? In the order of Aaron were many priests, who, like other mortals, resigning their breath by the stroke of death, their priestly honor was laid in the dust with them. We know from whence they arose, with what carnal ordinances and ceremonies they receive their inauguration, what sacrifices they offered, in what holy places they officiated, who assisted them in their various functions, and who succeeded them when they either died or were deposed from their office. But the priest "after the order of Melchizedek" (Ps. 110:4), being possessed of immortal life and called of God without external ceremonies to His high office, Himself was the sacrifice, Himself was the altar, Himself was His tabernacle and temple, assisted by none nor succeeded by any. In Melchizedek, whom Moses speaks of as though he had been immortal, we have but indeed a faint shadow and not the very image of the things themselves that are found in Jesus Christ. But let the faintness of the resemblance remind us of the greatness of the mysteries, for "who shall declare his generation?" (Isa. 53:8).

4

Isaac
Genesis 22

Next we shall glance at a very extraordinary piece of history, of the most difficult commandment that was ever given to any of the human race, yet was it punctually obeyed, and the obedience amply rewarded. It is the story of Abraham's offering up his son Isaac at the commandment of the Lord (see Gen. 22). The famous patriarch had endured many trials and proved the sincerity of his faith by a long course of obedience and a steadfast dependence on the divine veracity from the time he was called to leave his native Ur in the land of Chaldea. Long did he count Him faithful who had promised, that he should have a son, in whom all nations should be blessed, even when the accomplishment of the promise seemed next to impossible (Heb. 11:8-12). At last the expected child is born, a son of his old age; he flourishes apace and is now flushed with the radiant bloom of youth, both lovely and beloved. The joyful father might now think that the most troublesome scenes of life were happily finished and that it remained for him only to die in faith and peace. But how greatly would he be mistaken. The sorest, the sharpest trial yet remained: "And it came to pass after these things, that God did tempt Abraham, and said unto him,… Take now thy son, thine only son Isaac, whom thou lovest, and get thee into the land of Moriah; and offer him there for a burnt offering upon one of the mountains which I will tell thee of" (Gen. 22:1-2). Shocking precept! Mysterious mandate! Did ever such a message from God wound a parent's ear! Had the voice from heaven denounced that Isaac was to die a natural death and to be snatched away by a sudden stroke, the tidings had been mournful and agonizing. But how much more when it is declared that the hand of violence must be lifted against him, that he must be offered up for a burnt offering, butchered, mangled, and reduced to ashes!

Must Isaac Die?
But the crowning circumstance sets forward the calamity and renders it worse than a thousand deaths: the father must be the priest to bind, to kill, to cut, to burn his beloved son. Abraham, what were the thoughts of thy heart when your ears first heard such dreadful orders? You were accustomed to hear the voice of God speaking in more soothing accents. Hadst thou not been an extraordinary believer, into what a tempest had all thy soul been tossed? How might reason, natural affection, and religion have all conspired to persuade thy disobedience? "Offer up thy son, thine only son Isaac, for a burnt offering! Can this be the voice of God? Sure it must be the voice of some wicked spirit that would impose upon my credulity and urge a father to imbrue his hands in filial blood! But stay: the revelation is unquestionable. It was the very voice of God. I am not permitted so much as to doubt of this. Surely then it must have some other meaning than I first thought. Surely the merciful God cannot mean that I should really kill my Isaac. Take now thy son, thine only son, and offer him up for a burnt offering. Alas! My Isaac, was it for this I received thee by special promise? Was it for this thy mother brought thee forth when she was past her age and I called thee by a name expressive of joy and laughter? How ill dost thou now answer thy name! Thou art not a son of laughter, but of sorrow. O God, why couldst Thou not rather have demanded all my numerous flocks and kids, to smoke in one great burnt offering? Or if a human sacrifice delighted Thee more, why should my Isaac, rather than any other, be the victim? O that I could redeem his life with my own blood!"

"And must I too be the priest? Must he bleed by a father's hand? Ah? What will the world say? They will never believe me when I tell them it was by Thy order I did it. What will Sarah say? But, chiefly, what will come of Thy own promise? How will he be the father of many nations when he is no more? O ye nations! I thought that in this my Isaac you would all be blessed; but now farewell forever all such pleasing hopes. Isaac must die and the promise fail forevermore!"

But so strong was the faith of this eminent believer that either such misgiving thoughts were altogether strangers to his mind or they were soon repelled. He wisely considered that what God had commanded could not be wrong, and what He had promised could not be false. "Be hushed all unbelieving fears, for He who gave an Isaac from the barren womb to fulfill His promise can, if He please, for the same reason restore him from the burning altar. Come then, without delay obey the high command, believing that what He has promised He is able also to perform."

A Ram in the Thicket
No sooner had the early dawn begun to appear in the eastern sky than the resolved patriarch springs from his couch, saddles an ass, and takes with him the intended victim and servants, as much wood as he thought necessary, and proper utensils for the future sacrifice. Three days they traveled on this strange journey, and all that space he looked on his son as dead, but the steady purpose of his soul was not shaken. On the third day the fatal hills of Moriah are descried at a distance, the servants are left behind, the wood is laid on Isaac, and Abram carries the fire and the knife. And now, after some endearing conversation, they are arrived at the appointed place. The altar is built, the wood is laid in order, the plot is doubtless revealed to Isaac by his sedate father, and Isaac, though fully able to have made resistance or delivered himself by flight, is not recorded to have attempted the one or the other: for the same Almighty power that touched the patriarch's heart and made him willing to give the deadly stab did also beyond all doubt make Isaac no less willing, cheerfully to receive it. He is bound like another victim, he is laid upon the altar, and the hand now grasps the fatal knife to be lodged in his guiltless breast, when lo, a heavenly voice forbids the bloody deed, and the patriarch's willing mind is accepted for the actual sacrifice. His fear

of God is highly applauded, and by his works his faith was proved to be perfect. "Abram, you spared not your son for the sake of My command, but I spare him for the sake of thy obedience. Receive him again with My blessing. He shall be the progenitor of the Messiah, and all the nations shall be blessed in him." A ram caught by the horns in the thicket supplies the room of Isaac, and the grateful patriarch acknowledges the happy providence in calling the name of the place JEHOVAH-JIREH,[1] and afterward it became a common proverb, "In the mount the LORD it shall be seen" (Gen. 22:14).

God Spared Not His Own Son
O the inconceivable power of faith that can render the most difficult duties so easy! Nor is there a better way for the children of Abraham to ensure their dearest enjoyments, and improve them to the highest advantage, than by resigning them, totally resigning them to the sovereign will of God. But surely a higher mystery was contained in this extraordinary occurrence. Who can forbear here to think of the adorable mystery of redemption by Jesus Christ, "For God who so loved the world, as not to spare his own Son, but delivered him unto the death for us all."[2] Methinks the language of this whole transaction was as if God had said, "Ye children of men, hear you what My faithful servant and friend has done upon this mountain in cheerfully sacrificing his only son to testify his love to God. By the same method I will declare My love to a perishing world by giving My only begotten Son to fall a sacrifice for sin. In this mountain shall the sword of justice awake against Him by His own consent; and what has now been done only in a figure shall be really transacted at the appointed time. Meanwhile let rams, and other beasts, be sacrificed as a memorial of this grand burnt offering, but let no human blood smoke on My altars."

---

1. Editor's note: Jehovah-jireh is generally interpreted "God sees," in the sense, in this case, that He provides a sacrifice that He sees to be necessary.
2. Editor's note: The author here conflates John 3:16 and Romans 8:32.

But more particularly to enumerate the important predictions of this prophetical history, it contained, first of all, a lively intimation that in the fullness of time *a human sacrifice should be offered up*. Indeed, it is but just and equal that the nature that sinned should suffer: for how can the blood of harmless beasts atone for the sins of guilty men? And this might seem to have been confessed by the horrible custom that obtained in the Gentile world of sacrificing men to appease the wrath of their deities. But the living and true God discharged such direful offerings under the severest penalties, not only for their evident barbarity but because they encroached upon the plan of His infinite wisdom and anticipated the great propitiation, who was to be a human sacrifice, although He was no ordinary person, as Isaac was not an ordinary son. Like Isaac He was a Son and heir, the Son of God, and the heir of all things—a *beloved Son*, for He was daily His delight, before the mountains were brought forth; and oftener than once it was declared by a voice from the excellent glory, "This is my beloved Son, in whom I am well pleased" (Matt. 3:17). An *only Son*; for angels and saints, though styled the sons of God, have no claim to such a sonship as the filial Godhead is possessed of. Isaac, thy birth was altogether extraordinary, both by the father's and mother's sides, surpassing the ordinary course of nature; but still more amazing is the generation of our atoning sacrifice, whose Father as God was the all glorious JEHOVAH and whose mother was a virgin. The event of His birth, like Isaac's, was long foretold and ardently expected before it happened; but though long delayed, the promise was punctually fulfilled at the appointed time. His name imported joy and gladness. In Jesus, the true Isaac, our mouths shall be filled with laughter and our tongues with melody (Ps. 126:2).

Ask you *the manner of His death*? Behold it in this lively type. For as Isaac carried the wood, so the beloved Son of God carried His cross. O ye children of men, your iniquities were the heavy load He bore in "his own body on the tree" (1 Peter 2:24; cf. Deut. 21:22). These, like the wood that was intended to reduce Isaac to ashes, rendered Him combustible to the fire of divine wrath.

It was *for no crime* that Isaac was to suffer death in this tragic manner; yet such was his filial piety, such was his reverence of the high command, that he made no attempt to save his life, though he was able to have done it, being arrived at his youthful prime. Even so, the innocent Redeemer, in whom was found no cause of death—no, not by His very judge—He abhorred not the ignominious cross, He spared to employ all the legions of angels that were ready at His beck, He never attempted to make His escape when His time was come, which He had often done before. Though He had thoroughly digested in His mind the doleful circumstances of His crucifixion, He betrayed not the least unwillingness to submit to His heavenly Father's will, even when His human heart shrank from the bitter cup. "I lay down," says He, "My life; no man taketh it from Me. This commandment have I received from My Father. Father, not My will, but Thine be done" (see John 10:18; Luke 22:42).

It was *by his Father's hand alone* that Isaac was to breathe out his soul by a mortal wound, and by him alone was the funeral pile to be lighted up. For these purposes, we are informed in the sacred history, he carried the fire and the knife. It was not the envy of the Jews, it was not the covetousness of Judas, and it was not the irresolution of the cowardly Roman judge that chiefly consigned our Isaac over to the tormenting cross: but being delivered by the determinate counsel and foreknowledge of God, these only proved the sinful executioners of the high decree. Thy burning anger against the sins of men, O heavenly Father, was the fire that preyed upon His holy soul. Thy justice, inflexibly severe, was the keen flashing sword which awaked against Him and drank His vital blood. "It pleased the LORD to bruise him; he hath put him to grief" (Isa. 53:10). And truly the sufferings of our dying Redeemer were many of them of such a nature as none but God could inflict, even as none but God could have endured them.

Beyond all peradventure, *the scene where these things were transacted* by Abraham, being in the land of Moriah, could not be far distant from the horrid eminence of Calvary or the lovely heights of Zion. It is a circumstance by no means unworthy of our careful attention that the true propitiation was offered up nearly in the same place where the beloved son of Abraham was to expire upon the altar. "And Abraham called the name of that place Jehovahjireh: as it is said to this day, In the mount of the LORD it shall be seen" (Gen. 22:14). Ye mountains of Moriah, your name may now be JEHOVAH-JIREH for better reasons than when the ram was caught by Abraham in the thicket, which he offered for his Isaac; for God has now provided Himself a Lamb, and in these mountains the Lord was seen to "put away sin by the sacrifice of himself" (Heb. 9:26).

God So Loved
It was not possible for a mortal creature to give a higher document of love to God than by sacrificing for His sake a dearly beloved and only son. The whole history is so amazing that we know not whether we should most admire the strange commandment or the unparalleled obedience. Even so, it was not possible for the immortal God to give a nobler demonstration of love to men than by delivering for their sake His only begotten Son to die for their offenses: "Greater love hath no man than this, that a man lay down his life for his friends" (John 15:13). The whole transaction, from first to last, is of such uncommon nature and so foreign to every human plan for acceptance with God that to the wise Greeks it was mere foolishness and to the Jews a stumbling block. As Abraham could not without faith have acquiesced in the precept, no more can we without faith acquiesce in the gospel plan. He consulted not with Sarah when he was called to obey; and when we are called to believe, we must not consult with vain philosophy.

Though in the mystery of redemption there is a depth of wisdom, thy line, O reason, is too short to sound its bottom. Reason, especially in its depraved state, may not unfitly be compared to the patriarch's ass, which stayed at the foot of the hill but ascended not with Isaac to the sacrifice. It is the province of faith alone to ascend this hill of the Lord and comprehend the love of God "which passeth knowledge" (Eph. 3:19). Isaac, it is true, was not sacrificed, and there was no need that God should raise him from the dead, as the patriarch perhaps expected. But as he was in a manner a dead man during all the three days that intervened betwixt the sentence being passed against him and the reversing of it by the heavenly voice, it may be truly said that "in a figure" he was received "from the dead" (Heb. 11:19). Exactly so, our true Isaac was received on the third day from the dead, not in a figure only. Like Isaac, He felt no harm, but, "O death, He was thy plague; O grave, He was thy destruction." Like Isaac, He returned to His Father's house from whence He came and became a Father of many nations, who are begotten again to a lively hope by His resurrection from the dead; for thus the prophet Isaiah foretells, with admirable plainness and propriety, "When thou [O heavenly Father] shalt make his soul an offering for sin, he shall see his seed, he shall prolong his days, and the pleasure of the LORD shall prosper in his hand" (Isa. 53:10).

Forbear, ye children of men, anxiously to inquire, "Wherewith shall I come before the LORD, and bow myself before the high God?... shall I give my firstborn for my transgression, the fruit of my body for the sin of my soul?" (Mic. 6:6–7). For lo, He has given His firstborn to atone for your transgression, and the Son of His love to expiate the sin of your souls by the sacrifice of Himself. "He hath shewed thee, O man, what is good; and what doth the LORD require of thee, but to do justly, and to love mercy, and to walk humbly with thy God?" (Mic. 6:8).

5

Jacob

Genesis 28:10–22

The history of Jacob's life is also stored with very remarkable incidents, not unlike to those which befell our Lord Jesus Christ or which have befallen the church, which is His body and His other self, in all ages of the world. The truth of this will easily appear in the following parallel:

Jacob and Jesus Compared

1. The patriarch Jacob was chosen of God, who loved him before he was born, to be the progenitor of the Jewish nation, who also was chosen in him, rather than the posterity of Esau, called in the style of prophet "the border of wickedness, and the people against whom the Lord hath indignation forever."	1. The Lord Jesus Christ, being from everlasting the peculiar object of the Father's love, was chosen by Him before the mountains were brough forth to be the Father of the nations of them who are saved, who are also chosen in Him, that they should be holy and distinguished from the world that lies in wickedness.
2. From this patriarch the Jews, the peculiar people of God, are Israelites.	2. From Jesus Christ, the chosen generation are named Christians.

3. From him sprung the twelve patriarchs who were the fathers of that holy nation according to the flesh.

4. Many and great were the hardships which this patriarch conflicted with during the course of his pilgrimage; for it appears that he was the most afflicted of all his race, both on account of the treatment he met with from Esau, from Laban, and from God Himself.

5. Very early he began to struggle with his rough brother Esau, who carried his enmity to such a pitch as the resolve to murder him, for no other fault than excluding him highly from the privilege of birthright, which he himself had justly forfeited by selling it for a morsel of meat; and therefore when he would afterward have inherited the blessing, he could not by all his tears induce his father to bestow it upon him.

3. And the twelve apostles of the Lamb are the fathers of the holy nation according to the spirit.

4. Behold and see, was ever any sorrow like unto His? For His whole life was a continual war with woe. He was afflicted by the world, harassed by the devil, and persecuted even by God Himself.

5. Early, very early He felt the effects of the world's undeserved malice. And His rough brethren the Jews were so incensed against Him as to imbrue their hands in His blood. And wherefore did ye thus hate Him, O ye malicious Jews? It was because you gloried in your birthright and could not endure that the kingdom of God should, according to His doctrine, be taken from you and transferred to the despised Gentiles, though you had justly forfeited all title to such a glorious prerogative by your great contempt of spiritual and heavenly blessings.

6. In vain shall you think, O profane Esau, to thwart the unalterable decree; for the elder shall serve the younger, and the posterity of Jacob shall put garrisons in thy stronghold.

7. With his staff he passed over Jordan, an exile from his father's house; he served for a wife and returned again with much substance, having multiplied into two bands.

8. He spoiled Laban of his substance and idols. But when he followed after him, to rummage Jacob's tents, he found nothing that belonged to him. And when he departed from Jacob, the angels of God met him, and he called the place Mahanaim. But the conflict which Jacob had with God was by far the most mysterious affliction. Never was the patriarch in greater distress. Retired from his family, and all alone, expecting his brother Esau to come upon him with four hundred armed men, he pours

6. But be of good cheer, ye children of Jesus Christ, our Lord and master has overcome the world. And the time shall come when the saints of the Most High shall take the kingdom; and it shall be said, "Who is this that cometh from Edom, with dyed garments from Bozrah?" (Isa. 63:1).

7. With the staff of His cross He passed over the Jordan of death; and wandering in exile from heaven, His father's house, He took on Him the form of a servant (such was His love to the church); and afterward she was followed by the two bands of Jews and Gentiles.

8. The devil suspecting that this was the strong man who was to spoil his goods and utterly abolish the idols, he fiercely assaulted Him; but when the prince of this world came unto Him in the day of His temptation, he found nothing in Him, and when he left our Savior, the angels came and administered unto Him. But the conflict which our Lord had with the wrath of God was the greatest of all His afflictions. It was the lively feeling of almighty anger that made Him sweat blood: when retired from His disciples,

out his prayer to God and there wrestled a man with him till the breaking of the day, to whom he wept and made supplication. But at last he is victorious, his life is preserved, and he obtains the blessing.	and expecting the multitude to come upon Him with swords and staves, He offered up prayers and supplications with strong cries and tears to Him that was able to save Him from death. But at last He prevails to obtain the blessing, having endured the wrath of God.

And as Jacob was obliged to go down to Egypt in his old age to preserve his life from a cruel famine, so Christ Jesus fled into Egypt when He was a child to preserve His life from a bloody tyrant. Afterward was the saying of the prophet fulfilled, "Out of Egypt have I called my son" (Matt. 2:15). And, lastly, as Jacob left the world blessing his sons, so Christ left the world blessing His apostles.

Jacob and His Seed
But he was also a type of the mystical body of Christ, and indeed of every saint—whether you view him as chosen in the womb, striving at his birth, buying the birthright, meeting the angels of God, wrestling with the angel of the covenant, or buried in Canaan after a troublesome life. Behold in all these an emblem of everyone who is an Israelite indeed.

His *election in the womb* signifies how all the seed of Jacob are chosen to salvation. "Was not Esau Jacob's brother," his elder brother, and indeed a stronger child? For his hairy skin portended the vigor of his constitution yet was he not chosen to inherit the patriarchal blessing. The happy persons whom He chooses to inherit the blessings of eternity are so far from being better than other of their fellow-creatures that, for the most part, they are greatly inferior, both in the endowments of the mind and outward worldly distinctions. "Even so, Father, for so it seemeth good in Thy sight!"

His *struggling at his birth*, when he took hold of his brother's heel, might be intended to signify that every true Israelite must strive before he come to the possession of those blessings that are designed for him in the purpose of God. Electing love indeed prevents, but not excludes, our fighting the good fight of faith and laying hold of eternal life. Miserably shall they be disappointed who dream of seizing the kingdom of heaven without violence. When the husbandman can reasonably hope that indolence will fill his barns with plenty, when the soldier can think that victory will present him with her palms without striking a blow, then may the yawning Christian, whom it grieves to work out his own salvation with fear and trembling, expect to reap fruit unto life eternal and tread upon the high places of his spiritual foes.

His *buying the birthright* for pottage, ludicrous as it seems, perhaps may denote the high esteem which all the true seed of Jacob have of spiritual blessings. O wretched exchange! To barter for the satisfaction of a moment what was more valuable than a hundred lives! Profane Esau, was it nothing valuable to inherit the blessing of Abraham, to be the progenitor of the Messiah, and to entail on thy posterity the true knowledge of God? All this was undervalued when the birthright was despised. Ye Esaus of the world, take to yourselves your present sensual gratifications and esteem nothing good but present satisfaction, fill your bellies with the hidden treasure of God, and for the short-lived pleasures of sin renounce your part in heavenly felicities, and bury, without one sigh, each glorious hope. But let the house of Israel labor for the meat that endures to everlasting life; let them implore the cheerful light of God's countenance; let them enjoy the vision of His face in righteousness; and when inspired with these blissful expectations, all sublunary joys shall in comparison be no more regarded than was thy pottage, Jacob, in comparison of the birthright.

His *receiving the blessing* from his father in the garments of Esau, which his mother arrayed him with, may be viewed as a faint shadow of our receiving the blessing from God in the garments of Jesus Christ, which all the children of the promise do wear. When found in Christ and clothed with the perfuming robes of righteousness imputed, the garments of our elder brother, our gracious God and Father will forget our sinful imperfections, and beholding no iniquity in Jacob nor perverseness in Israel will bless us with all spiritual blessings in Christ Jesus. It was not the feigned venison, but the borrowed garments, that procured the blessing. Even so we are not blessed by God for our good works, however pleasing unto Him, but for the righteousness of our Redeemer. For should we presume to appear in the presence of Jehovah without this most necessary precaution of putting on the Lord Jesus Christ, our performances, however specious, could meet with no acceptance, but the evil which Jacob greatly feared would come upon us; we would procure to ourselves a curse and not a blessing.

His *meeting the angels* after his interview with Laban, when he called the name of the place *Mahanaim*, was not only designed to animate his courage amid the dangers that surrounded him in that journey but also to hint unto us what is the distinguished privilege of all the children of Jacob in their militant state, for "the angel of the LORD encampeth round about them that fear him" (Ps. 34:7). The despiser of his birthright, whose resentment Jacob dreaded, comes indeed escorted by four hundred men. But what were these to Jacob's invisible guard? This honor have all His saints, who come to the "innumerable company of angels," the ministrant spirits of the heirs of salvation and the bright guardians of the just (Heb. 12:22).

His *wrestling with the angel* (who doubtless was the Captain of the host that appeared to him in the likeness of a man—a prelude of His future incarnation—over whom he obtained the victory, and from whom he received the blessing when he wept and made supplication)[1] may be considered as a figure of that great fight of affliction which the beloved of the Lord may lay their account with in the night of this world. Even the Lord Himself may seem to stand against them with His right hand as an adversary. But as the mighty wrestler with Jacob assumed no greater strength than might be overcome,

---

1. Editor's note: See Joshua 5:14–15.

so God, that is faithful, will proportion the trials of His people to the strength He has given them. And by their strength (which yet is not their own) they shall prevail; for He that is in appearance against is really for them, and stronger for them than against them. If He casts down, it is but with His left, but He upholds them with His right hand. Mysterious but comforting truth! Hard to express but sweet to know. Jacob was never happier than when he seemed most miserable, nor more strong than when he seemed most weak; for at once he was lamed and blessed, conquered and victorious. A lively emblem this of what usually befalls the remnant of Jacob! For "happy is the man whom God correcteth" (Job 5:17). The love of the Lord toward the children of Israel is written in the most rigorous dispensations: when they are weak, then are they strong; and what He takes away from them in one way, He restores to advantage in another. O happy they who think it no solitude to be alone with God! Glorious things are spoken of thee, O duty of prayer! He who can prevail with God needs not fear that man should prevail against.

His *burial in Canaan*, the land of promise, after a life of singular affliction, may represent the distinguished lot of all the faithful, chosen, and called, who, after a short course of pilgrimage, harassed, with anxious cares and sorrows, do rest in the promised land of the heavenly Canaan. And truly, the beloved Jacob had shared no happiness to be compared with hated Esau's if in this life only he had hope. Who would not rather judge that Esau was beloved of God, and Jacob hated, if love or hatred could certainly be known by that which happens under the sun? And were the Christian to bind his views by the grave, should his hopes terminate in death? Ah! Then he were the most wretched of his race, and at his best estate he were altogether vanity.

Eternal Joys Above

O eternal joys above, O glorious rewards, reserved in heaven for those who seek for glory, honor, and blissful immortality, by patient continuance in well doing; without you, even pure and undefiled religion could scarce compensate the afflictions of this present life, to which we are exposed as men and Christians. But these assert the glorious prerogative of religion and the superior happiness of saints. Though the days of their pilgrimage, like Jacob's, be few and evil, yet still they are a people saved by the Lord, who has blessed them, and they shall be blessed.

6

Joseph
Genesis 37:1–11; 49:22–33

The history of Joseph's life is doubtless one of the most entertaining and eventful which all antiquity can boast of. Upon it are inscribed in most lively characters at once the terrible effects of malice and envy and the watchful care of providence over the cause of injured virtue and innocence. But the most remarkable thing that claims our attention here is the surprising likeness betwixt the whole narrative and the history of Jesus Christ, of whom it may truly be said, "The archers have sorely grieved him,…but his bow abode in strength, and the arms of his hands were made strong by the hands of the mighty God of Jacob" (Gen. 49:23–24).

Beloved Son but Hated Brother
He was the beloved son of his father Jacob, and truly he seems to have been worthy of his paternal favor; for, detesting the wickedness of his brethren, he reported their faults. This, with his prophetic dreams which he told them of, so stung them with envy and resentment that they could not speak peaceably to him nor look at him but with disgust and aversion. Their causeless anger is turned into obdurate hatred of their brother, and soon they find an opportunity of wreaking their bloody rage. He is sent by his father to inquire of their welfare when feeding their flocks in the wilderness, and dreading no harm as he was innocent, and stranger to offense, he carefully inquires after them till at last he finds them out. But ah! He looked

for brethren and beholds murderers. "Wrath is cruel, and anger is outrageous: but who is able to stand before [baleful] envy?" (Prov. 27:4). Transported with this blind fury, they forget at once that they were brethren, children, and men, and take horrid counsel against the darling youth, to imbrue their hands in his guiltless blood. One more merciful than the rest moves that they cast him into a pit rather than murder him outright, for he intended by this artifice at once to indulge their fury and to elude it by finding means to restore him again to his father. The motion takes. They strip him of his garment of many colors and, regardless of the anguish of his soul, they let him down into the pit; but themselves—O cruel monsters!—"sat down to eat and to drink," for they were "not grieved for the affliction of Joseph" (Ex. 32:6; Amos 6:6). Here they designed to leave him perish miserably in mournful solicitude, but Providence reserved him to better things: for lifting up their eyes, they see approaching a company of merchants who were of Ishmael's race and carried balm and myrrh from Mount Gilead into Egypt; and Egypt's future lord is sold unto the merchants for twenty pieces of silver, by his savage brethren, who dipped his garment in blood to show it to their father and cloak their matchless villainy by pretending that some wild beast had devoured him. Such were once the men, O ye Jews, in whom ye glory as your progenitors! The innocent sufferer is sold a second time to Potiphar in Egypt, in whose service he acquitted himself so well as to gain the good graces of his master, who reposed in him the most entire confidence and entrusted him with the sole management of his affairs. But soon, alas! The temptations of his mistress are likely to prove no less dangerous than the malice of his brethren. He preserved indeed his chastity by the fear of the Lord, but incurring the undeserved suspicion of a base crime, he is committed to the dungeon by his too partial master as before he had been cast into the pit by his cruel brethren. But "the king sent and loosed him; even the ruler of the people, and let him go free" (Ps. 105:20). For as he exposed himself to all his troublesome adventurers by telling his own dreams, so by his interpreting the dreams of others he laid the foundation of his subsequent grandeur. On a sudden his prison is turned a palace, his irons a chain of gold. Potiphar's servant is become Potiphar's lord. He "whose feet they hurt with fetters" now binds the "princes at his pleasure" and teaches "his senators wisdom" (Ps. 105:18, 22). And as he moves along the crowded streets, a herald proclaims before him, "Bow the knee" (Gen. 41:43). And now he feeds from his hoarded granaries the starving nations, for he wisely provided against the approach of the famine he foretold. The subjects of Pharaoh acknowledge him the savior of their lives. His unkind brethren, impelled by hunger and hard necessity, come also among the supplicants, to fulfill his dreams, which they vainly imagined to render forever abortive. He remembered the traces of their countenances, and by various harsh methods he explores the sincerity of their repentance and acquaints himself with the circumstances of their family. At last his bowels yearning toward them, and piteous of their misery, as being sufficiently chastised, he makes himself known to them, buries in oblivion their past misdemeanors, and transports them to dwell with him, where he nourishes them like a father in the midst of a terrible and extensive famine. And thus what was intended by the wickedness of men as means of extirpating the name of Joseph out of the earth was overruled, by the wisdom of God, for bringing about his glorious exaltation, for saving the lives of much people, and even the lives of those who sought his death.

Jesus the True Joseph
Which things are an allegory, for Jesus Christ is the true Joseph if you view Him as a beloved Son, an affectionate brother, a trusty servant, an illuminated prophet, a resister of temptations, a forgiver of injuries, but chiefly if you consider Him as an innocent sufferer, an exalted prince, and a universal Savior.

Like Joseph, he was a *beloved Son*, whom God the Father has blessed above all His brethren. Jacob made for Joseph a garment of divers colors, and God prepared for Christ a body curiously wrought in the lower parts of the earth.

Like Joseph, He is an *affectionate brother*. He came to seek His brethren in the wilderness of this world, though they received Him not. He knows them when they know not Him, and His bowels yearn toward them, even when He seems severe. He may deal roughly with them at first, but He will have mercy upon them at last. He liberally supplies their wants without money and without price, and at last will bring them to dwell with Him in the heavenly Canaan, where they shall behold His glory and be abundantly satisfied with the fatness of His house.

Like Joseph, He was a *trusty servant*, acquitting Himself dexterously in every part of the work that was given Him to do, even as the prophet also foretells, "Behold, my servant shall deal prudently, he shall be exalted and extolled, and be very high" (Isa. 52:13).

Like Joseph, He is a *most illuminated prophet*, in whom the Spirit of God is, none so discreet and wise as He, the true Zaphnath-paaneah,[1] or revealer of secrets, who is worthy to take the sealed book of God's decrees and open its seven seals (Rev. 5:5).

Like Joseph, He was a *resister of temptations*, for He was solicited in vain to spiritual adultery by the great enemy of salvation when he said unto Him, "All these will I give Thee, if Thou wilt fall down and worship me." Though this harlot world hath cast down wounded and slain many strong men, our Joseph overcame her. His heart declined not to her ways; He went not astray in her paths, though in the encounter He was stripped of His mortal life, which He willingly resigned.

Like Joseph, He was and is a *forgiver of injuries*: for as on the cross He implored forgiveness to His murderers with His expiring breath, so on the throne He gave repentance unto Israel and remission of sin, many of them whose hand had been very deep in that bloody tragedy of His crucifixion being brought to a sincere profession, that "[they were] verily guilty concerning [their] brother" (Gen. 42:21), and the blood which they impiously shed spoke "better things than that of Abel" (Heb. 12:24).

---

1. Editor's note: *Zaphnath-paaneah* is the name given to Joseph by Pharaoh (Gen. 41:45). The etymology is obscure, but it is taken by most commentators to mean "the one to whom mysteries are revealed."

Jesus the Innocent Sufferer
But chiefly let us view Him as an *innocent sufferer*, whose sufferings issued in glory to Himself and universal good to men. Joseph is mortally hated of His brethren, and the butt of their envy, because He exposed their wicked courses and foretold His own advancement. For these same reasons was Jesus Christ hated by the Jews, and Pilate knew that for envy they delivered Him. Joseph was derided of his brethren as an idle fantastic dreamer, and Jesus Christ was esteemed a doting enthusiast, a madman, and one beside Himself. Joseph, his brethren conspired against him to take away his life; and of Jesus Christ it is prophesied, "Why do the heathen rage, and the people imagine a vain thing?… against the LORD, and against his anointed?" (Ps. 2:1–2). Joseph's brethren stripped him of his garment which his father made for him, and of Jesus Christ it is said, "They parted my raiment among them, and for my vesture they did cast lots" (John 19:24, quoting Ps. 22:18). Joseph was cast into a pit, but he remained not long there; Jesus Christ was laid in the grave, but He saw no corruption. Joseph was sold for a servant by the advice of the patriarch Judah, and Jesus Christ was, by the apostle Judas, sold for thirty pieces of silver, the price of a slave: a goodly price He was prized at by them! Joseph was unjustly accused in Egypt and cast into a dungeon with two noted criminals, Pharaoh's butler and baker; Jesus Christ was unjustly condemned in Canaan and crucified between two thieves. Joseph adjudged the one criminal to death and the other to life from the same omens; Jesus Christ adjudged one of the thieves to everlasting life, while the other was allowed to perish after the same deserts. Joseph entreated the person whom he delivered to remember him when he came to his glory, but the person whom Jesus Christ delivered prayed Him, "Lord, remember me when thou comest into thy kingdom." Joseph indeed could but foretell his companion's deliverance, but Jesus Christ effected by His own power what He foretold: "Today shalt thou be with me in paradise" (Luke 23:42–43).

Jesus the Exalted Prince
Such were the patriarch's unparalleled afflictions. But as he soon emerged from these deep plunges of adversity, becoming of a forlorn prisoner a prime minister of state, so Jesus Christ was "taken from prison and from judgment" (Isa. 53:8) and receives from God the Father honor and glory and "a name which is above every name: that at the name of Jesus every knee should bow, of things in heaven, and things in earth, and things under the earth; and that every tongue should confess that Jesus Christ is Lord, to the glory of God the Father" (Phil. 2:9–11). Behold, ye mistaken Jews, how vain were all your machinations to frustrate His predictions. Even you yourselves became subservient to fulfill the grand design when you killed the Prince of life, who was, by suffering death, to enter into His glory. Here the patriarch's speech to his penitent brethren may fitly be applied: "As for you, ye thought evil against me; but God meant it unto good, to bring to pass, as it is this day, to save much people alive" (Gen. 50:20).

Jesus the Savior of the World
For as the sufferings and glory of Joseph issued in the common salvation of the lives of Pharaoh's subjects and the family of Jacob, who was "a Syrian ready to perish" (Deut. 26:5), even so Thy sufferings and Thy glory, O Thou once humbled but now exalted Redeemer, were ordained for the salvation of the world, both Jews and Gentiles, from a far more dreadful destruction than a famine of bread or water (John 4:42; 1 John 4:14)! Go unto this Joseph for the supply of your numerous wants, ye that are ready to perish. His fullness shall never be exhausted, be their number ever so great who receive out of it. O that His glory might be the joy of our heart and the grand theme of every tongue. With what cheerfulness ought we to forsake the stuff of all terrestrial things, when Joseph is alive, that we may be with Him where He is and enjoy these blessings that are "on the head of" *Jesus Christ* "and on the crown of the head of him that was separate from his brethren" (Gen. 49:26)!

Moses
Exodus 3

Though Christ and Moses may seem indeed, in one view, to be as unlike one another as the gospel and the law, as the ministration of righteousness and the ministration of condemnation, we may, however, observe in the character and history of this extraordinary man a great resemblance to that of Jesus Christ, whether we consider him as a deliverer, a mediator, a lawgiver, or a prophet.

Moses the Deliverer
First, let us view Moses as a deliverer of his nation from the bondage of Egypt. To this end he was born, and when his life was sought by a bloody tyrant, who murdered his fellow-infants, he was miraculously preserved by his reputed mother, who gave him a royal education. But when he was come to years and capable of judging for himself, he despised the pleasures of a court and chose rather to claim kindred with oppressed slaves, because they were the people of God, than with the daughter of Pharaoh, by whose right perhaps he might have inherited the crown of Egypt. At last, though his very brethren thrust him away, saying, "Who made thee a ruler and a judge?" (Acts 7:27), he accomplishes their rescue from the land of Nile, spoiling the Egyptians of their gold and silver, destroying their firstborn, and drowning in the Red Sea the flower of their army—and all this by means of the blood of a lamb which he shed and by his wonder-working rod.

Even so the birth of the deliverer, who came to Zion to rescue from the oppression of far worse enemies than the Egyptians or the Romans, was signalized with the cruel butchering of the infants in Bethlehem by Herod's ministers of blood. But the persecuted babe finds a safe retreat in Egypt, whither He was conveyed by the guardian care of His supposed father. And when He was come to years he disdained an earthly crown, when the Jews would have taken him by force, and made him a king, as before he had in a sort left for a time the court of heaven, the bosom of his Father, and the songs of hymning cherubims, to endure, in these regions of mortality, affliction for the people of God: for as Moses had a respect to the recompense of reward, so He, for "the joy that was set before him endured the cross, and despis[ed] the shame" (Heb. 12:2). And though His brethren "understood not…at the first" (John 12:16) that "God by his hand would deliver them" (Acts 7:25), and refused Him as an imposter, at last He accomplishes their redemption from the cruel bondage of the devil, whose power He destroyed by shedding His own blood and by sending the rod of His strength out of Zion (Ps. 110:2). By these despised means does the Captain of salvation bring many sons to glory, through racing sea of affliction, through waste and howling wildernesses of various temptations, till they arrive in that happy country which God has espied for them, which is the glory of all lands (Heb. 2:10).

Moses the Mediator
As by a prophet the Lord brought Israel out of Egypt, it is further to be observed that he acted the part of a mediator between God and Israel, both when they fought with Amalek, when they received the law, and when they made the calf in Horeb: in all which instances he may be viewed as a lively type of the one mediator between God and man, the man Christ Jesus.

When the militant church is fighting in the valley of this world, as an Amalek shall never be wanting from generation to generation, their victory depends not so much on their own prowess and skill as on the lifting up the hands of our great Intercessor, who, like Moses, appears in the presence of God upon a high mountain and eminent, even far above all heavens. Behold, all ye who are fighting the good fight of faith, how your great Mediator's hands are lifted up toward the throne of God. The hands of Moses could not long endure to be stretched out; they were heavy and weak and behoved to be strengthened and supported. But Jesus Christ, He faints not, neither is weary, though His hands be stretched out still: therefore shall ye prevail who fight under His banner, and have reason to say, "Thanks be to God, which giveth us the victory through our Lord Jesus Christ" (1 Cor. 15:57).

And as the law was ordained by angels in the hand of Moses as a mediator (for they to whom it was published were afraid by reason of the fire and dreadful sound which they heard, and went not up to the mount), so Jesus Christ our Lord stands betwixt the terrible majesty of an angry God and feeble guilty man, unable to appear in the presence of His glory. Like Moses, He engaged His heart to approach unto God. *But Moses only reported the law to the people; He fulfilled the law.* Moses quaked, and Christ was sore amazed, insomuch that He sweated blood from all the pores of His body. Be not afraid, ye redeemed of the Lord: Jesus tells you, "Ye believe in God, believe also in me" (John 14:1). Though our God be a consuming fire, the all-gracious Mediator hath quenched the flames and hushed the storm of wrath by His seasonable interposition, and the fiery law is now turned into a directing light.

And, lastly, Moses acted the part of a mediator when they made the calf in Horeb. When the anger of the Lord was justly incensed against them for that enormous crime, Moses said unto the people, "I will go up unto the LORD; peradventure I shall make an atonement for your sin. And Moses returned unto the LORD, and said, Oh, this people have sinned a great sin.... Yet now, if thou wilt forgive their sin—; and if not, blot me, I pray thee, out of thy book which thou hast written" (Ex. 32:30–31, 32). Perhaps he intended to seek that the almighty vengeance might rather fall on his own head than that the whole nation should perish, though he was not certain whether the offered propitiation would be accepted. But Jesus Christ has not only offered Himself to die for the guilty race but has actually made the atonement which Moses proposed to make and is set forth for a propitiation through faith in His blood.

Moses the Lawgiver

Next, let us view him as a lawgiver, as the children of Israel sung, "Moses commanded us a law, even the inheritance of the congregation of Jacob. And he was king in Jeshurun" (Deut. 33:4–5). But we Christians may say, in the language of the prophet, "The LORD is our judge, the LORD is our lawgiver, the LORD is our king; he will save us" (Isa. 33:22). A law is now gone forth of Zion, but Moses, not like thine, consisting of carnal ordinances—a law not of works but of faith, a law for which the isles of the Gentiles shall wait (Isa. 42:4; 66:19), a law which is not so much obeyed by doing as by believing and which will never stand in need of reformation or repeal.

Moses the Prophet

But, lastly, let us view him in his prophetic character, of whom it is testified, "There arose not a prophet since in Israel like unto Moses, whom the LORD knew face to face" (Deut. 34:10). Yet Moses truly said unto the fathers, "The LORD thy God will raise up unto thee a Prophet from the midst of thee, of thy brethren, like unto me; unto him ye shall hearken" (Deut. 18:15). Though we had not the express authority of an apostle for the application of this prediction to the Apostle and High Priest of our profession, we can scarcely be at loss to see how it can agree to none other. He, He is that prophet that should come unto the world, of whom Moses wrote, and who is like unto him, if you consider:

The stock from whence He sprung; for He was raised from among His brethren, not assuming the nature of angels but the nature of man, and of the seed of Abraham.

The meekness of His temper, which excelled the meekness of Moses, as far as the meekness of Moses excelled the meekness of other men (Num. 12:3). The Hebrew lawgiver, meek as he was, cannot be altogether free from sallies of impatience; but the meek and lowly Jesus, who calls us to learn of Him, was never indecently transported with rage, nor uttered one word unadvisedly with His lips, though upon the most provoking occasion.

The luster of His face. For not to mention His transfiguration on the mount, when His face did shine as the sun (Matt. 17:2), He is in His divine person the brightness of His Father's glory (Heb. 1:3), which, like Moses, He covered with the veil of His flesh when He descended into our world, that He might be qualified for holding familiar converse with men upon earth, His terror not making them afraid. For if the face of Moses the servant did shine with such dazzling glory by a short abode in the presence of Jehovah on an earthly mount that the Israelites could not endure to behold him without a veil (Ex. 34:29–33), how much less could the feeble eyes of mortal men have endured the face of Christ the Son, who abideth from everlasting in the presence of Jehovah, was daily His delight, had He shone forth, in all the blaze of deity, without the thick veil of His flesh?

The clearness of His manifestations. Of Moses indeed it is said, "With him will I speak mouth to mouth," even apparently, and not in dark speeches, and the similitude of the Lord shall he behold (Num. 12:8), whereas it was usual for the prophets of inferior rank to receive the intimations of the divine will in dreams when they were asleep, and ecstasies when awake. But of this prophet in the New Testament church His harbinger declares, "No man hath seen God at any time; the only begotten Son, which is in the bosom of the Father, he hath declared him" (John 1:18).

His fidelity in executing His commission, for the words the Father gave unto Him, He gave unto them; and as the Father gave Him commandment, so He spake. "Moses verily was faithful in all his house, as a servant...but Christ as a son over his own house" (Heb. 3:5–6).

The opposition He met with from Jews and Gentiles. He endured the contradiction of sinners against Himself, even as Jannes and Jambres withstood Moses (2 Tim. 3:8). And as His nearest relations quarreled with Him for marrying Zipporah, the Ethiopian woman (Num. 12:1), so did the Jews with Christ for espousing the Gentile church.

The miracles He wrought. "It was never so seen in Israel" (Matt. 9:33). Like Moses, He fed the Israelites in the wilderness, and their living was as miraculous as their eating.

Moses and Christ
What Moses did literally, the same Christ does spiritually for the beloved Israel. He sweetens their bitter waters, cures their diseases, and supplies their wants. Like Moses He fasted forty days, and like Moses He died at the commandment of the Lord.

8

The Priesthood
Exodus 29

As the sun paints the clouds with a variety of glorious colors, which in their own nature are but dark and lowering vapors exhaled from the earth, so when the Son of righteousness arises, even the carnal ordinances and commandments of the law, dark and earthly as they seem, are gilded by His beams and wear a smiling appearance. By His kindly influence, who is the Light of the World, the most barren places of the Scripture rejoice and blossom as the rose.

What portion of sacred writ is more apt to be perused without edification and delight than what relates to the Levitical priesthood: the qualifications of their persons, their apparel, their consecration, and the different parts of their function? And indeed it must be confessed a very hard task to reconcile with the wisdom of God the enjoining such numberless rites, purely for their own sake. But when we consider that Aaron, and his successors, were figures of our Great High Priest, we must acknowledge that these injunctions are neither unworthy of God nor useless to man but are profitable for doctrine and instruction in righteousness. We shall instance in a few things.

The Aaronic Priesthood and Christ
And, first, we shall take notice of the laws relating to the persons of Aaron and his sons. Whosoever he was that approached to God in the character of a high priest, he behoved according to the law of Moses to be of the stock of Israel, the tribe of Levi, the family of Aaron:

his genealogy, well attested; his body, sound; his life, temperate (for he was not to drink wine or other intoxicating liquors); his wife must be either a virgin or the widow of a priest but by no means a divorced woman or a harlot; and, lastly, it was absolutely forbidden that he should go out of the sanctuary to mourn for the dead, unless they were his nearest relations.

Let us apply these things to our High Priest. It must indeed be acknowledged that Jesus was neither of the tribe of Levi nor family of Aaron, *for it is evident our Lord sprang out of Judah, and Moses says nothing of the priesthood belonging to that tribe*. In this respect, to be sure, He differs from them in a very essential point, which, however it disqualified Him from officiating in the temple (for if He were on earth He should not be a priest) yet does not in the least infer His incapacity to be a priest of higher order than the order of Aaron—namely, the order of Melchizedek, *who joined in one person the priest and the king*. Jesus never assumed the character and office of a Levitical priest when He was upon earth, as indeed He could not have any claim upon it. What shall we say then? That He is inferior to Aaron and his successors upon this account? Nay, *the difference of His tribe is the most convincing proof of the supereminence of His order*. Like Aaron, He was taken from among men and was a Hebrew of the Hebrews, and never any priest of them all could boast of such illustrious pedigree as Jesus Christ. Which of them all was born of a virgin? And to which of them said God at any time, "Thou art my Son, this day have I begotten thee" (Heb. 1:5, quoting Ps. 2:7)?

The *genealogy* of the ancient priests behoved to be firmly documented, but they had no such illustrious proofs of their being the sons of Levi as Christ had of His being the Son of God, which His Father attested, both by the voice from heaven and by the mighty works He enabled Him to do.

The *soundness of their body* was no doubt intended to prefigure the integrity and perfection of Jesus Christ in His soul, for the least deformity here had rendered Him utterly incapable of propitiating the deity by the sacrifice of Himself: for such a high priest became us, who though falsely accused of many sins was never convicted of any but was holy, harmless, undefiled, separate from sinners, and "a lamb without blemish and without spot" (1 Peter 1:19), even in the pure eyes of God.

Their *restriction to marry a wife in her virginity* may perhaps denote that the human nature which our Great High Priest, Jesus the Son of God, deigned to wed to His divine person was not deflowered with sin, but a pure, incorruptible, and holy thing. But, beyond all doubt, we are naturally led to think of the whole church, and every member of that society, being presented as chaste virgins unto Christ. In vain does the Church of Rome claim the high prerogative of being the only spouse of Christ. Hear what the apostle declares of the followers of the Lamb: "These are they which were not defiled with women; for they are virgins…. These were redeemed from among men, being the firstfruits unto God and to the Lamb" (Rev. 14:4).

The *abstinence from wine and strong drink*, which was commanded, was not only designed to inculcate the strictest temperance (which is a most necessary virtue to the discharge of any important trust that requires the faculties of the mind to be in their most vigorous state), but it may be also viewed as an implicit intimation of that perfect command of Himself which our High Priest had in the discharging of His office, never forgetting what He was about in the smallest instance, being always found of quick understanding in the fear of the Lord, but by no means a gluttonous man and "a winebibber" as the hypocritical Pharisees maliciously affirmed (Matt. 11:19). The prohibition of going out of the sanctuary to mourn for the dead (Lev. 21:11–12) was a prediction that when Jesus Christ should pass into the heavenly sanctuary, He should leave all His sorrows behind Him and dwell forever in the presence of God, where there is fullness of joy. Moreover, it clearly signifies that He was to abolish death and the grave. Henceforth let no unmanly tear be shed for the blessed dead who die in the Lord (Rev. 14:13). That most calamitous event to the eye of sense is to the eye of faith the most happy revolution in the lot of the just.

The Significance of the Priestly Garments

Nor are the laws about their priestly garments less instructive and significant. The curious materials of the *ephod* of gold, blue, purple, and scarlet might represent the unsearchable riches of Christ and the luster of those divine graces which adorned His sacred humanity.

The names of the twelve tribes he bore first upon his shoulders and then upon his *breastplate*, as a memorial before the Lord continually, engraved on precious stones and disposed in comely order, is no obscure emblem of the saints, whom our High Priest carries both on the shoulders of His Almighty power and on the breast of cordial love, according to the most pathetic prayers of the spouse, "Set me as a seal upon thine heart, as a seal upon thine arm" (Song 8:6). These names were engraved on precious stones: for such are all His saints, though disallowed of men and trampled underfoot as naughty pebbles, yet are they chosen of God and precious, and they shall be His in the day that He makes up His jewels (Mal. 3:17; 1 Peter 2:4). No tribe was wanting in that most costly breastplate: for Jesus Christ knows them by name whom He redeems, both great and small, and there is no respect of persons. They were arranged in comely order, for He is not "the author of confusion, but of peace, as in all the churches of the saints" (1 Cor. 14:33). They were firmly set, and not slightly put into the breastplate, for all the faithful are so firmly united unto Jesus Christ that not the smallest jewel can be picked from the breastplate of our Aaron by the joint efforts of earth and hell. It was not lawful for the Israelites to enter into the Most Holy Place in their own persons, but in the person of their high priest they entered every year, as their names were graven on his shoulders and heart and presented unto Jehovah. Even so, in Jesus Christ the holy Christian nation who live upon the earth are entered into the holiest of all and even set down with Him in heavenly places.

Shall we mention next the *Urim and the Thummim* that Moses was commanded to put into the breastplate of Aaron (Ex. 28:30)? If we cannot certainly determine the nature or form of this divine workmanship denoted by such an uncommon phrase, we are certain however that in Jesus Christ we have that priest who stands up with Urim and Thummim and bears the judgment of Israel before the Lord continually. In Him are found the clearest light of wisdom and the greatest perfection of holiness. In Him that prayer is fully answered, "Give the king thy judgments, O God, and thy righteousness unto the king's son" (Ps. 72:1). The curious girdle signifies the alacrity wherewith our High Priest discharged every part of His office; for girding up the loins of His mind, He did with all His might what His hand found. Aaron's girdle was indeed of costly texture, gold and purple, blue and scarlet. But of Jesus Christ it was prophesied, "Righteousness shall be the girdle of his loins, and faithfulness the girdle of his reins" (Isa. 11:5). The beloved apostle John beheld Him equipped with this priestly ornament when he saw Him in the visions of God walking in the midst of the seven golden candlesticks, clothed with a long white garment down to the foot, and girt about the chest with a golden girdle (Rev. 1:12–13).

The *golden bells* suspended around the hem of Aaron's under robe may signify the sweet sound of the gospel which is gone into all the earth. O greatly blest are the people who hear this joyful sound, sweeter to the ear of faith than music in its softest strains to the ear of the body, an undoubted sign that our High Priest is alive though we see Him not and lives forever in the presence of Jehovah to make intercession for us. The *pomegranates* that were curiously wrought betwixt the bells, and equal to them in number, may be an emblem of those fruits of righteousness with which the preaching of the gospel is attended.

The fair *miter* that adorned his head, with *the venerable inscription on the plate of gold* surrounding his temples, may put us in mind of Jesus Christ, who is the only crowned priest, and not only holy but holiness itself unto the Lord; yea, He is Himself the holy Jehovah and fountain of holiness unto His people, for "this is his name whereby he shall be called, The LORD OUR RIGHTEOUSNESS" (Jer. 23:6).

Such were the garments for glory and beauty that the typical priesthood was commanded to wear, and such their mystical signification. Let us come next to the manner of their consecration.

The Consecration of the Priestly Garments

The Hebrew lawgiver is directed to bring Aaron and his sons to the door of the tabernacle of the congregation, where they were washed with water; arrayed with the priestly vestments; anointed with the costly oil, which it was death to counterfeit; and lastly, sanctified by the offering up of peculiar sacrifices, whose blood was put upon the extreme parts of their bodies.

Though every minute circumstance in these venerable rites may not be capable of application to Jesus Christ, it is sufficient if we can observe a general analogy. Aaron was washed in water to signify that he was before polluted, and Christ was baptized, not indeed because He was Himself polluted but as it became Him to fulfill all righteousness. Aaron was arrayed with the appointed vestment, and Christ was clothed with the garment of our flesh, curiously wrought in the lower parts of the earth. Aaron was anointed with oil, wherewith the inferior priests were but sprinkled, but Christ is anointed with the Holy Spirit, which God gives not by measure unto Him. Aaron was consecrated with the blood of beasts, but Christ was sanctified by His own blood and made perfect through sufferings, by which He learned obedience, though He was the Son of God.

The Roles of the Priestly Function

The different parts of their function is the last thing that demands our attention. Every high priest taken from among men in the manner above described is ordained for men in things pertaining unto God and to offer both gifts and sacrifices for sin. This indeed was the most distinguishing part of their office and fundamental to all other functions that are appropriated to them. However, they were also appointed to bless the people, to pray for them, to instruct them in the knowledge of the divine will, to oversee the service of the tabernacle, to blow the trumpets both in peace and war, and to judge betwixt the clean and the unclean.

But we see Jesus our high priest giving Himself an offering and a sacrifice of sweet-smelling savor, more graceful unto God and more appeasing to His incensed justice than all the victims that ever smoked in the worldly sanctuary or than all the gifts that were ever presented there or than all the incense that ever fumed from the golden censer. Put off your robes, ye legal priesthood; your work is finished, your office entirely superseded. What ye could not do by multiplied oblations, Jesus Christ has done by one sacrifice. The veil is now rent and the temple now destroyed. The shadow has given place to the substance. Perhaps it was not without a mystic signification that Zacharias, a priest of Aaron's order and the father of John, the harbinger of Christ, was struck dumb when officiating in the temple so that he could not speak unto the people when he came forth of the Holy Place. Might it not be a silent omen that a dispensation was now commencing in the days of Messiah wherein none of Aaron's order should open their mouths any more to bless the people, saying, "The LORD bless thee, and keep thee: the LORD make his face to shine upon thee, and be gracious unto thee: the LORD lift up his countenance upon thee, and give thee peace" (Num. 6:24–26)? Jesus is that priest whom God hath sent to bless us, who prays for His people, whose lips keep knowledge to instruct us in the will of God. Jesus is that priest who oversees the service of the tabernacle, being head over all things to the church, which is His body. Jesus is that priest who now blows the great trumpet of the gospel and who shall descend shortly from heaven with a shout, with the voice of the archangel, and with the trump of God (1 Thess. 4:16) to gather the congregation of the righteous. Then all who have Him not for their priest to wash and sprinkle them with His hyssop and blood (Ps. 51:7) shall have Him for their priest to pronounce them "utterly unclean" (Lev. 13:44).

Joshua

Joshua 1:1–9

The name of Joshua and Jesus are scarcely more like than their achievements. This captain, so famous in the sacred history, was nominated to be the successor of Moses and ordained of God's command to this high post in the presence of all the congregation of Israel. He received the name of Joshua before, when sent to spy out the land, his former name being Oshea (Num. 13:8, 16), and he is the first of the typical persons who was called by the very name, by which, in future ages, a greater Savior than he was commonly known (Matt. 1:21). Perhaps it was not without its meaning that he was the servant before he was the successor of Moses, for it might signify that our Jesus was the first to become the servant of the law before He should abolish it. But passing this, let us take a more particular notice of the most memorable passages of that marvelous campaign.

Crossing the Jordan
And the first thing that presents itself to our view is his passing the Jordan, which was miraculously driven back to afford a safe passage to the chosen people. In this river God was pleased for the first time to magnify His servant Joshua in the sight of all the tribes of Israel, and in this river it pleased God to give the first most public testimony to Jesus Christ, when the heavens seemed to open at His baptism, and the Holy Spirit descended in the likeness of a dove, and "a voice from the excellent glory" proclaimed His high character:

"This is my beloved Son, in whom I am well pleased" (2 Peter 1:17). But the chief thing to be observed here is the resemblance betwixt the passage of Israel over Jordan into the Promised Land under the conduct of Joshua and the passage of all the redeemed through death into the heavenly inheritance. Long had they traversed the vast and howling wilderness, the haunt of ravenous beasts and poisonous serpents, where their hearts many a time were like to faint for thirst and hunger; but now the land flowing with milk and honey receives them, and their wanderings in the pathless desert are forever ended. Though Jordan overflows his banks, their march is not obstructed. O powerful presence of JEHOVAH! "The sea saw it, and fled: Jordan was driven back" (Ps. 114:3). And now that they have taken their farewell of the weary wilderness, we hear no more of the miraculous cloud that conducted them nor of the manna that fed them forty years.

Such is the safety of all true Israelites when marching to their promised rest under the conduct of the Captain of their salvation. Death is the Jordan through which they pass from the wilderness of this world into the blissful regions of immortality. But when they pass through these waters, they shall not overflow them; for He who dries up the waters of the sea by His rebuke will be graciously present with them till they gain the safe shore of Immanuel's land. Then shall the ordinances be discontinued and the Bible superseded, which are so necessary in their wandering state to support their lives and guide their paths, as the cloud vanished and the manna ceased when the fine wheat of Canaan supplied the Israelites with food, according to the promise. It is not Moses, but Joshua, who leads them through Jordan. Jesus, Thou art the only conqueror of death. What will they do when they come to the swellings of Jordan, who are not under Thy auspicious conduct? Thanks be to God who gives us this victory over death, not through Moses, or the law, but through Jesus Christ our Lord. Twelve stones are left by the Hebrew captain as a memorial of this great deliverance, and twelve apostles were appointed by the Captain of our salvation to be witnesses of all things which He did both in the land of the Jews and in Jerusalem.

The Walls of Jericho

From the banks of Jordan let us now come to the walls of Jericho, the accursed city. Never was town or garrison besieged in such a manner before or since; no mounds are raised, no battering rams are applied to the walls, no attempts are made to sap the foundations, but, by the direction of the Lord of Hosts, the army marches in silent parade round the walls. Their martial music is not the sound of their silver trumpets but of ram horns blown by their priests. Ridiculous, weak, and foolish as this new method of assault might seem to the unbelieving sinners of Jericho, they soon found that the weakness of God is stronger than men and that the most contemptible means, when God ordains them, shall gain their end in spite of all opposition. "What ailed thee, O thou sea, that thou fleddest? thou Jordan, that thou wast driven back?" (Ps. 114:5), and ye walls of Jericho, that ye fell flat to the ground when compassed seven days? It was not owing to the sword of Israel, nor even to the sound of the trumpets, but to the power of Israel's God accompanying this feeble mean prescribed for the trial of their faith and proof of their obedience. For—O the power of faith!—had their walls threatened the clouds and been harder than adamant, firmer than brass, down must they tumble on the evening of the seventh day. Thus are the strongholds of sin, and every high thing that exalts itself against the New Testament Joshua, cast down by the mighty weapons of the Christian warfare, which are not carnal. The feeble voice of the gospel when faithfully preached, though not with a silver sound or with excellency of speech, shall be mighty through God to triumph over all opposition: so it was in the days of the apostles, so it has been in every distant age, and so it shall be till the victory is complete. Thus, Babylon, shall thy proud towers be leveled with the ground, though seemingly fearless of assaults: "For the day of the LORD of hosts shall be upon every one that is proud and lofty, and upon every one that is lifted up; and he shall be brought low," and "upon every high tower, and upon every fenced wall" (Isa. 2:12, 15). Though the kings of the earth should give their "power and strength unto the beast" (Rev. 17:13), our Joshua shall prevail, by the foolishness of preaching, and the sound of the gospel-trumpet; and at the appointed time the strong-lunged angel shall cry, "Babylon the great is fallen, is fallen" (Rev. 18:2).

The Saving of Rahab

The saving of Rahab and her household is the next remarkable occurrence. Who would have expected to find in this city of destruction even a strong believer, whose faith should be celebrated by one apostle and her works by another? And who should have also the honor to make one of that illustrious hue from whence the Messiah should arise? But so it was. Though once a notorious sinner, and called *Rahab the harlot* to this day, yet she was a believer of the promise that God made to Israel and proved by her works that her faith was genuine: for protecting the messengers of Joshua, at the hazard of her life, she preferred the interests of the church of God to those of her country, which she knew very well was impossible to be saved. Though we can by no means justify the dissimulation by which she saved the spies from the pursuivants[1] of the king of Jericho, yet God has forgiven those blamable parts of her conduct of which she has long since truly repented.

Jesus Our Better Joshua

Well does Joshua answer his name, in saving not the race of Israel only, but Rahab, though a cursed Canaanite, with all her household, though sinners of the Gentiles. Was it not a dark prelude of Jesus Christ, our better Joshua, His saving the Gentile world from the wrath to come as well as the preserved of Jacob? Might it not portend that publicans and harlots and such notorious sinners should be received among the first into His heavenly kingdom? And that the harlot Gentiles, who formerly were serving divers lusts and living in the most abominable idolatries, should be incorporated into the holy society of the church and espoused as a chaste bride to Jesus Christ,

---

1. Editor's note: "Pursuivants" are junior officers of heraldic authorities, such as the College of Arms in England or the Court of the Lord Lyon in Scotland.

as Rahab became a proselyte to the Jewish religion and the wife of Salmon (Matt. 1:5), an illustrious prince in the chief of their tribes? Perhaps the scarlet thread which, at the direction of the spies, she hung forth of the window as a discriminating signal by which all under her roof were exempted from the dismal desolation, perhaps, I say, it might be an intimation, though a very obscure one, that the shedding of Christ's red blood should prove the means of salvation to the Gentile world and of making peace betwixt the Jews and them, who were formerly at variance and harbored mutual hatred. Red was the color of salvation to Israel in Egypt, when sprinkling their doors with blood protected them from the destroying angel's sword, and red is the color of salvation to Rahab in Canaan, when the hanging a scarlet thread over her windows was her security from the destroying sword of Israel. Happy they who have the blood of Christ upon them, and not *for destruction* (as the Jews who murdered Him and imprecated this dreadful vengeance on themselves, Matt. 27:25) but *for salvation* (as all them who believe). Rahab's safety was confirmed by the oath of men, but theirs by the oath of God, for whom it is impossible to lie (Heb. 6:18). Destruction approaches not these doors; death enters not these windows where the blood of Christ is found.

Promised Land and Promised Rest
In vain did the kings of Canaan conspire to oppose the victorious Joshua after the destruction of Jericho, for at last he bids his captains set their feet upon the necks of their hostile princes, in token of full conquest. Nor was it strange he should be able to do this, when the very heavens befriended him by casting down prodigious hailstones to kill his flying enemies and their most glorious luminaries, the sun and moon, were obedient to his voice and stood still in their habitation, till the vengeance written was executed upon the devoted nations. Such is that complete victory over all the enemies of God and His people which he shall gain who goes forth conquering and to conquer. It is the distinguished honor of all His faithful soldiers to tread upon the devil, the world, and the lusts of the flesh. These are

the dragons and the lions which they trample under their feet; these are the kings they bind with chains; these are the nations they shall dash in shivers as a potter's vessel with a rod of iron. And a time is coming when the upright shall have dominion over the wicked, for so is His will whom not only the sun and moon but all the numerous hosts of heaven and earth obey.

At last the favored nation of the Jews are brought into their promised rest, under the conduct of their valiant general. He puts them in quiet possession of that happy country which He had before spied out for them. This Moses could not do. So Jesus Christ hath introduced us not into a temporal rest, like thine, O Joshua, but into a spiritual and eternal rest, an incorruptible and undefiled inheritance, which the law could not do, having become weak through the flesh.

10

Samson

Judges 16:23–31

Let us now glance at the prodigious feats of Samson, that mighty and renowned judge of Israel, whose birth, life, and death were all so extraordinary that, as some suppose, the fabulous tales of Hercules, so famous in Greece, are but this true history metamorphosed and dashed with fiction. It may indeed seem odd to insert a person whose vices were so glaring and unmanly in the catalogue of the illustrious types of Jesus Christ, for the hints of his religious and saintly disposition in the history of the judges are so dubious and sparing that one would be tempted to suspect whether he was a saint at all. But the honorable character he was vested with by God, and the signal deliverances of his people he was enabled to achieve, afford us more than a presumption that he was not wholly a stranger to the fear of the Lord. Above all, his reputation as a believer is firmly established by a New Testament writer, who ranks him among the eminent worthies who lived and died in faith, "who through faith subdued kingdoms, wrought righteousness, obtained promises, stopped the mouths of lions, quenched the violence of fire, escaped the edge of the sword, out of weakness were made strong, waxed valiant in fight, turned to flight the armies of the aliens" (Heb. 11:33–34). Be it so that, on account of the criminal weakness of his mind, which wrought his own destruction, he is rather a figure of the sinner, yet if we consider the prodigious strength of his body, which wrought salvation in Israel, he is justly esteemed a figure of the Savior.

The Circumstances of Samson's Birth

The circumstances of Samson's birth so much resemble those of Jesus Christ that we can scarcely pass them over in silence (Judg. 13). Both Jesus Christ and he were conceived in an extraordinary manner beside the course of nature; their birth and future importance were declared by a messenger from the invisible world, to their female parents, that they should be Nazarites unto God and saviors of Israel. Only whereas Samson's mother was but a barren spouse, the mother of Jesus was an unspotted virgin. The angel that appeared to Manoah's wife refused to tell his name when importuned, but the angel who appeared to the wife of Joseph declared who he was without being asked. Samson was but a legal Nazarite from the womb, and many a time he seems to have acted a part very unworthy of such a sacred name.

But Jesus Christ was that in substance which Samson, and other Nazarites, were only in shadow: "holy, harmless, undefiled, separate from sinners" (Heb. 7:26) and "purer than snow,…whiter than milk,…more ruddy in body than rubies, [and] their polishing was of sapphire" (Lam. 4:7). He was, during His whole life, dedicated to the service of God, abstracted from the affairs of the world, denied to the gratifications of sense, and pure from all uncleanness. And, lastly, that the resemblance betwixt Him and that religious order might be more complete, whereas, at the expiring of their vow they were obliged by the divine law to offer as many sacrifices as though they had been lepers, even though they had fully complied with all their restrictions, so Jesus Christ, that He might fully pay His vow to the mighty God of Jacob, offered Himself a sacrifice, though He had no sin of His own to be expiated. And perhaps it is more than a conjecture that His education in the village of Nazareth which occasioned His being called a Nazarene, in the common style of His country, was intended, in the secret providence of God, to be an intimation to all that He was the true Nazarene in whom the ancient laws of Nazariteship were to receive their end; and thus, according to the holy evangelist, it was fulfilled that is written in the prophets, "He shall be called a Nazarene" (Matt. 2:23).

Singular Actions of Samson
We shall now come to take notice of some of the most singular actions of this illustrious Danite, which are as uncommon as his extraordinary birth presaged. Whether his marriage with a Philistine was any dark figure of the calling of the Gentiles, I will not determine.

But his *encounter with the young lion* that roared against him when he had no defensive weapon in his hand (Judg. 14:1–7), in which he was victorious (a prelude of his future victories), seems not unlike that first prelusive battle our Redeemer had with the roaring lion of hell, who met Him in the wilderness and roared against Him by three most hideous temptations but was totally routed and overcome by the lion of the tribe of Judah (Matt. 4:1ff.).

> "Hail Son of the Most High, heir of both worlds,
> Queller of Satan, on thy glorious work
> Now enter and begin to save mankind."
> —Milton[1]

And whereas the *dead carcass of the lion is recorded to have become a hive of bees*, who, by some strange instinct, chose here to make their honey (Judg. 14:8–20), this may at least put us in mind what are the happy effects of the conquests of our Redeemer. The law roared against Him by its threatenings, but He overcome it by His complete satisfaction. Death roared against Him and thought to swallow Him; but, O death, He was thy plague. Be not afraid of the condemning law, ye that believe in the Son of God, tremble not at the thoughts of death. These roaring lions are quelled by your Redeemer, who has seen the travail of His soul and is satisfied, as Samson did eat of the honey which he found in the carcass, and who also invites His people to partake with Him in His repast as it is said, "Eat ye that which is good, and let your soul delight itself in fatness" (Isa. 55:2). To have beheld a flight of eagles alighted on the carrion would have been no uncommon occurrence, for "wheresoever the carcase is, there will the eagles be gathered together" (Matt. 24:28).

---

1. Editor's note: John Milton, *Paradise Regained*, book 4, lines 633–35.

But for bees to take up their quarters in a dead carcass, and there to deposit their delicious stores, is so unlike the natural disposition of these clean and prudent insects as to afford the matter of that famous riddle which this great champion propounded to his friends on the occasion of this extraordinary adventure, and which they were not able to guess the meaning of, till according to the proverb then used they ploughed with his heifer. That swarms of Christians should be associated together and live by the death of Jesus Christ, the Lion of the tribe of Judah, whose flesh is meat indeed; that glory should come to us by His dishonor, riches by His poverty, strength by His weakness, life by His death; that the most unlikely means should bring about the most glorious and beneficial ends; that our most terrible enemies should be meat for us; that what promises nothing but stench and putrefaction should yield sweet comfort and refreshment—these are the things which by the gospel are declared unto us. Here Samson, thy riddle unfolds itself which none can understand aright who plough not with God's heifer—that is, the Spirit of God, who searcheth all things and reveals what the natural man receiveth not nor knows (1 Cor. 2:14).

It was strange *the Israelites did not join together under such a redoubtable champion to shake off the shameful yoke of the Philistines.* But they were so lost to all sense of shame and gratitude as to treat the deliverer of their country like the betrayer of it. They bind (by his own consent) their judge and avenger and traitorously deliver him up to their tyrants and oppressors (Judg. 15). But their joy was short in their prisoner. For bursting their bands and casting away their cords, with a very contemptible weapon he deals death and desolation at every blow and makes a most terrible carnage. For the Spirit of the Lord came upon him and stung his arm with more than mortal vigor. And the promise was literally fulfilled, that "one…shall chase a thousand" (Josh. 23:10). Even so, the avenger of the human race, the Lord Jesus Christ, was basely delivered up by His own countrymen, who had received many favors from Him, into the hands of the Gentiles. But without His consent, Judas, with all his rout, could not have bound Him. O Savior of the world! Thy love to men and obedience to God were the invisible but mighty cords that held Thee fast. These, and not the nails that transfixed Thy hands and feet, hindered Thee to save Thyself and come down from the cross. But the triumphing of the wicked was short, for when they vainly imagined they had Him sure and safe fastened on a cross and laid in the grave, He starts up a dreadful adversary. The cords of death are not able to hold Him; out of weakness He is made strong; and though all nations compassed Him, yet in the name of the Lord He did destroy them. And how contemptible was the instrument He used in this mighty work! As when Samson, who wanted not spears and swords, was directed to use no other weapon but the jaw bone of an ass, so Jesus Christ, who could have commanded the secular arm to spread the conquests of His gospel, or have ordained strength out of the mouths of eloquent orators or profound philosophers, yet chose contemptible fishermen and perfected praise out of the mouths of babes and sucklings.

I might mention, in the next place, *His marvelous escape from Gaza* (Judg. 16:1–3), where He was watched all night by His enemies, but He eluded their vigilance, and unhinging their massy gates He took away upon His shoulders part of the battlements of that strong city, for they were not the Lord's, and carried them to the top of a hill, the enemies having no power either to resist or to pursue. An emblem of our mighty Savior sleeping in the chamber of the grave where He was watched by the jealous Scribes and Pharisees who vainly imagined to hinder His resurrection. But when they least expected, He arose, He burst the gates of death, and leading captivity captive, He ascended on high.

But *the manner in which he died* is perhaps what most entitles him to be the type of Jesus Christ, who, like Samson, was betrayed and sold by a pretended friend, bound, blindfolded, insulted, and made His grave with the wicked (Judg. 16:23–31). Like Samson, He willingly resigned His breath; but by His death, death was abolished, principalities and powers were spoiled, and, O ye enemies of salvation, destructions have a perpetual end. Thy death, O Jesus, is our life, and by Thy cross we triumph over these wicked lusts that have shorn the locks of our strength, have bound us with fetters of iron, have put out the eyes of our mind and made us dwell in darkness and toil at the abhorred drudgery of the devil. Happy they who are avenged of these cruel enemies, though like thee, O Samson, they should die with them.

11

David
2 Samuel 7:1–29

There is scarcely a more amiable and consummate character to be found in the compass of sacred history than David's, notwithstanding some blemishes with which it is tarnished. What mouth is not opened in the praises of this good king, the first of the kind that swayed the Jewish scepter, who is honored to be the penman of these devout and rapturous compositions styled the *Psalms*, where the graces of poetry strive with the beauties of holiness and which are justly esteemed the treasure of the world and a complete system of revelation in miniature? When we consider that fervent devotion, that submission to the divine will, that delight in God's law and zeal for His worship, that spirit of forgiveness in the case of personal injuries, and the other lovely graces that breathe through all his writings and history, we must certainly allow him to have been a saint of the first magnitude. But it is chiefly to be observed, to the honor of this illustrious king much talked of in the Bible, that he was at once a prophet, a progenitor, and a figure of the Messiah. The last particular is so evident from innumerable places, where David and his Lord exchange not only words and speeches but also names, that taking for granted this obvious truth, we shall briefly hint at the most remarkable parallels betwixt them.

Born in Bethlehem
Perhaps his very name, *David*, which signifies "beloved," may

intimate that Christ his antitype should be the beloved of God and of men. But it is certain the place of his birth was always held to be the same where Christ should be born. Might not this be one reason why David (who was a prophet and knew that himself was a type of Christ and that he should be born in the same village) discovered such a fondness for Bethlehem as to be seized with ardent longing even for a draught of water from its well? Much was this little village aggrandized by giving birth to King David, but more by giving birth to Jesus Christ, for so the prophet sings, "But thou, Bethlehem Ephratah, though thou be little among the thousands of Judah, yet out of thee shall he come forth unto me that is to be ruler in Israel; whose goings forth have been of old, from everlasting" (Mic. 5:2).

A Man after God's Own Heart
From the place of his birth let us come to the qualifications of his persons both in body and mind. The ruddiness of his complexion is very particularly noticed by the sacred historian. And besides the comeliness of his person, his prudence and valor recommended him at court when he had no higher title than *the son of Jesse the Bethlehemite*. But above all, his character is crowned by the most ample commendation God was pleased to give him when He removed Saul: "I have found…a man after mine own heart, which shall fulfil all my will" (Acts 13:22). And where shall these illustrious endowments be found in their highest perfection but in the person of the Son of David, who is "white and ruddy, the chiefest among ten thousand" (Song 5:10), "fairer than the children of men" (Ps. 45:2), "the mighty God" (Isa. 9:6), the prudent servant of the Lord (Isa. 52:13), and lastly, who came "to do thy will, O God" (Heb. 10:7), Thy law was in the midst of his heart (Ps. 40:8)?

Sufferings
Let us next compare their sufferings, and we shall find a surprising resemblance.

We might, first, take notice of his lurking in *obscurity* for a long time in his father's house, where he tended the flocks of sheep before he was a shepherd of men. But though the like obscurity was the fate of Jesus Christ for a long track of years when He dwelt in His father's house, perhaps it is not so proper to mention this particular under the head of David's afflictions, for we can scarce doubt but it was the most happy period of his life when he followed the ewes with young.

From the time David began *to attract the observation of the world*, what was the greatest part of his life but a continual war? His own brother made him a very surly speech to deter him from his first public adventure in encountering Goliath, insinuating that the sole motive he had in visiting the camp at that juncture was pride and naughtiness of heart. Which puts us in mind of the coarse reception our gracious Redeemer met with from His brethren according to the flesh, who received Him not but loaded Him with the most odious imputations, and virulent reproaches, and always put the worst constructions upon His words and actions. We are also told that some of His nearest relations believed not on Him.

As to the *persecutions* he endured under the tyrant reign of Saul (which were the occasion of many sweet psalms, transmitted even to our times), the likeness betwixt them and those of Jesus Christ, under the tyrant reign of Herod, is greater than one would think at first view. David's life is sought after by his own king, and what was the quarrel? It was the fear that David would succeed to the crown, as was revealed to the prophet Samuel: so Jesus Christ is persecuted by Herod, king of Judah, from a foolish supposition that he could elude the high decree of heaven and falsify the Scriptures of the prophets. In David's quarrel the innocent priests in Nob were cruelly butchered, and the innocent babes in Bethlehem in the cause of Jesus Christ. *Cursed be their anger, for it was cruel.* But both the bloody tyrants shared the same success, for as all attempts to seize the person of David were vain, so Herod's bloody plot against the life of Christ proved abortive.

Betrayal

But when we are remembering David and all his afflictions, we must not forget that very singular one which befell him when he was compelled, by an unnatural son and rebellious subjects, to fly from his royal city and with his sorrowful friends passed over the brook Kidron in a melancholy plight (2 Sam. 15). It was over this same brook the Son and Lord of David passed to that fatal garden where He was apprehended, in company with His sorrowful apostles (John 18). And what was no small addition to David's distress, his own familiar friend, in whom he confided, and servant that ate of his bread played the traitor and lifted up his heel against him (Ps. 41:9), a circumstance which was not wanting in the case of Jesus Christ, betrayed by one of His apostles. Who knows not that the same Scriptures are applied to Judas in the New Testament that are in the Old spoken of Ahithophel? "Let their habitation be desolate"; "his bishoprick let another take" (Ps. 69:25; Acts 1:20). It is true, the Son of David knew from the beginning who should betray Him, which David knew not; but in other respects the parallel is very near, for both these cursed traitors were alike in their former character and trust, alike in their execrable villainy, and alike in their tragic end.

Renowned Achievements
Having enumerated some of David's typical afflictions, let us come to his renowned achievements both in war and peace, wherein also he seems to have been designed an emblem of the same glorious person. His victory over that proud, insulting Philistine who defied the armies of the living God is none of the least exploits for which he stands recorded in the rolls of fame (1 Sam. 17). He heard his blasphemous railing; he saw the unmanly terror of the Israelites, who all declined the single combat of this vain boaster; he was informed of the great rewards the victor should receive from the king, and not in the least intimidated by his fierce appearance, he resolves to accept the challenge in the name of the insulted God of Israel. Armed with no weapons but his staff and sling, he lays the vaunting warrior prostrate in death, adding withal this indignity to his huge corpse, to sever his head from the body with his own sword.

Let the vaunting Goliath be an emblem of *the devil*, who has the power of death. A great reward is proposed to the person who shall encounter and overcome this formidable enemy, by the King of heaven. No man, no angel, dared the arduous enterprise. But Jesus Christ, descending to visit His brethren, and see our camp, and moved with a becoming zeal for the glory of God and the salvation of the human race, and for the joy that was set before Him, He prepares Himself for the mortal combat. His brethren indeed despised Him and used Him rudely, but He was not deterred from His merciful design. He borrowed no armor from us, for He only partook of our infirm fleshly nature: but by His own strength and wisdom He obtained the victory with the staff of His cross—a most unlikely weapon! For God was His shield and glory and the lifter up of His head. "Through death," which was like the devil's sword, "he [destroyed] him that had the power of death" (Heb. 2:14). And so the saying of the prophet is fulfilled: "I will…save them by the LORD their God, and will not save them by bow, nor by sword, nor by battle, by horses, nor by horsemen" (Hos. 1:7).

The Gentile Church
We might also observe how his taking the stronghold of Zion from the Jebusites might be an emblem of Christ's conquering the Gentile church. His desiring to find a place for the God of Jacob to rest in may be considered in the same light (Ps. 132:5). This, O Savior, was Thy glorious design in visiting our regions of mortality, to find a place of rest among the sinful race of men for that God whose throne is the highest heaven, and His footstool the earth—to find not a shadowy rest upon an earthly mountain or in a material structure but a real, a glorious, an everlasting rest in the temple of Thy body, the church, that God the Lord might dwell forever among them.

Great was the glory to which the king of Israel was raised from small beginnings; and the prudence of his administration when he was lifted out of the dust proved him not to have been unworthy of such high dignity. It is true, we must allow him to have committed no small errors in some particular acts of governments, but as to the main of his conduct, he received this honorable testimony: "He fed them according to the integrity of his heart; and guided them by the skilfulness of his hands" (Ps. 78:72). Even so the humble Savior, who might truly say, "My heart is not haughty, nor mine eyes lofty" (Ps. 131:1), was exalted from His state of low debasement to the highest pinnacle of glory, to become not only the head of His church but of the heathen, and the people who knew Him not are made to serve His will. But in this He far excels the type, that the annals of His reign are not stained with any of the smallest blots, and "of the increase of his government and peace there shall be no end" (Isa. 9:7).

Christ the King
We shall but mention, in the last place, the covenant of royalty which God was pleased to make with David and his seed forever: an emblem of that covenant which God hath made with Christ as the representative of His chosen people. This covenant, O David, was thy consolation in all thy family trials and under the melancholy apprehensions of thy successor's apostacy. O may it also be our consolation, and let all the children of Zion "be joyful in their King" (Ps. 149:2).

12

Solomon

1 Kings 2:1–12

The next illustrious personage we shall mention is Solomon the son of David: the wise, wealthy, magnificent, and peaceful monarch of Jerusalem, who like his father was honored to be the penman of a very considerable and useful part of the inspired writings, by which he may be justly reckoned to have made abundant compensation to the church of God for the great offense he was left to give to all good men by the sad apostasy of his advanced years. That he was a figure of the Messiah seems evident from what God said concerning him by the prophet Nathan, which is applied by a New Testament writer to Jesus Christ: "I will be his father, and he shall be my son" (1 Chron. 17:13; Heb. 1:5); from what David said in the Seventy-Second Psalm; and from the most excellent Song of Songs composed by Solomon, not concerning himself but Jesus Christ, the glorious Bridegroom of the church, under a borrowed name. Nor is it difficult to find out several things in Solomon's character and history that greatly resemble the character and history of a far greater person than he.

Wisdom

We shall first take notice of that wisdom and sagacity for which he was so much celebrated. It pleased God to confer upon this beloved king a very uncommon measure of intellectual endowments to fit him for discharging the high office to which he was raised. He asked wisdom from God as the best and most perfect gift; nor did he ask in vain, for God gave him a wise and understanding heart, as never monarch had before. His wisdom far excelled that of the most renowned sages of his time. The world of nature was all his own. He spoke of plants and animals from the triumphant cedar down to the humble moss, and from the soaring eagle to the creeping insect. As a scholar no question was too hard for him to resolve, and as a judge no cause too intricate to decide. The wisdom of his proverbial sayings, and the sublimity of his poetical compositions, may be most certainly inferred from those specimens which have reached our times.

He was not only revered as the oracle of his country, but even princes neighboring and remote courted his friendship and were ambitious of his acquaintance. His very servants that ministered unto him were pronounced happy by a great queen, who, fired with the love of wisdom, undertook a large and expensive journey, leaving for a time the delights of her court and the cares of state to pay him a visit of whom she had heard so much, though still, as she afterward acknowledged, the half had not been told her (2 Chron. 9:1–8). Therefore shall she rise up in judgment against the men in every generation who refuse to hear the wisdom and receive the instruction of a greater than Solomon (Luke 11:31), who is the wisdom of God itself (1 Cor. 1:24) and in whom are hid treasures, all treasures of wisdom and knowledge (Col. 2:3), who instead of waiting till we come to seek Him has come from heaven to us and cries in the chief places of concourse, in the openings of the gates, in the city He utters His words, "How long, ye simple ones, will ye love simplicity?...and fools hate knowledge? Turn you at my reproof" (Prov. 1:22–23).

What was thy wisdom, Solomon, to His on whom, as the prophet testifies, the Spirit of the Lord did rest—the Spirit of wisdom, counsel, and knowledge—to make Him of quick understanding in the fear of the Lord? Admire we the vast extent of Solomon's erudition? There is no creature that is not manifest in the sight of Jesus Christ from the greatest unto the least. It is recorded of Him that with the utmost facility He answered the hard questions that were put to Him. Neither can the wisdom of Jesus Christ be nonplussed to answer the most puzzling query, when that most difficult of any has been resolved by Him: Wherewith shall a guilty sinner come before the Lord? And how shall he bow himself before the high God (Mic. 6:6)?[1] Was Solomon an acute, penetrating judge, judging his people with righteousness and his poor with judgment? Of Christ it was declared, "He shall not judge after the sight of his eyes, neither reprove after the hearing of his ears: but with righteousness shall he judge the poor, and reprove with equity for the meek of the earth" (Isa. 11:3–4). He discerns at first view a Nathaniel and a Judas and will separate the righteous and the wicked. And what are the wise speeches of Solomon to those of Jesus Christ, by whose Spirit the whole Scriptures were dictated and Solomon himself inspired?

Wealth

To the wisdom let us subjoin the wealth of Solomon, who made even silver in Jerusalem as the stones of the street (2 Chron. 9:27). But how shall this agree to our Lord Jesus, who was Himself a poor man, without a fixed dwelling place, and whose followers most generally are the poor among men? True, indeed, He neither possessed the riches of the world Himself nor can His subjects boast that they have amassed huge quantities of white and yellow earth, called silver and gold: yet are Thy riches, Lord Jesus, unsearchable; eternity itself is too short to count them. The arithmetic of angels would not be able to cast up the mighty sum. These riches hast Thou purchased by Thy poverty; and what is said of money, we still more truly affirm of Thy inexhaustible fullness: "It answers all things." If Solomon made silver as the stones, Jesus Christ renders the most admirable vanities of the world but loss and dung. O the immense value of the riches of Christ, of whom it is said in the prophet, "For brass I will bring gold, and for iron I will bring silver, and for wood brass, and for stones iron" (Isa. 60:17). Even such amazing wealth is scarcely fit to be an

---

1. Editor's note: The author's quotation of Micah 6:6, like many of his Scripture quotations, is adapted to a hortatory mode of address. The actual text of this verse reads, "Wherewith shall I come before the LORD, and bow myself before the high God?"

emblem of the true riches, for a New Testament writer rises in the description and talks of a city whose habitations are kings, whose walls are jasper, whose gates are pearls, whose streets are paved with gold (Rev. 21:18–21). Here that precious metal on which the men of the world set their hearts is trodden with the feet. How diminutive is the splendor of earthly courts! How despicable is a Solomon, though seated on his ivory throne, in comparison of such stupendous magnificence, which never indeed existed in the world of nature but has a true, though spiritual, existence in the kingdom of Jesus Christ! To conclude then, as the wisdom of Solomon was but folly to the wisdom of Jesus Christ, so in comparison to His riches, his wealth was poverty.

Dominion
From his wisdom and wealth, let us come to the extent of his dominion, which we are told was very wide. And if in the multitude of people is the king's honor, the King Messiah equals and far excels the king of Israel. What was it to reign over all kingdoms from the Euphrates to the midland sea, and to the corner of Egypt, to His extensive sway whose kingdom rules over all?

Peace
But what was a most singular recommendation of Solomon's happy reign, for the most part it was not disturbed either with civil wars or foreign war; for, as his name imported, he was a man of rest, and, except toward the latter end of his days, his subjects enjoyed the most profound tranquility. This was designed to be a faint representation of the government of the Prince of Peace, whose gospel is a doctrine which, if sincerely believed, effectually reconciles men to God and one another. Therefore the ancient prophets, speaking of these peaceful times when the Messiah should reign, have collected the most striking and amiable images of peace that can well be conceived. They talk of nations beating their "swords into plowshares, and their spears into pruninghooks" (Isa. 2:4; Mic. 4:3)—that arts of death and mutual destruction shall no more be learned as

an useful science; that the most ravenous beasts shall be as tame as those with which mankind are most familiar (Isa. 11:6; 65:25); that the most envenomed serpent shall cease to be pernicious; that bows and swords, and such like instruments of death, shall cease out of the earth, and the odious din of battle shall be heard no more. If now these charming prophecies have not received their full accomplishment, our wars and lightings, O Prince of Peace, are not the native result of the gospel, but they come from the lusts that war in our members. To this original they may all be traced. O shame to men who are called by the Christian name, to act a part so unlike their sacred profession by waging horrid wars with one another and rejoicing in mutual slaughter to make their swords drunk with blood! Nevertheless we, according to His promise, expect more happy times when the import of the predictions shall be more fully known and of the increase of His government and peace there shall be no end (Isa. 9:7). For here indeed the order is inverted in Solomon and his antitype. Whereas the beginning of Solomon's administration was the most peaceable part of it, the latter end of the Messiah's government shall be the most serene and happy period.

God's Building
To pass over the foreign match of the Israelite monarch, which some have supposed a prelude of calling the Gentile church to the fellowship of Jesus Christ, we shall only take notice of the magnificence of Solomon's building. He was pitched upon by the great God to build a house for His name, and under His direction, that sacred structure was reared at an immense charge. The workmen were foreigners and many of the materials fetched from abroad. The stones being all prepared and fitted to each other beforehand, the noise of hammers was not heard as the building advanced. Who knows not that the ancient temple was a figure of the church which is His body? Christ Jesus is the true Solomon, who builds this holy and beautiful house not with dead but with living stones, which are hewed by the law and polished by the gospel; and being thus fitly framed, they become a spiritual building and grow into a "holy temple in the Lord"

(Eph. 2:21). Even sinners of the Gentiles are employed in this honorable work of building up the church, and of them it may be said, "Ye are God's building" (1 Cor. 3:9). The doctrine of the apostles and prophets is the foundation, and Jesus Christ Himself the chief cornerstone (Eph. 2:20–22).

13

Jonah
Jonah 1:17–2:10

The comparison which our Lord was pleased to make of Himself and the prophet Jonah, when an evil and adulterous generation sought after a sign from heaven, forbids us to pass over in silence this short but strange history, which is doubtless one of these passages in the Old Testament to which the apostle refers when he speaks of Christ's dying for our sins, according to the Scriptures, and being buried and rising again the third day, according to the Scriptures: "For as Jonas was three days and three nights in the whale's belly; so shall the Son of man be three days and three nights in the heart of the earth" (Matt. 12:40; cf. Luke 11:29–32; Acts 10:40).

Jonah and the Gospel for the Nations
That we may have the fuller view of the resemblance, let us briefly recollect what we are told of this prophet in the book denominated from him. He is charged with a commission by the great God to denounce the vengeance of heaven against the great and sinful city Nineveh, the metropolis of the mighty Assyrian Empire. This is the first time we read of a prophet sent to reform a Gentile nation and doubtless was a prelude of His granting to the Gentiles in future times repentance unto life. It was God who commanded, and the prophet ought to have been all submission. But as Simon the son of Jonah long after disputed the command of God when he was sent for the first time to preach unto the Gentiles (see Acts 10:14ff.), so

Jonah, though a prophet of the Lord, who ought to have known better things, resolves to play the fugitive and, like Cain, to go out from the presence of the Lord and be an exile from the church where God was worshipped, expecting to hear no more such troublesome orders from above if he was once on some foreign ground. He finds at Joppa a ship bound for Tarshish, and thinking it a fair opportunity of carrying his scheme into execution, he enters himself a passenger.

But, ye mariners, little did you think what a dangerous cargo you were taking on board, for soon a tempest from the Lord embroils the ocean, and death sits threatening on every wave. Every mariner betakes himself to his prayers, but Jonah, the cause of the storm, is fast asleep. He is seasonably reproved by the master of the ship for his untimely security and earnestly invited to join with them in calling also upon his God. A good advice, to be sure, but, alas, Jonah's heart condemned him, and though his God was the God of gods, he had little ground to hope that his prayer would be heard. Alas! The guilty person was most unfit to become a mediator for the rest of the crew. They rightly judged that this preternatural storm was sent by angry heaven to punish some notorious offender; it was put into their hearts to find out by lot who he was. And, O surprising! a professor of the true religion, and a prophet of the Lord, is singled out in a crew of heathen sailors as the greatest sinner in the ship. His iniquity, which he thought to have kept a profound secret, is revealed in the most public manner, and he himself is obliged to confess his crime at large, that being a servant and a prophet of the God who made heaven and earth, and the sea, and the dry land, he had presumed to fly His presence and disobey His positive command.

What shall they do? Their case seems desperate. They ask his counsel whom they now esteemed a prophet. And, though at the expense of his life, he gives them the best direction that could be thought of: to cast himself forth into the sea. But though he was willing to die, the good-natured mariners were not willing to put him to death till they had exerted their utmost efforts to save themselves and him. Till at last they found their labor in vain and with great reluctance they heaved overboard the guilty prophet, having first fervently deprecated the guilt of his blood. And now at last the tempest ceased to roar, and the sea laid aside its rage, when the criminal they demanded was surrendered to the ocean, which had such a good effect upon the mariners as, it is hoped, they proved sincere worshipers of the true God, whom the winds and seas obey.

Who would expect to hear of Jonah anymore? But, strange to say! a huge fish, which the Creator had commanded to be ready, receives the astonished prophet in its belly, where he lives three days and three nights, being supported by an almighty power. In this dreary mansion he finds time to meditate his past folly and cry unto the Lord in the language of sincere repentance. And after he had been sufficiently punished, the obedient fish returns him safe and sound on the dry land on the third day. The commission is renewed; and, wiser than before, he obeys, goes to Nineveh, and preaches the doctrine of repentance, threatening them with destruction in forty days. The men of Nineveh repent, and God also delays to strike the blow and repented Him of the evil.

But what we intend chiefly to observe in the whole of this uncommon transaction: a greater than Jonah is here pointed forth in His death, burial, resurrection, and preaching to the Gentiles.

Jonah Consigned to a Watery Grave

The casting forth of Jonah into the sea bears no small resemblance to the *death of Christ*, though in some circumstances there is a considerable difference: for the prophet Jonah was, for his own offenses, delivered into the hands of mariners, who, without being guilty of murder or thirst after his blood, did, with great reluctance, throw him overboard for their own preservation, earnestly beseeching that his blood might not be laid unto their charge; but Jesus Christ, being delivered, not for His own but our offenses, unto the Jews and Gentiles was taken, crucified, and slain with wicked hands, while His bloody murderers imprecated the direful vengeance of His innocent blood to be on them and their children. In other respects the case of Christ and Jonah was more alike.

With his own consent the prophet is cast forth into the sea after he had acknowledged that he himself was the man for whose cause the storm was sent and whom the angry ocean demanded; so Jesus Christ laid down His life in the most voluntary manner and boldly offered Himself to the multitude who were sent to apprehend Him, saying, "I am the man whom ye seek; and if ye seek Me, let these go their way." And as the sufferings of the prophet, who was plunged into the ocean, were attended with the most happy consequences, the stilling of the tempest, the preservation of their lives, and, as is hoped, the salvation of their souls, even so, when Jesus the Son of God expired on the cross, this event, though in appearance tragic, was productive of the most blessed effects, appeasing the tempest of God's anger and saving from destruction the many for whom He gave His life a ransom, some of whom were the instruments of His death.

Jonah Three Days and Nights in God's Great Fish
His lodging in the belly of the fish three days and nights most certainly corresponds to the *burial of our Redeemer in the grave*, a part of three natural days (Jonah 1:17). Never did that monster of the deep swallow such a morsel before. Nor did ever the grave enclose such a prisoner as Jesus was. Jonah, it is true, was not really dead as Christ was when in the heart of the earth. But as that dismal place of darkness and corruption did much resemble the gloomy horrors of the loathsome grave, and is even styled the belly of hell by the prophet himself, perhaps the circumstance of Jonah's being alive in that living sepulcher may put us in mind that Jesus Christ was the living God, even when He was a dead man; for, O death, you were able indeed to rend His soul and body from one another, but neither soul nor body were dissevered from His divine person. And as Jonah received no harm in that horrible prison—which was miraculous if we consider the strength and heat in the stomach of so large a creature—so Jesus Christ, when lying in the grave a pale and bloody corpse, saw no corruption.

Jonah Washed Up on Dry Land

His casting forth on dry land on the third day after his imprisonment, at the commandment of the Lord, answers to the resurrection of the Son of God, who, at the commandment of His Father, was on the third day taken from prison and from judgment (Jonah 2:10). When Jonah was saved from the fish, he was also saved from the sea, revisiting at once the light of day and the dry land. When Christ was rescued from the grave, He at the same time emerged from under those billows of His Father's wrath which all passed over His head. It was not possible that Jonah should be detained in his ugly dungeon when the Lord spoke to the fish. It was not possible that Christ should be held by the cords of death longer than the appointed time; and He may truly say, "Yet hast thou brought up my life from corruption, O LORD my God" (Jonah 2:6). Nevertheless, in all things Jesus must have the preeminence, and we must certainly acknowledge that a greater than Jonah is here. For whereas Jonah did not contribute in the least toward his own restoration but would have forever continued in that melancholy prison if he had not been miraculously delivered from it, our Redeemer, on the other hand, as He had power to lay down His life, so He had power to take it again. The fish that swallowed Jonah might, for aught we know, receive as little harm by the prophet as the prophet by the fish; but, O grave, He was thy destruction. This hungry monster had gorged all the race of Adam and never said, "It is enough." Never any descended into the grave but it was able to digest them, till Jesus Christ died and was buried. This grand devourer snatched the bait of His human body, was not aware of the hook of His divinity, and was forced to surrender her prey, having received such a deadly wound as never shall be healed.

Preaching to the Lost

His preaching to the Ninevites, and saving them from imminent destruction, corresponds to Jesus Christ's *preaching to the Gentiles by His apostles after His resurrection from the dead*. For the gracious design of preserving a guilty city by turning them from their evil ways was the prophet preserved in the monster's belly and revisiting the light on the third day. And for the same merciful purpose was Jesus raised from the dead: to save a guilty world from death and to bless them in turning every one of them from their iniquities.

The belief those poor Gentiles gave to the threatening prophet, and their speedy repentance, was it not a prelude of that quick reception the doctrine of Jesus Christ should meet with among them that were aliens from the commonwealth of Israel? On this occasion the prophet acted a most unworthy part and evidenced a greater regard to his own reputation than the salvation of his hearers. Sure never man suited his name worse; for he is more like a vulture than a dove.[1] In this Jonah is not a type of Jesus Christ, who wept over Jerusalem, not because they repented but because they repented not and knew not the thing that belonged to their eternal peace. On this account, as well as those formerly mentioned, we may truly say that "a greater than Jonas is here" (Matt. 12:41).

---

1. Editor's note: The name Jonah means "dove."

BOOK 2
Typical Things

1

Jacob's Ladder
Genesis 28

In the multitude of dreams, divers vanities are not lacking; yet God is also in our sleep and has conveyed to the human mind notices of the last importance in a dream, in a vision of the night, when deep sleep falls upon us in our slumberings upon the bed, so great is that power He has over us, both when we wake and when we sleep. A pregnant instance of this we have in Jacob's night vision, which God granted unto him in Bethel to cheer his drooping heart when as an exile from his father's house he wandered all solitary to avoid the resentment of his brother. The sun was set, and the lonely traveler not being able to reach the next town, or on some other account not known to us, resolves for one night to make the great God his landlord, the earth his bed, the stones his bolster, and the canopy of heaven his covering. For though he was delicately brought up by his fond mother, whose darling child he was, the tender usage he received had not so far unmanned him as to betray undue softness and effeminacy, for upon this occasion he could put up with very coarse accommodation. There is no doubt his working mind would be fertile of melancholy thoughts as he lay thus in the open air, exposed to the chill damps of the night and other dangers. Perhaps he might compare his dismal solitude with the happier lot of Esau, who was enjoying himself at home with his father. Who knows but he might begin to think that the birthright and blessing he was so fond of obtaining were not such great matters as that he needed for their sakes to have exposed himself to such hardships as he presently felt and might still expect to meet with? But if any such pensive thoughts disturbed his mind, they are soon chased away by the welcome approach of sleep, and the delightful vision he saw, together with the friendly words he seemed to hear from the mouth of God Himself, for "he dreamed, and behold a ladder…the top of it reached to heaven: and behold the angels of God ascending and descending on it. And, behold, the LORD stood above it," not silent, but speaking words full of inexpressible consolation (Gen. 28:12–13). The meaning of this emblem is the present subject of our thoughts, and perhaps it will be found, on a nearer inspection, both to represent the mystery of providence and of redemption.

A Vision of Providence
And, first, it was a vision of providence and might be intended to suggest to the patriarch's mind the following important and interesting truths:

That though God be in the heights above, He *forgets not the affairs of mortals below*, as though the interposing clouds could veil them from His sight or the huge distance of heaven and earth could be an objection against His superintending care.

That though He is able, by Himself alone, to govern the whole world without the help of any created beings whatever, yet He is pleased to use *the ministry of angels*, which walk invisibly through the earth and are continually passing from heaven to earth, to fulfill the pleasure of Jehovah, and from earth to heaven, to receive the commands of their eternal Sovereign.

That the regards of Providence, and the kindly offices of these spiritual creatures, are not confined to large societies and the grand revolutions that happen in the world, but are even extended to the most *private interests* of every individual, for none but Jacob was present in the place where the ladder seemed to stand.

And lastly, that the divine Providence exercises the most tender care when *one's situation is most deplorable, destitute, and afflictive*, for Jacob saw this vision when his head was lying hard and his heart perhaps tormented with anxious care—when he was leaving a kind mother, a religious father, and the place where he was born and educated, uncertain of the reception he would meet with from his relations or if he should ever see his dear parents anymore. But as his affliction abounded, his consolation did much more abound (Rom. 5:20).

An Emblem of Christ
But perhaps we shall not think amiss, though we consider this emblematical ladder as a figure of the Messiah Himself, who is the blessed medium of communication between heaven and earth—the way without whom no man comes to the Father and "the one mediator between God and men" (1 Tim. 2:5; John 14:6). We can scarcely find a fitter explication of what Christ Himself promised to Nathaniel, that Israelite indeed, "Hereafter ye shall see heaven open, and the angels of God ascending and descending upon the Son of man," than by comparing it with this wonderful ladder, which He seems to hint was Himself (John 1:51). And there is no contemptible analogy, for at least five reasons:

For, first, whereas the foot of this ladder was on earth, and the top reached to heaven, this may both represent what is *the constitution of His person* and what are the blessed *fruits of the mediatorial interposition*. As the ladder seemed to unite the heaven and earth, the most distant extremes, so the person of Immanuel unites the human nature and the divine, though the distance between them is infinitely great. And as the ladder opened a path from God to man, and from man to God, by reaching from heaven to earth, so the mediation of Jesus Christ has paved a way both for the approach of the deity to sinners, that He may dwell with them, and for the access of sinners unto God, that they may dwell with Him and have their conversation in heaven. O merciful and faithful High Priest, by Thy incarnation and satisfaction a friendly correspondence is established between the heaven and earth, for Thou hast laid Thy hand upon us both and art Thyself our new and living way to everlasting bliss and the channel of conveyance to every spiritual blessing.

Whereas the angels of God were seen to *ascend and descend* upon the ladder, this may both signify that *in Jesus Christ* angels and men shall be united in one society and that *by Jesus Christ* they are upheld from falling and supported in their happy state. Were they not the friends of men, why should they be represented as running on our errands? Were they not confirmed and supported by Jesus our mediator, why should spiritual beings and winged messengers be said to ascend and descend upon the Son of Man, as on a ladder?

Whereas the Lord stood *above* this ladder, and from its top spoke good and comfortable words to His servant Jacob, *confirming the gracious covenant made with his fathers*, is not this a clear intimation that "God [is] in Christ, reconciling the world unto himself" (2 Cor. 5:19), confirming His covenant and uttering His gracious promise as well pleased in His beloved Son?

Whereas Jacob alone was at the *foot* of the ladder, on whose top the Lord seemed to stand, might not this have been considered by the adoring patriarch, after he awoke, as a comfortable intimation that *the glorious person who was signified by the vision should spring out of his loins* and be made of his seed according to the flesh as the true possessor of the birthright and inheritor of the patriarchal blessing (Rom. 1:3)?

And, lastly, whereas he saw but *one* ladder, Jesus Christ is *the alone mediator*, without whom the Father comes to no man, and no man comes to the Father: "No man can come to me, except the Father which hath sent me draw him: and I will raise him up at the last day…no man can come unto me, except it were given unto him of my Father" (John 6:44, 65). Jesus is the gospel ladder, and by Him only you may be saved now and ascend to glory hereafter.

2

The Burning Bush
Exodus 3

The last emblematical vision was seen in a night dream by Jacob. But that which we are now to consider was shown unto Moses in the daytime, when he was broad awake. This future lawgiver was now of a prince in Egypt, become a shepherd in Midian; and as it was the purpose of God to send him to Pharaoh with a commission to demand the release of His oppressed people, He was pleased to grant him an illustrious manifestation or prodigy to rouse his attention to what God should speak and to presage the success of his negotiation and his own future dignity. At the time when he saw the heavenly vision, he was tending the flock of Jethro, as honest industry, and the moderate exercise of the thoughts about the lawful affairs of the world is no obstruction to divine communications. And the place in which he received it may also be worthy of our notice: he led his flock to the backside of the desert and came to the mountain of God, even to Horeb; for solitude and retirement from the hurry of the world has always been a friend to holy meditation and intercourse with God. So Moses found on this occasion: for the angel of the Lord, not a created angel but the uncreated Angel of the covenant, who assumed to Himself the high title of "the God of Abraham, the God of Isaac, and the God of Jacob" and "I AM THAT I AM" (Ex. 3:6, 14) and who required of Moses the tokens of the most profound respect and religious subjection—to be short, the Messiah Himself—appeared in a flame of fire out of the midst of a bush, and "behold, the bush burned with fire, and the bush was not consumed" (Ex. 3:2). The novelty of the sight induced him to satisfy his curiosity by a nearer approach, but he was stopped short by the voice of God, which sufficiently explained the prodigy. Should it now be inquired why the divine Majesty chose to appear in this manner?

Though we could assign no other reason but His sovereign pleasure, it were sufficient. But most generally, the appearances and manifestations of the deity, in that age of types, were vouchsafed in such a manner as to represent some hidden mystery or important doctrine of the gospel. They who think that the flame of fire might signify the pure and spiritual nature of God, who appeared in it, of which no similitude can be made, are certainly not mistaken. And it is also not unfitly observed that the burning bush may represent the state of Israel at that time, who were entangled in the thorny bush of adversity and encompassed with the fire of affliction, in which they were like to be consumed. But let us draw near and consider with Moses this great sight with a closer attention, and perhaps it will be found a most significant emblem, both of Jesus Christ, who was in the bush, and of the church, which is His body, in every age of the world. And, first, it seems very probable that this was a prelusive[1] vision both of the future incarnation and sufferings of Jesus Christ.

A Vision of the Incarnate Christ

That the bush may represent His *human nature* is not unlikely, especially as the prophet Isaiah compares Him to a tender plant and root out of a dry ground, in which, to the eye of sense, no form, comeliness, or beauty should be found (Isa. 53:2).

That the flame of fire may adumbrate His *divine nature* will be no less evident when we consider how often the fiery element is, in the Scripture style, an emblem of the deity; yea, it is expressly said, "Our God is a consuming fire" (Heb. 12:29; cf. Deut. 4:24).

---

1. Editor's note: *Prelusive* means "constituting or having the form of a prelude."

That the union of the flame of fire with the bush may denote the *union of the Godhead and the manhood* is not at all absurd to suppose, for why should Moses in his dying benediction be directed to speak of the goodwill of Him who "dwelt in the bush" (Deut. 33:16)? May it not signify that the continuance of the flame of fire in the bush for a short time was a type of the fullness of the Godhead dwelling forever in the man Christ Jesus (Col. 2:9)? As the bush was in the fire, and the fire was in the bush, yet still they were distinct things, though enjoined thus in one: even so the man Christ Jesus is in the God, and the God is in the man, though both these natures, so mysteriously united, do still retain their own distinct properties.

A Vision of the Sufferings of Christ

And if Moses was struck with admiration that the bush was not consumed, though in such near neighborhood with ruddy flame, much more may we be overwhelmed with amazement to think how a portion of our frail humanity lives forever in a state of the nearest approach unto and most ineffable union with the glorious Godhead in whose unveiled presence we mortals could not live, and even the angels cover their faces with their wings.

Here also may be discerned a shadow of those *direful sufferings* by which the Son of God was to expiate our sin. For the wrath of God is everywhere in Scripture compared to fire the most fierce and dreadful of all the inanimate creatures, which with severe impartiality devours all combustible things. Who of all the human race could dwell with this devouring element? Far less could any abide with the everlasting burnings of the Almighty's indignation. But Jesus Christ who dwelt in the bush dwelt also with these fierce flames, and though He endured the wrath of God, which flamed most intensely against Him as He bore the sins of many, though He was compassed by this fire all the days of His humbled life, yet He was not consumed, because His deity, like the angel in the bush, supported His humanity and bade Him be a glorious conqueror.

A Vision of the Sufferings of the Church
From the sufferings of the head, let us descend to the sufferings of the body, who are predestinated to be conformed to His image (Rom. 8:29).

Let the bush be an *emblem of the church*, to which it may be compared on account of its weak, obscure, and contemptible state in the esteem of worldly men, who are taken with nothing but what dazzles the eye of sense. For though there is a real glory and a spiritual magnificence in this holy society, she cannot compete with earthly kingdoms in outward splendor any more than a bush in the wilderness can vie with the cedar in Lebanon; for besides the paucity of her true members, they are commonly to be found rather in smoky cottages than proud palaces, and sometimes they have been found in prisons, dungeons, dens, and caves of the earth (Heb. 11:38; Isa. 2:19).

Let the fire in which the bush burned signify the *fiery trials* to which the church has been no stranger in all ages. Sometimes she has burned in the fire of persecution and sometimes of division.

But as the bush was not consumed, so *neither shall the church be finally destroyed*. In vain shall the great red dragon persecute this woman clothed with the sun and watch to devour her offspring; for a place is prepared for her in the wilderness by the great God, and there no necessary provision shall be wanting. How many times have bloody and deceitful men conspired her destruction? When were incendiaries wanting to foment and kindle those fires, which, without the immediate interposition of the Keeper of Israel, would certainly have wasted unto destruction and completed the utter extinction of this humble bush? What society but this alone could have subsisted to this day in the midst of a hating world? Where are now the mighty empires of antiquity? They are but an empty name, live only in history, having fallen to pieces by their own weight or been crushed by bloody war. But the church of Christ, though she has undergone many revolutions, remains, and will remain, when the consumption determined by the Lord of Hosts shall come upon all the earth.

A Vision of the Salvation of the Church
Ask you the reason? The angel of the Lord is in the bush, and though persecuted, the church is not forsaken; therefore shall the fiery trials, instead of consuming her, serve to refine her and add unto her glory, as the bush was only brightened by the flame.

Does not the famous history of the three Hebrew worthies, who by faith quenched the violence of fire, attest this whole matter in the most literal sense (Dan. 3)? Nebuchadnezzar, the mighty king, takes it into his head to erect a monstrous golden image to be worshipped by all his numerous subjects. The dedication of this new god is celebrated by a prodigious concourse of people, who, by the king's proclamation, assembled in the plains of Dura. A severe edict is issued forth against any person who should refuse to pay religious homage to the molten deity. He must be cast alive into a burning fire, for was it ever heard that cruelty and idolatry were separated? The noise of every musical instrument is the signal for beginning the detestable rites of adoration.

What a parade to establish this silly superstition! And now the music sounds; see how the foolish people fall down in adoration to a senseless statue! Yet there are found among the captives of Judah, who dare dispute the royal order. O faith, how dost thou extend thy triumphs! Who can sufficiently admire the excellent spirit and the undaunted resolution of these heroes! They stand before a sovereign and angry majesty, they see the vast pomp of his courtiers, they hear the sonorous peals of the music sent from a thousand instruments, they behold the prodigious furnace gleaming to the clouds, yet are they not appalled by any—by all—of these things so apt to strike terror into vulgar minds, but despise them as ludicrous and puerile. They boldly tell that the God they adored was able to deliver them from his furnace, if He pleased, and though He should not, they would not comply to worship another god. The music that resounded through all the spacious plain was not half as melodious as their answer to the king's menaces. The enraged tyrant orders, and without delay they are cast bound hand and foot into the burning flame. But mark the amazing event! A marvelous thing is presented to the eyes of the king, for looking narrowly he beholds not three men melting but four men walking in the fire, and the form of the fourth is like the Son of God.

These servants of the Lord were not ashamed of Him, nor is He ashamed of them, but descends in a bodily shape (a prelude of His incarnation), looses their fetters, makes a covenant for them with the flames of fire, and walking with them openly in the furnace proclaims to all spectators, "Inasmuch as ye have done it unto…these my brethren, ye have done it unto me" (Matt. 25:40). Go now, mighty monarch, and glory in thy despotic sway, but remember there is a King more sovereign than thou who can make the flames of fire harmless as the morning light, who can bid that fierce and dreadful element spare them whom thou biddest it to devour, though in the very heart of the oven, and destroy them whom thou wished it would not touch, though standing without. Thus wherein any deals proudly, God is above them. The king, and all his councilors, see with their eyes this extraordinary miracle and that the faithful servants of God had not received the least damage by the fire, and are ashamed for their envy to the people. Thus was the promise fulfilled, "When thou walkest through the fire, thou shalt not be burned; neither shall the flame kindle upon thee" (Isa. 43:2). And so the bush, though burning, is not consumed in the fire.

3

The Pillar of Cloud and Fire
Exodus 13:17–22

The sojourners of Goshen were now escaped from the land of Egypt and about to enter into the vast wilderness of Arabia that interposed between them and the Promised Land. The Lord, who makes "the clouds his chariot" and "darkness…his pavilion," was pleased to go before them in a marvelous pile of cloudy vapor resembling a pillar, ascending from their camp (see Pss. 104:3; 18:11). Here he dwelt, not for a short time, as in the bush, but for the space of forty years. A most extraordinary thing to be sure it was, and none of the least of the standing miracles which He showed to the chosen seed. The fame of this strange phenomenon was spread abroad among the nations, who heard that the cloud of the Lord stood above them and might very well be supposed to move the question, "Who is this that cometh out of the wilderness like pillars of smoke?" (Song 3:6).

The Cloud as a Complication of Miracles
For this cloud differed so much from all others that ever were seen as it may justly be reckoned a complication of miracles. It was miraculous that its form was never changed, when there is nothing more variable than the appearance of the ordinary clouds that sail through the airy regions. It was miraculous that it should always maintain its station over the tabernacle, when other clouds are carried about by tempests and driven with fierce winds from the one extremity of heaven to the other. It was miraculous that it should preserve its consistency forty

years, whereas all other clouds are dissipated by the wind, exhaled by the sun, or dissolved in rain and dew and in a very short time are blotted from the face of the sky. It was miraculous that this cloud should move in such peculiar direction, as it had been endued with instinct and intelligence, for it was carried about by His counsels in a more immediate way than can be said of the other clouds of heaven. But especially it was miraculous that contrary to the nature of all other clouds, it should be brighter by night than by day, when it had the appearance of the shining of a flaming fire.

The Cloud as a Prelude to the Incarnate God
As to the particular meaning of this cloud wherewith the Lord covered His Israel, not in His anger but in His love, it was without all doubt a visible symbol of a present deity, God hereby condescending to adapt Himself, as in many other things, to the rude taste of that ancient people and perhaps to signify the dark and cloudy nature of the legal dispensation under which they were. But the principal reason I would suggest is the following. His appearing to Israel in a veil of cloud might be a prelude of His appearing in a veil of flesh. What though we should say, this pillar of cloud and fire is an emblem of that glorious person in whom the brightness of divinity is joined with the darkness of humanity! For as there were not two pillars, the one of cloud and the other of fire, but one pillar both of cloud and fire, so there are not two persons of Immanuel, the one God and the other man, but one person, who is both God and man. An adorable mystery this, strange indeed, and beyond measure surprising. But it is so far from being only a vain speculation that it is deservedly esteemed a fundamental article of the Christian faith; and truly, without admitting it, the Scriptures themselves will be darker than this cloud ever was to the Egyptians.

John, the beloved apostle and great New Testament prophet who saw the visions of God and who talks in many places in the Old Testament dialect, speaks of a glorious angel arising out of the East, who certainly was Christ Himself: He was clothed with a cloud, and "his feet [were] as pillars of fire" (Rev. 10:1), a description which might very probably allude to this same cloud and fire. But if we take a more particular survey of the uses for which it served in the wilderness, we shall see with what admirable propriety they all may be affirmed of Jesus Christ, who indeed was the angel that resided in the cloud and is that unto His church in every age, in their bewildered state, which the cloud was to the twelve tribes till they reached the earthly Canaan. In whom but Jesus Christ can we suppose that great and precious promise made to the universal church to have received its accomplishment, "And the LORD will create upon every dwelling place of mount Zion, and upon her assemblies, a cloud and smoke by day, and the shining of a flaming fire by night: for upon all the glory shall be a defence" (Isa. 4:5)? What then were those uses for which this cloud served the Israelites?

The Cloud as the Guide to Israel
It was *their guide* that went before them in the vast, pathless desert, where they wandered in a solitary way. So great was the regard they paid to all its motions, which they continually watched, that when it moved they struck their camp at any hour of the day or of the night; when it halted they pitched their tents and there abode till its next remove, whether the time was short or long. The times and seasons of their marching were not, as in other armies, adjusted by their counsels of war, nor left to the regulation even of Moses himself, for God put them wholly in His own power. However, it would appear that its motions were properly timed and mercifully proportioned to the strength of the weak and the convenience of all. Nor did it ever leave them, for all their provocations in the wilderness, till they arrived at the land that flowed with milk and honey. Just such a general, unerring, gentle, and perpetual guide is Jesus Christ by His example, Word, and Spirit to all the travelers for the better country through the wilderness of this world; for "it is not in man that walketh to direct his steps" (Jer. 10:23), by his own wisdom, in the way that leads to life. Who can recount the wanderings of miserable sinners till Jesus Christ was given a leader and a commander to the people? He it is who teaches to profit and leads in the way wherein

we should go. Nor is it possible that any should miss eternal glory who walk after Him in the wilderness, conforming themselves to the dictates of His holy Word with the same care the Israelites observed the motions of the miraculous cloud. O ye followers of the Lamb, you shall not err under the conduct of your celestial guide; you shall be led forth in the way that is right, even where there is no way, till you come to the city of habitation (Ps. 107:7).

The Cloud as the Guard of Israel

It was *their guard* that protected them when their Egyptian pursuers were pressing on their rear, for it removed on that occasion from their van and went behind them, forbidding by its darkness the approach of the hostile army all that night on which they traveled through the flood on foot. On this occasion we are told that the Lord looked through the pillar and troubled the Egyptian host at the hour of midnight. "The waters saw thee, O God, the waters saw thee; they were afraid: the depths also were troubled. The clouds poured out water: the skies sent out a sound: thine arrows also went abroad. The voice of thy thunder was in the heaven; the lightnings lightened the world: the earth trembled and shook. Thy way is in the sea, and thy path in the great waters, and thy footsteps were not known. Thou leddest thy people like a flock by the hand of Moses and Aaron" (Ps. 77:16–20). Such is that protection Jesus affords to His militant people, who being rescued from the bondage of sin are marching forward to their goodly inheritance. Though Satan, with his infernal host, like the tyrant of Egypt, pursues after them and fondly thinks to reclaim the lawful captives, "the glory of the LORD shall be thy reward" (Isa. 58:8); Jesus is unto them for "walls and bulwarks" (Isa. 26:1), forbidding the approach of mortal danger. He is their hiding place, in whom they are preserved (Ps. 32:7), like Israel in the cloud, being "kept by the power of God through faith unto salvation" (1 Peter 1:5).

The Cloud as a Candle to Israel

It was *their candle* that enlightened their darkness, that smoothed the rugged brow of the night and served to abate the horrors of the wilderness after the sun was set; for it reserved its shining appearance to the season when the Israelites were most in need of its cheerful aspect. Nor dost Thou, O Thou "true Light" (John 1:9), suit Thyself to the case of Thy people with less condescension. Without Thee this world were a dark place and, to the eyes of our mind, more dismal than the dreary wilderness would have been in the blackest night to the Israelites without their kind, officious cloud. Blessed be God for the sun, the moon, the stars, but more for Jesus Christ, who delivers from "the blackness of darkness for ever" (Jude 13) and who, like the cloudy pillar, is always most liberal of His lightsome manifestations, when His people are sitting in the darkness of adversity. House of Israel, let us walk in this light of the Lord, whilst the way of the wicked, like the way of the Egyptians, is as darkness.

The Cloud as an Umbrella over Israel

It was *their umbrella* or screen to shade them from the sultry beams of the sun in that torrid wilderness. A most grateful service! And whereas an apostle speaks of our fathers being "baptized…in the cloud" (1 Cor. 10:2), it would seem that on some occasions this beneficial cloud refreshed the Israelites by shedding kindly dews upon their camp. So Jesus Christ is to His people as a refreshing "dew upon the grass" (Prov. 19:12; Mic. 5:7) and as "a cloud of the latter rain" (Prov. 16:15). Under His shadow they sit down with great delight and find cool shelter from the scorching beams both of divine wrath and worldly tribulation. Happy souls who have thus the Lord for their keeper and for their shade on their right hand (Ps. 121:5). "The sun shall not smite [them] by day, nor the moon by night" (Ps. 121:6); even that great and terrible day, which shall burn like an oven (Joel 2:31; Mal. 4:1), will be to these favored of the Lord as "the times of refreshing…from the presence of the Lord" (Acts 3:19).

The Cloud as an Oracle for Israel

It was *their oracle*, for "he spake unto them in the cloudy pillar" (Ps. 99:7). And it was their ornament, for He spread this cloud for their covering, or cloth of state, making darkness not only His own but their pavilion. How fitly both these may be applied to Jesus Christ is not difficult to see. Who but Christ is the oracle of His church, in whom God speaks unto His people, both as a promising and prayer answering God, without whom we would not have heard His voice at any time but in the language of terror? Who but Christ is their ointment, who makes them "terrible as an army with banners" (Song 6:4) and comely as Jerusalem? The pillar of cloud and fire was not half so adorning to their camp as is Thy gracious presence to every assembly and every dwelling place of Mount Zion, O Thou glorious Redeemer. Even now Thou art the "light to lighten the Gentiles, and the glory of thy people Israel" (Luke 2:32). But how much more when this imperfect scene shall pass away and they shall know the import of that most gracious promise, "The LORD shall be unto thee an everlasting light" and "thy God thy glory" (Isa. 60:19).

4

The Manna in the Wilderness
Exodus 16

We have seen how the horrors of the wilderness were considerably abated by their miraculous cloud. But soon the provision they brought from Egypt is spent, and unless some new miracle is wrought for them, they have nothing before their eyes but the melancholy prospect of perishing with hunger. The faithless multitude, forgetting their late deliverance at the Red Sea, fall to murmuring against Moses and wished they had never stirred from the house of bondage. Had they got what they deserved on this occasion, the Lord had sent fire from heaven upon them instead of food; but God, who is rich in mercy, chose to still the fretful murmurs of His firstborn with the breast rather than with the rod. He bids the heaven supply by its bounty what the earth denied by its barrenness, and without their toil or sweat gives them plenty of bread, even in a land that was not sown: He "rained down manna upon them to eat, and had given them of the corn of heaven. Man did eat angels' food: he sent them meat to the full" (Ps. 78:24–25). How happy are they who are walking after the Lord, though in a wilderness! It was a convincing proof that man does not live by bread alone. But God intended by this good gift not only to supply their present necessity but also to prefigure that spiritual meat presented in the gospel. In this interpretation we cannot possibly be wrong when we have no less an authority for it than Jesus Christ Himself, who, speaking to His hearers on this very subject, says, "Moses gave you not that bread from heaven; but my Father giveth you the true bread from heaven. For the bread of God is he which cometh down from heaven, and giveth life unto the world.... I am the bread of life" (John 6:32–33, 35). Having, therefore, such infallible testimony to the general meaning of this heavenly food, let us try to find out the principal traces of resemblance between it and Jesus Christ. In order to this we shall shortly attend to the following things about the manna: its falling, its gathering, its distribution, its preparation, its taste, its putrefaction when improperly used, its despising by the people, and its preservation.

The Source of the Manna

The manna *fell* from heaven (Num. 11:9); Christ is He that comes down from above (John 3:31; 8:23). It fell round about their camp. Christ is to be found in the visible church and nowhere else: with the dew when they slept (Jesus Christ is purely the gift of God, who descends like dew upon the grass, for whom we toil not, sow not, reap not); when they were in the most absolute need, and ready to perish ("when we were yet without strength, in due time Christ died for the ungodly" [Rom. 5:6]); when they were not at all deserving it, but grievously sinning, by preferring the flesh-pots of Egypt to the prospects of Canaan; and Christ laid down His life when sinners were preferring the pleasures of sin, and vanities of the world, to all the things above. In a word, it fell in such large quantities as to suffice that numerous host; in Jesus Christ there is enough to supply every want.

The Gathering of the Manna

Its *gathering* by all the Israelites may signify the improvement we all should make of the offered Savior. It was gathered every day, so Christ should be daily improved by faith. It was gathered in the morning, for we must devote the best part of our time to seeking His face, as it is said, "O God, thou art my God; early will I seek thee" (Ps. 63:1). It was gathered outside the camp, so must the soul that seeks Him retire from the hurry of the world, or, to use the expression of the sacred page, "go forth into the field" and "lodge in the villages" (Song 7:11). It was gathered a double portion on the sixth day, but on the seventh, which was the Sabbath, they stirred not from their tents but lived on what they laid up the day before. So in the season of this mortal life must we labor for "that meat which endureth unto everlasting life" (John 6:27) in the believing improvement of the means of grace, and when the eternal Sabbath comes, we shall enjoy the hidden manna without means or any painful endeavors.

The Distribution of the Manna

Its parting among the Israelites seems not to be without its meaning. Some gathered less, some more, in proportion to their ability and diligence, but all received a homer (a large allowance) from the common heap. By which means, as Moses relates, "he that gathered much, had nothing over" because he gave to him that gathered less, and "he that gathered little had no lack" because he received from him that gathered more (Ex. 16:18). Was the manna parted liberally unto all? None are straitened in Jesus Christ: "They shall be abundantly satisfied with the fatness of thy house; and thou shalt make them drink of the river of thy pleasures" (Ps. 36:8). Was the manna equally distributed among the Israelites? So all believers—of every sex, of every age, of every nation, strong or weak, eminent or obscure—do equally partake in the common salvation, for all are "one in Christ Jesus" (Gal. 3:28).

The Preparation of the Manna

Its *preparation* in mills, mortars, and pans, where it was ground, beaten, and baked to make it fit for digestion and nourishment, may put us in mind of the various sufferings of Christ's body and soul. The bread of God is He which came down from heaven; but ere He could prove the bread of life, He behoved Himself to die. That His flesh might be meat indeed, He behoved, as it were, to be beaten in the mortar of adversity, ground in the mill of vindictive justice, and baked as in the oven of the wrath of God.

The Taste of the Manna

Its *taste* is so sweet when thus prepared (for it resembled the fatness of oil and the lusciousness of honey) and its proving so wholesome and nutritive to all, though of different constitutions, may it not signify that Jesus Christ is to the soul both sweet and wholesome food and adapted to the taste of all, of young men, of children, and of fathers? As the manna is supposed to have needed no other ingredients to make it palatable, no more does Jesus Christ, or the doctrine of His gospel, need any foreign recommendation to the spiritual taste. "O taste and see that the LORD is good," says the sweet singer of Israel (Ps. 34:8), and in another place, "How sweet are thy words unto my taste! yea, sweeter than honey to my mouth!" (Ps. 119:103).

The Putrefaction of the Manna
If kept contrary to God's command, its *putrefaction* was the invariable result, for what was not used today bred worms and stank tomorrow. Might this not denote that when the wholesome doctrines of Christ's gospel are hoarded up in idle speculation—without being otherwise received in love or digested in spiritual nourishment—they end up so far from being the savor of life unto life that they become "the savour of death unto death" (2 Cor. 2:16)? And does this not breed the worms of various lusts and a condemning conscience, on which account it may be said here, "He that increaseth knowledge increaseth sorrow" (Eccl. 1:18)?

The Despising of the Manna
Its despising by the multitude as light food, by which their soul was dried away, in comparison with their rank Egyptian fare, renders it a proper emblem of Jesus Christ, the true bread, who is "despised and rejected of men" (Isa. 53:3). Though the pure doctrine of Christ is, like the manna, angels' food—for into these things they desire to pry (1 Peter 1:12)—yet are there found to whom the word of the Lord is a reproach, and they have no delight in it. A romance, a philosophical disquisition, a moral declamation, a political harangue is far more grateful than a sermon whose theme is a crucified Redeemer. What is this but to prefer the fish, the melons, the cucumbers and onions of Egypt to the corn of heaven? For their contempt of this celestial food, the Lord sent fiery serpents to plague the murmurers and complainers. Nor do the despisers of Jesus Christ expose themselves to less

dreadful strokes, though they should not be of a corporeal kind: for all these things happened unto them for ensamples [i.e., types]; and "they are written for our admonition, upon whom the ends of the world are come" (1 Cor. 10:11).

The Preservation of the Manna
Its preserving it in a golden pot, where, for a number of ages, it was deposited in the Most Holy Place and remained without corruption, was it not a representation of Christ's ascension into heaven, where He appears in the presence of God, death having no more dominion over Him, and where He will be contained till the time of the restitution of all things? Why else should communion with Christ in glory be spoken of in terms alluding to this very thing? For thus it is promised, "To him that overcometh will I give to eat of the hidden manna" (Rev. 2:17) in the words that the Spirit says unto the churches.

The Provision of the Manna
The continuance of this heavenly bread for the space of forty years (for so long they were in the wilderness), does it not clearly intimate that Jesus Christ will never forsake His people while they are here below? Still shall the bread of God descend in the dispensation of the everlasting gospel while the necessities of His people call for it: for so He promised when about to depart from the earth. He says to His apostles, "Go ye therefore, and teach all nations, baptizing them in the name of the Father, and of the Son, and of the Holy Ghost" and "Lo, I am with you alway, even unto the end of the world" (Matt. 28:19-20).

The Ceasing of the Manna
May the ceasing of the manna upon their tasting the corn of Canaan not be viewed as a figure of ordinances ceasing when the wandering tribes gain their promised rest? Or shall we say that as their heavenly provision failed when they tasted the bread that comes out of the earth, so when the children of God themselves begin to relish overmuch of the things of the earth, they may expect that heavenly

consolations will be suspended in proportion? When they are on the worst terms with the world, or when it is unto them as a wilderness and a land not sown, then truly God is good to Israel. Know your mercy, ye distinguished favorites of heaven, nor envy their happiness who "eat the lambs out of the flock, and the calves out of the midst of the stall," but are not fed with "the heritage of Jacob" (Amos 6:4; Isa. 58:14). Let the sensual voluptuary glut himself with the impure pleasures of sin, which, like the little book that John did eat, are sweet to the mouth but bitter in the belly (Rev. 10:9) and to whom we may adapt the significant words in Job, "His meat in his bowels is turned, it is the gall of asps within him" (Job 20:14). Let the rapacious worldling, who is smitten with the dull charms of gold and silver, who is all hurry, hurry about the business of this transitory life, let him fill his belly with the hidden treasure of God, which never yet did satisfy a soul immortal. Let the legal self-justifier, who is perhaps called by the name of Christ but eats his own bread, and wears his own apparel, and trusts in his own righteousness, in whatsoever shape, as the ground of his acceptance with God, let him also spend his money for that which is not bread and his labor for that which satisfieth not (Isa. 55:2).

But let the Christian who knows the gift of God, and the excellence of the heavenly provision, let him "labour not for the meat which perisheth, but for that meat which endureth unto everlasting life, which the Son of man shall give unto you" (John 6:27). Hungry and starving soul, you ask for bread, the world gives you a stone; what else are worldly riches? You ask a fish, the world presents you with a serpent; what else are sinful pleasures? But hearken diligently unto Him who is Himself the living bread: "Eat ye that which is good, and let your soul delight itself in fatness. Incline your ear, and come unto me: hear, and your soul shall live" (Isa. 55:2–3). What is a happy old age to a happy eternity? This, O Jesus, is thy "unspeakable gift" (2 Cor. 9:15). He that eats Thee by faith shall live forever. He that comes to Thee "shall never hunger" (John 6:35), and what is more, he that believes on Thee "shall never die" (John 11:26). O Lord, deny us what Thou wilt, but give us this bread forevermore.

5

The Rock in the Wilderness
Exodus 17

Bread shall be given them, says the prophetic voice; the proof of this we have already seen. Their water shall be sure, the proof of which we shall presently see: For "he clave the rocks in the wilderness, and gave them drink as out of the great depths. He brought streams also out of the rock, and caused waters to run down like rivers" (Ps. 78:15–16). What cannot this mighty God do, at whose command the clouds shall yield bread, which usually comes out of the earth, to appease the hunger of His beloved people, and the rocks shall send forth water, which usually falls from the clouds, to satisfy the thirst of His chosen race? "Tremble, thou earth, at the presence of the Lord, at the presence of the God of Jacob; which turned the rock into a standing water, the flint into a fountain of waters" (Ps. 114:7–8). Let us briefly recollect this memorable event and its mystic signification.

The Rock Was a Test of Faith
The ransomed tribes are, for the trial of their faith, conducted by the Lord, who alone did lead them to a dry and thirsty spot in the wilderness at the rock Rephidim, where there was no water to drink. They ought to have recollected on this occasion that the God who brought them here would most certainly extricate them from their present difficulties, as He had done often before. But, O impatience, how absurd and unreasonable art thou! Instead of betaking themselves to God by humble prayer and quietly waiting for the salvation

of the Lord, they impiously demand of Moses to give them water. They reproach him with decoying them out of Egypt, where they were living so happy, with no other design than to famish them in the wilderness. In vain does this meek and gentle servant of God remonstrate the injustice and impiety of their outrageous conduct. They are at the very point of stoning their deliverer and rewarding with a cruel death the good offices he had done for them. He flies to God as his sanctuary and invokes the almighty aid, not to revenge the affront offered him by the rude multitude but to relieve them in their present straits. The prayer is no sooner made than answered. He is directed to take with him the elders of Israel and the wonder-working rod, with which he smote the rivers: "Behold, I will stand before thee there upon the rock in Horeb; and thou shalt smite the rock, and there shall come water out of it, that the people may drink" (Ex. 17:6). Moses obeys, and the event crowns his wishes. But long after, when the people were in Kadesh and reduced to the same straits they were in at Rephidim, the unbelieving race relapsed into their old rebellious murmurs. Moses is directed to nearly the same method of relief but does not acquit himself with the same temper and moderation. For they angered him at the waters of strife and provoked his spirit so, that he spoke unadvisedly with his lips, betraying at the same time, in presence of the whole assembly, his own diffidence in the promise of Jehovah; for being commanded to speak to the rock, and assured that it would obey his voice, he seems to have exceeded his commission by addressing the host in the language of wrath and doubting, and smiting the rock more than once. The miracle indeed was wrought but the worker, though dear to God, severely punished for his offensive behavior and unbelief, being involved in the same fate, together with Aaron, as the rest of the generation, to die in the wilderness, without entering into the Promised Land.

The Rock Was Christ

That more was meant than to give water for their thirst might be presumed from the naked history in Moses. This God could do without a miracle. He could have opened the bottles of heaven or led them to another Elim (cf. Ex. 15:27; 16:1; Num. 33:9–10). Or if He had chosen the miraculous method, why should the rock be smitten with a rod to give streams in the wilderness and waters in the desert while God Himself was standing on its summit? But the great apostle of the Gentiles puts it beyond all doubt, and warrants us to say without faltering, that this rock was Christ (1 Cor. 10:4). Having therefore such an infallible guide to our meditation, let us reflect a little what was the rock, what was the smiting, and visit the water that issued from it and followed them in the way.

The *rock itself* might be an emblem of His person, in whom is everlasting strength, to whom we may fly as a refuge, and upon whom we may build as a foundation. There is not, perhaps, a metaphor more frequent in the book of God than this: God is a rock. Though never once used before this remarkable occurrence, yet soon after it is adopted by Moses in his dying song (see Deut. 32:4, 13, 15, 18, 30–31; see also Pss. 18:2, 31, 46; 42:9; 62:7; 78:35; 89:26; 94:22; Isa. 17:10; Ezek. 26:14).

The *smiting of the rock* might prefigure Jesus's satisfactory sufferings, who was stricken, smitten of God, and afflicted; and one of the soldiers opened His side with a spear, and there came out blood and water. The rock was smitten with the rod of Moses, the type of the law, and it was the curse of the law that subjected Him to the ignominious cross, who redeemed us from "the curse of the law, being made a curse for us" (Gal. 3:13). The rock was smitten in the presence of the elders and people of the Jews with noise and tumult. So Christ was wounded for our transgressions at Jerusalem, the most public place, and at the Passover solemnity, the most public time. Then and there He endured the cross and despised the shame (Heb. 12:2). At the commandment of the Lord the Rock was smitten, and by the commandment of the Lord was the Captain of our salvation made perfect through sufferings (Heb. 2:10). It was smitten but once with approbation, and when Moses smote it twice, the Lord was angry with him for doing it. Might not this be an obscure intimation that Christ by one offering should finish the work of our redemption? For He needed not often to suffer from the foundation of the world. But whoever they be that crucify to themselves the Son of God afresh, they shall not go unpunished (Heb. 6:6).

The *water* that issued from the rock, what might it signify? Shall we say it is an emblem of *the glad tidings of the gospel of Jesus Christ*, which are to the distressed conscience as cold water to a thirsty soul? In vain did the poor and needy seek water to refresh their troubled minds in the legal doctrine of the Scribes and Pharisees or in the philosophical disquisitions of the Gentile sages. Still their souls failed them for thirst. But the Lord heard them, and the God of Jacob did not forsake them. For in the preaching of the everlasting gospel both to the Jews and Gentiles, the charming promise received its accomplishment in the most simple of manners: "I will open rivers in high places, and fountains in the midst of the valleys: I will make the wilderness a pool of water, and the dry land springs of water" (Isa. 41:18). "The beast of the field shall honour me, the dragons and the owls: because I give waters in the wilderness, and rivers in the desert, to give drink to my people, my chosen" (Isa. 43:20). Or shall we say that the water from the rock is an emblem of the *influences of the blessed Spirit*, that, like a river pure as crystal, issues from the throne of God and of the Lamb (Rev. 22:1)? To this refreshing, cleansing, and prolific element, our Lord Himself compares this glorious person, when on the last day of the feast He stood and cried, "If any man thirst, let him come unto me, and drink. He that believeth on me,…out of his belly shall flow rivers of living water. (But this spake he of the Spirit, which they that believe on him should receive)" (John 7:37–39). Or shall we say that this water may be an emblem of that "precious blood of Christ" (1 Peter 1:19), which cleanses from all sin, and except we drink it in a spiritual manner, we can "have no life in [us]" (John 6:53)? Or, lastly, shall we say that the water that issued from the smitten rock did represent all the blessings of redemption, the salutary effects of His sufferings and death? For to Him we may apply what the prophet foretells, "And a man shall be as…rivers of waters in a dry place, as the shadow of a great rock in a weary land" (Isa. 32:2).

The Rock Gave an Abundant Provision

These waters flowed not till *the rock was smitten* with the rod of Moses. Nor could we have derived these gracious benefits from Christ, which we do partake, if He had not suffered. The striking of a flint, one should think, would rather bring fire than water. But it was of the Lord of Hosts, who is wonderful in counsel and excellent in working. Who would imagine that the Redeemer's sufferings, which in themselves were tragic and melancholy, should prove so consolatory to the believing soul? O Christian, it is thine to extract joy out of sorrow, happiness out of misery, glory out of ignominy, life out of death, though these things seem as impossible as to fetch "oil out of the flinty rock" (Deut. 32:13).

The waters flowed when the rock was smitten, not in scanty measure but in *large abundance*. The miraculous stream was not exhausted, though many hundred thousand men with their herds drank of it. Nor were the dry places of that sandy desert able to imbibe the copious moisture. So inexhausted is the fullness of Jesus Christ, from whom all sorts of men—the Jews, the Gentiles, the barbarians, the Scythians, the bond, and the free—may receive all sorts of blessings. You are not straitened in Him, O children of men; this river of God, which is full of water, can never run dry nor be exhausted, however abundantly we drink of its refreshing streams.

The waters that flowed from the rock were not only sufficient to supply the present straits of Israel but, as the sacred story tells, they *followed them in the way* for some considerable time, at least after the rock was smitten. So Jesus Christ imparts the blessed fruits of His satisfactory death, not only to the first ages of Christianity but to the most distant ages of the world. Never shall this goodness and mercy cease to follow all that are Israelites indeed, till mortality shall be swallowed up of life, till the wilderness be exchanged for Canaan and the militant resign to the triumphant state. The winter shall not arrest this river in icy fetters, and the drought of summer shall not drink it up like a brook; for thus the promise runs, by the mouth of the prophet Zechariah, "In summer and in winter shall it be" (Zech. 14:8).

The Rock Who Loves Us

Blessed be our rock, who consented to be smitten, that we might drink abundantly of the river of pleasures. Great was the love of David's three worthies, who hazarded their lives to purchase for their longing general a draught of water from the well of Bethlehem (2 Sam. 23:16). But greater was the love of Jesus, who lost His life and poured His precious blood that we might draw water with joy from "the wells of salvation" (Isa. 12:3) when "hungry and thirsty, [our] soul fainted in [us]" (Ps. 107:5). "Oh that men would praise the LORD for his goodness, and for his wonderful works to the children of men!" (Ps. 107:8, 15, 21, 31). May this river, "the streams whereof shall make glad the city of God," be your consolation in this "dry and thirsty land" (Ps. 46:4; 63:1). Ye "broken cisterns" of this world—sinful pleasures, vain comforts and delights, and our own legal righteousness—can you supply the place of this "fountain of living waters" (Jer. 2:13; 17:13)? How miserably are they disappointed who exchange the one for the other! They shall come back with their pitchers empty; they shall be ashamed and confounded and cover their heads. How justly they deserve that God should bring upon them the waters of the river, strong and many, and pour upon them the fury of His anger who refuse these "waters of Shiloah that go softly" (Isa. 8:6)! Open, O Lord, the ears of sinners to hear Thy gracious invitation, "Ho, every one that thirsteth, come ye to the waters" (Isa. 55:1). Open their eyes to see this well, as once Thou opened the eyes of Hagar in the wilderness (Gen. 21:19), lest in hell they lift up their eyes in torment, without a drop to cool their tongue (Luke 16:23). O grant us to believe on Christ, that we may never thirst!

6

The Brazen Serpent
Numbers 21:4–8

The host of Israel had long traversed the desolate wilderness, and finding no end of their wanderings, instead of accepting this punishment of their iniquity from the hand of the Lord, again they murmur, against Him and Moses, and undervalue their heavenly provision, though the food of angels. The incensed Jehovah commands the serpents to bite them. The serpents obeyed, and many of the people died. The survivors, convinced of their error, confess their fault and beg that Moses would intercede for them with their offended God. Moses listens to the people, and the Lord is entreated by him. But observe the strange manner wherein the cure was wrought. Does He kill these poisonous and fiery flying serpents outright? No. Does He drive them to some distant region of the earth or remote corner of the wilderness where the Israelites would be annoyed with them no more? Nor this either. Or does He restrain these noxious creatures from stinging them, which was also possible, though they swarmed in the camp? None of all these. The serpents are suffered to live, suffered to remain in the camp, and suffered to bite as before. But a brazen serpent is by God's command lifted upon a pole, that it might be conspicuous from afar; and whoever snatched a look of this lifeless serpent need not fear the bite of the living ones, for the wound was not mortal. "Happy art thou, O Israel…O people saved by the LORD" (Deut. 33:29). They were hungry, and they had miraculous bread; thirsty, and they were supplied with miraculous drink; now they are sick and wounded, and they are favored with miraculous medicine. Here indeed the Scripture was fulfilled in the most literal sense: "Fools because of their transgression, and because of their iniquities, are afflicted. Their soul abhorreth all manner of meat; and they draw near unto the gates of death. Then they cry unto the LORD in their trouble, and he saveth them out of their distresses. He sent his word, and healed them, and delivered them from their destructions" (Ps. 107:17–20).

Let us behold in this eminent figure at once our miserable state by sin and the method of our recovery by Jesus Christ, who from this very thing preached to Nicodemus the doctrine of His cross: "As Moses," said He, "lifted up the serpent in the wilderness, even so must the Son of man be lifted up" (John 3:14).

The Serpent as the Emblem of Our Sinful Condition

The devil and his angels, these are the fiery flying serpents who, though invisible to the eye, have stung the race of Adam and have insinuated their deadly poison through the whole mass of human nature, for which we may take up the prophet's lamentation, "The whole head is sick, and the whole heart faint" (Isa. 1:5). Ever since we broke through the hedge of the divine law, these serpents have incessantly bitten us. This makes the world a terrible wilderness indeed, a land of trouble and anguish, whence come the viper and the fiery flying serpent. It is true, the wounds that are made by the scorpions of hell may seem but slight at the first, for many a time they have stricken us and we were not grieved. But as the unhappy Israelite soon perceived the deadly venom drinking up his vitals, so shall the devil's fiery darts, sooner or later, inflame the conscience and never fail to enkindle in the heart a burning fever of unsatisfied and irregular desires. It was only the death of the mortal body that threatened the stung Israelite. But the soul—the immortal soul—is endangered by the bite of the infernal serpent unless an antidote can be found. And this antidote is the Lord Jesus Christ, of which Moses's serpent was a figure.

The Serpent as the Emblem of Our Savior
It may perhaps seem odd at first that so noxious and hateful a creature as the serpent should be made an emblem of the amiable and beneficent Redeemer, especially when we consider that "the serpent" is a name commonly appropriated to the grand adversary of God and man (Gen. 3:1ff.). In the Scripture style, wicked men are called "serpents" and a "generation of vipers" (Matt. 3:7; 12:34; 23:33). But let us reflect *to whom* He is a serpent, for He is to the devil what this malicious spirit is to us—that is, his destroyer. Why should it not be equally proper to compare the gracious Redeemer to the serpent as to the lion, both which are names of his great enemy? What is the strength of the roaring lion of hell to His strength who is the Lion of the tribe of Judah? And what is the subtlety of the devil, the old serpent, to the wisdom of Jesus Christ, the new? Besides, the serpent being the first cursed creature may even on this account be pitched on as a type of Him who was to become a curse for us. But whereas the serpent of Moses was void of poison and wore no sting, for it was only the form of a serpent, it is natural here to think how Jesus Christ only appeared in the likeness of sinful flesh but was utterly a stranger to the venom of sin, though in all other things made like to us, whose poison is as the poison of a serpent. Whether the strength and luster of the brass might be a faint shadow of the strength and glory of that wonderful person, the God-man, I shall not affirm.

The Serpent's Lifting Up Anticipates Christ's Death on a Cross
But the lifting up of this serpent seems an evident prediction of that death which Christ should die. Here He is evidently set forth crucified before us, as we are taught by Himself who is the end of the law for righteousness, when speaking of the death He should die: "And I," says He, "if I be lifted up from the earth, will draw all men unto me" (John 12:32). The serpent was lifted up on a pole, and Christ was lifted up on the accursed tree. The serpent was lifted up by Moses, the figure of the law, and Christ was by the law subjected to enduring the cross. The serpent was lifted up in the most conspicuous manner amid the camp of Israel, and the crucifixion of the Son of God was

transacted in the most public manner at Jerusalem, the metropolis of Judea. It was God who commanded the serpent to be lifted up in the wilderness, and it was God who commanded our Lord and Savior to lay down His life, and adjusted, by His determinate counsel, all the shameful and all the painful circumstances of that awful and amazing scene. If it had not been with a view to its elevation on the pole, Moses had not been ordered to make this brazen image, nor would the Son of God have appeared in the likeness of a man but with an intention to expire on the cross and give His life a ransom for many. The serpent was lifted up, that whosoever beheld it might be healed and live, and Christ was crucified, that whosoever believeth in Him might not perish but have everlasting life.

Looking to the Serpent Pictures Saving Faith in Christ

That a wounded Israelite should be saved by looking, and a perishing sinner by believing, are things that bear no small resemblance to each other. For what is believing on Him but seeing Him who is invisible, that, like Moses, we may endure? What is it but looking on Him whom we have pierced, that we may mourn? How fitly may the glorious words in the prophet Isaiah come from the mouth of the crucified Redeemer, "Look unto Me, and be saved, all ye ends of the earth; for I am God, and there is none else; besides Me there is no Savior" (see Isa. 45:22)? Let us more particularly observe the likeness of their remedy to ours.

It was a method of cure *solely contrived and appointed of God*, from whose ordinance alone it received its efficacy. Who would so much as have imagined in a dream that to look at a dead serpent of brass would cure the bite of a living serpent? Should reason be allowed to give her verdict, she would perhaps be so far from pronouncing it a proper expedient that she would rather judge it a gross absurdity, especially if it be true what some affirm, that the sight of burnished brass is naturally pernicious to them who are bitten of serpents, and if it be true what is also asserted, that to see but the shape of any venomous creature increases the torment of the unhappy sufferer whom it bit. Exactly so, the method of our recovery by the cross of Jesus Christ is a device that claims God Himself for its only original. The world by wisdom never would have arrived at the knowledge of it; nay, it is a thing they are highly offended with, for it is in them that perish foolishness, but to them that are saved it is the wisdom of God, and the power of God unto salvation to everyone that believeth. Though reason would not have thought, God has ordained it. To this alone must all its efficacy be ascribed, for it is the will of the Father that "every one which seeth the Son, and believeth on him, may have everlasting life" (John 6:40).

It was a method of cure that *never failed*, being no less sure than strange. Not an Israelite died, as Moses assures us, who looked at the brazen serpent. Where were they ever ashamed that put their trust in Christ? Were they ever disappointed in their expectations, those that believed in Him for everlasting life? "For God so loved the world, that he gave his only begotten Son, that whosoever believeth in him should not perish, but have everlasting life" (John 3:16).

It was a method of cure that might be *easily put into practice* by an Israelite if he was not blind. Perhaps he might happen to receive his wound in some remote place of the camp, and though it should have affected him in such a manner that he could neither move hand nor foot, yet without stirring from the place where he was, without sending for physicians to apply their medicines, he was saved by one glance of his eye. In like manner, if the god of this world has not blinded our minds, we are saved not by working but by believing. The works of the law are physicians of no value to the distressed conscience, but Christ is a present help, and to find Him we need neither climb up into heaven nor descend into the deep.

It was a remedy that might be *repeated as often as there was occasion for it*. So Christ is the propitiation for our sins, to whom we may warrantably have recourse as often as we are wounded by hellish temptations and in every time of need. Yet let no abuser of this heavenly doctrine infer that because the remedy is at hand, they may be careless and secure and expose themselves at random to the painful stings of the infernal serpents. What Israelite would have been so mad as to handle these hateful creatures and court them to instill their venom, with no other design than to try the experiment of the brazen serpent's virtue? Would not this have been a horrid perversion of that healing ordinance and at least a tempting of the Lord? But the truth is, the human race does not more abhor the touch and neighborhood of serpents of every kind than an Israelite indeed, or a sincere believer, when acting up to his character, will abhor even all approaches to temptation. It is every whit as reasonable to suppose that because the serpents in the wilderness were not permitted to destroy the Israelites, by reason of their heavenly antidote, therefore they loved the serpents, and delighted in their society, as it is to suppose that the true Christian can be encouraged to sin, or love that which he hates, because of abounding grace.

It was a remedy that, without all doubt, proved *effectual to the Israelite who used it, though his eyesight had been ever so weak.* So the weakest faith, if genuine, is as saving as the strongest because its object is the same.

It was, in short, a remedy that *ascribed the whole glory to God,* even as in the work of our salvation by Jesus Christ all boasting is excluded. While the believing soul treads upon the adder and tramples the dragon under feet and says, "O death, where is thy sting?" (1 Cor. 15:55), O Satan where is thy power? let him also say, "Thanks be to God, which giveth us the victory through our Lord Jesus Christ" (1 Cor. 15:57).

7

Thoughts on the Veil of Moses
Exodus 34:29–35

The lawgiver of the Jews having ascended the second time to Mount Sinai—where he obtained a sight of the divine glory and got the second tables inscribed anew with the finger of God after the first were broken—he now descends to the camp with the tables in his hand but is greatly surprised to see his brother Aaron, and other Israelites, filled with perturbation at his approach and afraid to look him in the face. Such horror might indeed have well become them the first time he descended, for they had, during his absence, been guilty of that almost unpardonable crime, the making the golden calf, which they could not but suspect would be highly resented both by God and Moses. But now their peace was made, and their prophet comes with the pledges of reconciliation in his hand, what can be the reason (might he say to himself) of my brethren's running away from me, as I were still their enemy? The face of Moses was equally meek as before, but though the features were the same, it shone with a glory visible to everybody but himself. This strange phenomenon was the cause of that awful distance they kept. But perceiving that his voice was the same, though his face altered, they resume their courage and venture to approach him, though still they dare not come to any close interview with their shining lawgiver till, in condescension to their weakness, he put a veil upon his glorious face. Such honor it pleased God to confer on his faithful servant, not only to inspire the minds of the Israelites with greater reverence for him but chiefly to dignify that dispensation of which he was the minister. We are not told how long this miraculous brightness lasted, but in all appearance it was not of long duration, and vanished gradually away, to signify the transient nature of that economy.

There Was a Veil upon the Hearts of God's People

Moses himself, perhaps, intended no more by veiling his face than what is expressed in the history. However, the wisdom of the Holy Spirit having given us a divinely inspired interpretation of this action by the mouth of the apostle Paul, let us dwell upon it a little.

The veil upon the face of Moses, according to that eminent apostle, did signify that, partly through the obscurity of their law and partly through the blindness of their hearts, the children of Israel could not steadfastly look to the end of that which was abolished. Now that which was abolished is their legal dispensation, and the goal of that which was abolished is Jesus Christ Himself, who is "the end [or goal] of the law for righteousness" as having fulfilled its meaning, canceled its authority, and introduced in its place a far more excellent economy (Rom. 10:4).

What, some may reply, did Israel not know the meaning of their law? Was it the intention of the Almighty to conceal from them a thing in which they are so highly interested? Had they no sufficient intimations that their ritual institutions did point at better things and were, in future time, capable of repeal and would actually come to an end?

In answer to this, it is not at all denied that there were many things in the writings and Law of Moses that not obscurely hinted at its true design. The veil of Moses was not so thick and broad but some rays of his light did actually pass through it, even as the darkness and blackness that enveloped the summit of Mount Sinai was interspersed with flashes of lightning and gleams of fire. The attentive Israelite, who meditated upon the law of the Lord day and night, might know that more was meant than was plainly expressed.

The *constant expectation of a Messiah*, which universally obtained in all ages of the Jewish church, might fully convince them of the weakness of their rites, to do what they seemed to promise, and that the ceremonial law was far from being the whole of their religion. They had it hinted to them, in the dying benediction of their great forefather, that their judicial law should not be always observed but that a period should arrive when the scepter should depart from the royal tribe: "The sceptre shall not depart from Judah, nor a lawgiver from between his feet, until Shiloh come; and unto him shall the gathering of the people be" (Gen. 49:10).

A small measure of acquaintance with their own hearts might have easily persuaded them that *the demands of the moral law*, or Ten Commandments, were too rigid for them ever to hope justification by their compliance with them. For however much it may be thought by superficial observers that the first nine precepts in the law may be fulfilled by an imperfect creature, yet it is evident that the very letter of the tenth commandment forbids the sins of the heart and all the motions of concupiscence. How can the proudest legalist plume himself with the foolish conceit of being able to conform himself in all respects to the very letter of the law when the very letter of the law says, "Thou shalt not covet" (Ex. 20:17)? If then there were many Israelites who rested in the law, without looking any further, and fondly imagined that it was able to give them eternal life, this fatal mistake was not chiefly owing to the obscurity of their dispensation but to the blindness of their own hearts that were hard as the stones on which their law was written and veiled as their lawgiver's face.

The Veil Lifted in the New Testament

But after all, it must be confessed, the law and holy books of Moses have much obscurity in them when compared with the great plainness of speech used by the apostles in the New Testament. They may be compared to a fine picture placed in a dark corner: though its principal figures may be discerned by a penetrating eye, it is, however, impossible the delicate touches of the pencil, the distributions of light and shade, the beauty of the tints, the elegance of the designs can be thoroughly perceived by the most vigorous sight till the finished piece is translated from its obscure situation and set in an advantageous light.

One that reads the writings of Moses and throws but a cursory glance over the moral, the ceremonial, and the judicial law, without remembering that, like Moses, they put a veil on their face, he would be very apt to mistake the true design of the whole system and to entertain many erroneous opinions that are really inconsistent with its original intention, though they seem to be founded upon it. One would think the ceremonial worship prescribed so minutely by Moses must certainly have been very acceptable to God even for its own sake, or He would never have been at the pains to adjust, by His express authority, the smallest circumstances relative unto it. One would almost imagine that God took pleasure to eat the flesh of bulls and drink the blood of goats, that He is displeased with outward corporeal uncleanness, that the beauty of His worship consists in the outward pomp of splendid rites, that the blood of slaughtered beasts was able to take away sin, that man has still a power to obey the moral law, that we must enter into life by keeping the commandments, that righteousness can come by the law, that the natural seed of Abraham could never be rejected from being the people of God, that their civil state should be unhinged and their ceremonies should never be abolished. These, and many such false opinions, might have been suggested by the terms in which the law is uttered. And many a carnal Jew was taken in this snare. "Even unto this day, when Moses is read, the vail is upon their heart" (cf. 2 Cor. 3:13–15).

The prophets labored in vain to pull this veil aside and reclaim from these vain imaginations that stiff-necked people, the bulk of whom, in our own day, persevere in their absurd prejudices and presumptuous expectations.

If any should inquire why the revelation of the divine will was not equally plain in the past as in the present age and why the God with whom light dwells would deliver a law to His people, of which the true design and genuine scope was not obvious at the first view, remember that it is not for us to dive into the eternal counsels. It was the will of God that it should be so, and who dares say to Him,

"What doest thou?" (Job 9:12). Let us rather observe how the veil was gradually removed till Moses stands confessed, and the design of His economy is no longer a mystery, since the revelation of Jesus Christ.

The Veil Is Lifted with the Coming of Jesus Christ
Much is said in the prophetic Scriptures that might have undeceived the blind Jews and taught them to abate their vain confidence in their national privileges, their ceremonial observances, and their moral righteousnesses (see Isa. 64:6). The grand doctrines of Christianity relating to the person, the character, and mediation of Jesus Christ are laid down in these venerable prophetic writings with greater perspicuity than in the books of Moses. But though the prophets harmoniously conspire in giving their suffrage to every Christian doctrine, yet still they put upon their face the veil of poetical figures and ceremonial phrases. They describe spiritual blessings by images of civil peace and plenty. With them the victory of Jesus Christ is treading of a winepress, in which the wine is the blood of slaughtered enemies, prayer is incense and a pure offering, conversion is going up to Jerusalem, gospel worship is the celebration of the festival of the Jews.

But now comes *John the Baptist*, the harbinger of Christ, who talks still plainer than Moses or the prophets, and instead of commending the Levitical sacrifices, he invites his hearers to regard that unknown person to whom he pointed as the completion of them all: "Behold the Lamb of God, which taketh away the sin of the world" (John 1:29).

But by the *ministry of Christ and His blessed apostles*, the law is wholly unmasked and the veil on Moses's face entirely done away. The lowly birth, indigent life, and ignominious death of the Messiah Himself was an incontestable proof that His kingdom is "not of this world," as the Jews expected (John 18:36). Though He was the Great High Priest, He gave no attendance at the altar, and His forerunner, though born a Levite, never officiated in the temple. This was a plain declaration that He was come to abrogate these ancient rites. But if we attend to the strain of His doctrine, it will appear how it was calculated to remove the veil and cure the prejudices of the mistaken Jews. He taught that a man is not defiled by what enters in at the mouth; foretold that their city and temple, the center of their worship, should be razed; and that a spiritual worship should be established over all the world and might be presented unto God in every place (Matt. 15:11; John 2:19; Mark 16:15, cf. Col. 1:23). That He might pave the way for explaining the grand doctrine of justification by His imputed righteousness, He expatiated upon the vast extent of the moral law and frequently inculcated the sad depravity of human nature (Matt. 5:17ff.). He spoke of Himself as the fulfiller of all righteousness (Matt. 3:15), the heavenly manna (John 6:58), and the antitype of the serpent lifted up in the wilderness (John 3:14).

But *after His ascension*, Christ inspires His apostles to finish what He had only begun and completely remove that veil which Moses put upon his face. By their apostolic decree, they instructed the Christian Gentiles in their New Testament liberty, and by their epistles addressed to the primitive churches, they entirely dissipated the obscurity of the Old Testament shadows. Now it appears that the kingdom of God is "not meat and drink; but righteousness, and peace, and joy in the Holy Ghost" (Rom. 14:17), that the Mosaic law was only a schoolmaster to tutor the church in her childish state and train her up for a more perfect institution. Now we plainly see that righteousness cannot possibly come by the law nor pardon by the sacrifices. If the veil is not still upon our hearts, we may in Christ behold "with open face…the glory of the Lord" and be "changed into the same image from glory to glory" (2 Cor. 3:18). Now "the face of the covering cast over all people, and the vail that is spread over all nations" is entirely destroyed (Isa. 25:7); and therefore, O house of Israel, "come…and let us walk in the light of the Lord" (Isa. 2:5).

8

The Sacrifices
Leviticus 1:1–9; Romans 12:1–2

Sacrificing is a religious action in which a creature devoted to God was in a solemn manner destroyed in His presence for sacred ends, and it was a mode of worship that obtained in the earliest ages of the world. It may not only be traced up to the famous era of giving the law from Mount Sinai, for the ancient patriarchs did commonly practice it. How many altars were built by Abraham and his grandchild Jacob? Melchizedek was a priest of the Most High God, Job offered sacrifices both for his children and for his friends, and God smelled a savor of rest when Noah sacrificed clean beasts and birds upon the altar which he built unto the Lord. But why do I mention these venerable personages as the most ancient practicers of sacrificial worship when it may be more than conjectured that Adam himself did use it? Can we think, when Abel offered unto the Lord the firstlings of his flock, that his father did not instruct him to testify in this manner his fear of the Lord?

And what shall we say of the coats of skins which the Lord made for them or directed them to make? The beasts to whom they belonged cannot so soon after the creation be supposed to have died of old age. They behoved, therefore, to be slain. How natural to suppose that they were slain in sacrifice rather than for any other use? Perhaps it was not without a mystery that the skins of these beasts should clothe their bodies, whose blood made atonement for their souls. To be short, then, though we can by no means assent that in the state of innocence there would have been the least occasion for them, they seem, however, to be as ancient as the promise about the seed of the woman, who was to have His heel bruised while He bruised the serpent's head (Gen. 3:15).

The Source of the Sacrifices

The antiquity of sacrifices being supposed, let us now see by whose authority they were first enjoined. And it will be certainly found that as their date is ancient, their origin is divine. That God prescribed them to His chosen people is not disputed, for a great part of Scripture is occupied in describing the various laws by which this species of worship should be regulated. But what shall we think of the sacrifices that were offered by the patriarchs before the giving of the law? Were they acts of will worship?[1] Did they contrive this mode of adoration from their own brains? Did the light of nature dictate that the Lord could be delighted with butchering, slaying, and burning a harmless brute or otherwise destroying creatures that were inanimate? No: neither did the light of nature dictate them, nor blind superstition, but *the sovereign will and positive command of God* is their original warrant.

Be it so, we read of the practice before we read of the precept. Still, from the former we may fairly infer the latter, for such eminent saints would never have adventured to express their devotion in such a strange manner if they had not been required to do so by the declared will of God. Indeed, without such a persuasion they could not have offered in faith, and we are assured by an authority too great to be controverted that the first man whose sacrifice is expressly mentioned in Scripture offered through faith a more excellent sacrifice than Cain, of which the deity was pleased to testify His acceptance by some distinguishing marks of regard (Gen. 4:4; Heb. 11:4). Now, let us even suppose these primitive believers might have been so

---

1. Editor's note: See Colossians 2:23, "Which things have indeed a shew of wisdom in will worship, and humility, and neglecting of the body; not in any honour to the satisfying of the flesh."

presumptuous as to invent or practice such bloody rites without the command of God, it can never be admitted that God, who has upon all occasions testified His displeasure against the inventions of men in His worship, would have smiled upon such self-devised modes of adoration. Instead of testifying of their gifts, accepting their burnt offerings, would He not rather have upbraided them, as in the words of that well-known reproof, "Who hath required this at your hand?" (Isa. 1:12). Upon the whole, then, it is easy to see that sacrifices were not offered without the command of God. And it is more than probable that the precept and the practice are of equal age; that these holy rites were commanded immediately after the readmission of our first parents into the divine favor upon the back of their apostasy; that the universal custom of sacrificing was received by tradition from the first man; and that after the true design of the institution was lost among the degenerate nations, the ceremony itself was still preserved.

The Goal of the Sacrifices

Well then, the custom was ancient, was divine, and surely it was for some important end God would command—and the best of men practice it—for the space of four thousand years. What could move the eternal Majesty to require for so long a time that sacrifices should be an essential part of His worship? Was there any real excellence in these actions that might render them pleasing to God for their own sake? Were they to be put on an equal or superior footing to acts of moral service? Not at all. God Himself declares in the most positive manner, even in the age of sacrifices, that to offer thanksgiving, to pay their vows, and to do justly and love mercy were actions far preferable to loading His altar with the most costly oblations. Even though men had been ever so punctual in this kind of worship, they were not immediately entitled to the character of saints, whatever course of action they steered in their other deportment toward God or their fellow creatures. Yea, so far were sacrifices from being able to recommend the persons of wicked sinners to God that, on the contrary, their sins, when resolutely persisted in, rendered not only their persons but also their sacrifices detestable to Him. He loathed, He despised, He abhorred, and His soul was weary to bear them. That they did really atone for *ceremonial* guilt, or sanctify to the *purifying of the flesh*, may indeed be allowed. But that they could *really atone* for moral guilt, *purge the conscience* from dead works, or *be acceptable to the divine Majesty* for their own sake is denied by Scripture, reason, and even by the sacrifices themselves.

It is denied by Scripture. For in the prophet Micah, rivers of oil and thousands of rams are denied to be an adequate propitiation: "Will the LORD be pleased with thousands of rams, or with ten thousands of rivers of oil?" And this needs not be wondered at, for what is still more, the firstborn, we are assured in the same place, would not be accepted for transgression, nor the fruit of the body for the sin of the soul: "Shall I give my firstborn for my transgression, the fruit of my body for the sin of my soul?" (Mic. 6:7).

It is denied by reason. For reason herself being judge, where were the justice to punish a harmless beast for the sins of its owner? What proportion can there be between the sin of a man and the sufferings of a brute beast? Can the Majesty of heaven indeed be prevailed upon to lay aside His just anger for such a puny satisfaction? Then, Sinai, thy thunders are vanished into smoke, and there was no occasion to publish with such solemnity and terror to the trembling Israelites that fiery law whose curses might be thus so easily avoided!

But let us ask even the sacrifices themselves, and they will confess their insufficiency to expiate moral guilt; for there were many sins that were not to be purged with sacrifice or offering. Let David bear witness, who says to God concerning his complicated crime of adultery and deliberate murder, "Thou desirest not sacrifice; else would I give it: thou delightest not in burnt offering" (Ps. 51:16). Besides, the repetition of these sacrifices is a most invincible proof that it was not in them to make perfect those that offered them: "for then would they not have ceased to be offered?" Surely they would, for "the worshippers once purged should have had no more conscience of sins" (Heb. 10:2).

Was it then impossible that the blood of bulls and goats should take away sin, notwithstanding the antiquity and divine original of the custom to offer sacrifice? Having removed the false end [i.e., goal] of their institution, let us look into the real intention, and we shall have a particular eye to the offerings under the economy of Moses.

Sacrifices under the Economy of Moses

And here it will not be contradicted if one should affirm that sundry circumstances in the law of sacrifices might be intended to convey moral instructions—for instance, that the brutish qualities of the sacrificed beasts might signify the vices or lusts which we ought to mortify for the honor of God or that the virtuous qualities of the victims (suppose meekness, patience, and the like) might denote those graces and virtues which the worshipper of God should cultivate in his own heart. It must not be denied that the ancient ceremonial worship might be a figure of that reasonable service which is ever due to the sovereign Creator in all the different states of the rational creature. But though these and other considerations may have their proper weight and place, we have not yet found out the adequate reason of these mysterious institutions.

That true reason may be confessed as follows: *In Thy bloody death, O Jesus, we see the great antitype of these legal oblations.* Most certainly, they were public acknowledgments of guilt and professions of faith in the grand propitiation which they believed should appear in the end of the world. Tell us, thou sweet singer of Israel, who is he that shall do for us what the law could not do? In the fortieth psalm, David, speaking not of himself but of a far more glorious person, has these most emphatic words: "Sacrifice and offering thou didst not desire:…burnt offering and sin offering hast thou not required. Then said I, Lo, I come: in the volume of the book it is written of me, I delight to do thy will, O my God" (Ps. 40:6–8). *It was not Christ who came to imitate the sacrifices, but the sacrifices were ordained to prefigure Him.* They were the "shadow" of future good things, "but the body [i.e., substance] is of Christ" (Col. 2:17). When Christ was first revealed, the sacrifices seem to have been observed, and when He died, they ceased to be offered. The temple heard His dying groan and rent her veil in presence of the priesthood as they offered the evening sacrifice (Matt. 27:51). From this time forth shall your office be vacated, ye legal priests! Ye beasts of the field, no more shall you smoke as victims on God's altar, for the merciful High Priest "hath loved us, and hath given himself for us an offering and a sacrifice to God for a sweetsmelling savour" (Eph. 5:2).

Now, if they began with the prediction of His death and ended with the accomplishment of His atoning death, what can be plainer than the relation between them as the shadow and the substance? Set this relation aside, and it is impossible to vindicate to any advantage the original appointment of sacrifices or to account for their abolition after they were enjoined. Should any be contentious in this point, we have an entire book in the canon of the New Testament in which the professed argument is the resemblance of the Old Testament sacrifices to the true propitiation. Let us here glance at some of the most luminous parallels only between the sacrifice of Moses and the sacrifice of Jesus Christ.

The Qualities of Sacrificed Creatures
We may first take notice of the qualities of the sacrificed creatures, especially of the animal kind. It was not left a matter of indifference, and wholly in the option of God's peculiar people, with what victims they should stain His altars.

According to the law, they were required to be *clean creatures*, fit to be eaten for the support of human life, and to be one with the offerer in some sense, by their aptitude for digestion into the substance of his body. This was an evident memorial of the sanctity of the great propitiation, and that He should be a partaker of the same flesh and blood with those for whom He should die, for it was requisite that both "he that sanctifieth and they who are sanctified [be] all of one" (Heb. 2:11). The integrity and perfection which God required in the bodies of these beasts may easily be accommodated to the glorious antitype, who would be wholly incapacitated from the discharge of His priestly function by the smallest blemish. For though it became the typical nation of the Jews to have a high priest involved in the same guilt of actual transgression with his brethren, who was therefore to offer first for his own sin before he presumed to offer for the errors of the people, yet "such an high priest became us, who is holy, harmless, undefiled, [and] separate from sinners" (Heb. 7:26).

They were, further, to be *valuable and beloved creatures*, as lambs that are for clothing and goats that are the price of the field, and he that offered them was put to cost and damage, as indeed in the first ages of mankind the riches of the most opulent possessor consisted chiefly in flocks and herds. What forbids us to think here of Jesus Christ being the darling of His Father and precious to them that believe? O the invaluable treasure of blood that was paid for the redemption of the soul! In comparison hereof, what is silver and gold and all corruptible things? Ransack the bowels of the mountains, for all the glowing gems formed there in dark retirements, when compared to the precious blood of the Lamb, they are poor and beggarly acquisitions, and converted into pebble stones fit to be trampled under feet.

Moreover, there behoved to be found in the destined victims some *amiable qualities resembling moral virtues*. They were not permitted to sacrifice the stupid ass or the sordid swine, though tame creatures; far less were the fierce inhabitants of the forest, as wolves, bears, lions, to come upon God's altar. But the sacrifices in which He delighted were the gentle dove, the patient and laborious ox, the meek lamb, and the sheep that is dumb before the shearer and the butcher. Who sees not in these characters the very picture of the meek, lowly, patient, and uncomplaining Savior of the world, who opened not His mouth when He was led as a lamb to the slaughter (Isa. 53:7; Acts 8:32)? This is a circumstance, which, next to the dignity of His person, did contribute to the value of His satisfactory death.

It is also worthy of notice that of all these beasts, the *firstborn* was most acceptable, and, according to the law, such were holy unto the Lord. Was not this a prelude that He whom God would give to expiate our transgression should be the firstborn among many brethren whom they should honor as the excellency of dignity and to whom they should owe their deliverance from death and their title to the inheritance?

I shall only further hint that whereas God was not only pleased when the rich men offered of their larger cattle but when the poor men brought turtle doves and pigeons, might not this put us in mind how the sacrifice which God accepts is *equally accessible to the poor and the rich*? And truly, as the legal sacrifices were chargeable, in less or more, to all that presented them, the real and better sacrifice costs us nothing; for we may buy it without money and without price (Isa. 55:1). From the qualities of the victims, let us go on to the sacred rites of oblation, and we shall find something in our great sacrifice corresponding to them all.

The Rites of Oblation
When the creature that was to surrender its life for its owner was pitched upon, it was brought unto the priest and solemnly *sisted*[2] *before the Lord*. But our Lord Jesus was not brought by others, like the irrational animal; but He voluntarily presented Himself before the Lord when His time was fully come. Fully apprised of what was to be done unto Him, He set His face to go up to Jerusalem and patiently expected in the melancholy garden the coming of the traitor and his band of armed men, to whom He was to deliver Himself. The sacred animal being sisted before the Lord was rendered ceremonially guilty by the imposition of hands on its head and by confessing over it the sins of the offerer. It was the Lord Himself that laid on Him the iniquities of us all. O Jesus, it is our guilt alone that can justify the Judge of all the earth in taking pleasure to bruise Thee! And this doubtless was one great reason why He opened not His mouth, while the Roman governor wondered at His silence. It was this consideration that fortified His mind at the approach of His inconceivably bitter agonies and held in His mouth as with a bridle when these astonishing words dropped from His lips, "Now is my soul troubled; and what shall I say?" (John 12:27).

---

2. Editor's note: An old Scots word (especially in law) meaning "to stop" (proceedings of one kind or another). Here it refers to death by sacrifice.

In the next place, *the blood of the innocent animal*, now made guilty by imputation, was shed, was poured out, and sprinkled around; for "without shedding of blood is no remission" (Heb. 9:22). Let there be no talk of an unbloody sacrifice of expiation. That it is the blood that makes atonement for the soul is asserted by the God of Israel Himself, who expressly assigns this reason of the strict prohibition given to His ancient people: "No soul of you shall eat blood, neither shall any stranger that sojourneth among you" (Lev. 17:12). It is easy to see how this prefigured the violent death of the Son of God, who poured out His soul unto death and whose blood cleanses from all sin.

The *pulling of the skin* from the butchered animals, dividing their bodies, and burning them with fire (Num. 19:5) are certainly intended to denote the exquisite torments He was to endure when the assembly of the wicked enclosed Him and His heart was melted in the midst of His bowels like wax before the fire.

The *towering of the smoke* to heaven, which was sometimes perfumed with burning incense, signified how acceptable the sacrifice of Christ should be to God and of what sweet-smelling savor.

In the time of offering, *prayers were offered up*. And we know that in the days of His flesh He offered up prayers, tears, and strong cries to Him that was able to save Him from death (Heb. 5:7).

The *blowing of trumpets* and praising God in the time of the holy rites, with music vocal and instrumental (Num. 10:10), which was often practiced, may no doubt put us in mind of that praise which waiteth for God in Zion on account of purging away our transgression by Himself, which would have prevailed forever against us (Ps. 65:1–3).

The *carrying the blood of the victims into the Holy Place*, the figure of the heavenly sanctuary (Lev. 16:15–16), corresponds to the intercession of our High Priest within the veil, where He appears as a Lamb that has been slain (Heb. 6:19–20; Rev. 5:12; 13:8).

Atonement Made

When the holy rites were finished, atonement was made. The guilt of the offerer was abolished when his victim was destroyed. The anger of God was in some manner appeased, and He gave signs of reconciliation. But as we showed before, it was not in these ceremonial actions to atone for any moral guilt, except in a typical way. But He whom God hath set forth for a propitiation hath, in the most proper sense, fully expiated the sins of all His people who have lived or shall live (Rom. 3:25; 1 John 2:2; 4:10). In His atonement the believers of ancient and later times have rejoiced as the sole foundation of their hope. And nations yet unborn shall be justified by Him from all things from which they could not be justified by Moses's law (Acts 13:39).

The fire that came down from heaven and consumed the sacrifices, which doubtless was kept alive by the priests upon the altar, was it not an emblem of that fierce burning wrath which preyed upon the soul of the incarnate Son of God? Or was it an emblem of the Holy Spirit, through whom He offered up Himself and who is styled "the spirit of burning" (Isa. 4:4)? Or else the fire might signify that fervent love to God and man, which many waters could not quench. It was love that wrought His death; by this holy and pure flame was our atoning sacrifice reduced into ashes.

The altar, what was it? His cross, say some. Nay, it was rather His divine nature, which like the altar supported, and like the altar sanctified, His holy humanity, which alone was destroyed. This the cross can scarce be said to do, which was but the instrument of man's cruelty and a despicable piece of timber, which neither sanctified the body which it carried nor received sanctification from it. Where, then, are they who address it with divine honors and pay even to its picture that homage which is due to Him alone that expired in agonies on that shameful tree?

9

The Ordinance of the Passover
Exodus 12:1–30

The fatal night was now arrived when the destroying angel was to smite all the firstborn of Egypt and the chief of their strength in the tabernacles of Ham. This last and sorest plague shall break the unrelenting heart of Pharaoh and dismiss the oppressed Israelites from his cruel yoke. But mark the goodness of their God in providing for their safety amid the general devastation! They are directed to sprinkle on their door posts the blood of a lamb, whose qualities, the manner of its death, and the rites wherewith they were to eat its flesh are very minutely prescribed and left upon the record for the generations to come. The messenger of death, they were assured, would not presume to enter these hallowed doors, though a thousand did fall at their side and ten thousand on their right hand (Ps. 91:7). Then it was that the Egyptian idols did also feel the vengeance of the true God, and so memorable was the night that the month in which it fell was, in all succeeding ages, to be the beginning of months, or the first month of the year. A ceremony indeed it was that seemed but weak, unmeaning, and unprofitable; but, penetrating the outward veil, let us try to discern the hidden mystery by that same faith through which Moses kept the Passover and the sprinkling of blood, that he which destroyed the firstborn should not touch him. Its meaning we are not now left to explore by our own wit, for that it was a prophetical type, and a very expressive image of the Lamb of God that takes away the sin of the world (John 1:29), an inspired apostle gives us to know by telling us that "Christ our passover is sacrificed for us" (1 Cor. 5:7).

A Lamb without Blemish
A lamb was chosen out of the flock, emblematic of Him who was taken from among men (Heb. 5:1) and raised up from among His brethren. And like that lovely creature did injury to none, though he received from many and is useful in life and death, being at once our clothing and our food, it was a male of the flock of a year old, for Christ is a Son given to us, to suffer in the flower of His age, but without blemish and without spot (Ex. 12:5; 1 Peter 1:19). Though descended from an impure race of ancestors, He brought no stain of sin into the world with Him. And though He long conversed with sinful men and grappled with strong temptations, He contracted not the smallest taint (Heb. 4:15). Even Judas and Pilate attested that He was just and upright—the last before he condemned, and the first after he betrayed Him (Matt. 27:3-4, 23).

A Lamb Slain and Roasted by Fire
On the fourteenth day of the month Abib, the lamb was fetched from the field, and on the nineteenth day at even it was killed by all the Jews in the place which the Lord chose (Ex. 12:6, 18). Even so He of whom these things were spoken went up to Jerusalem five days before the Passover, where with wicked hands He was taken, crucified, and slain (John 12:1, 12ff.).

The lamb was *roasted with fire*. O immaculate Lamb of God, it was the fire of the Father's wrath that forced Thee to complain, "My heart is like wax; it is melted in the midst of my bowels. My strength is dried up like a potsherd; and my tongue cleaveth to my jaws" (Ps. 22:14-15).

A bone of the lamb was *not to be broken*, and none of it was to be left until morning. To accomplish the first, the soldiers brake not His legs, as was usual, and to fulfill the last, He was taken down from the cross the same evening in which He died.

The Blood of the Lamb Sprinkled

In vain had the Israelites killed the lamb if they had not also *sprinkled its blood* with the hyssop upon the doorposts (Ex. 12:22). And Christ is to us dead in vain unless applied by faith to the conscience (Heb. 10:22). His blood must not be sprinkled behind the door, for we must publicly profess that we are not ashamed of the cross of Christ, nor below the door, for it must not be trodden under foot, but above and on every side—on all that we are, on all that we have, and on all we do. Indeed, by His all-penetrating eye the doors of the house and heart are seen with equal clearness. Had a presumptuous Israelite despised this ordinance of God and neglected to sprinkle his doors with blood, he was not within the limits of the divine protection; yea, had he ventured abroad in that perilous night, the angel was not bound to spare him. *So when the arrows of destruction are flying thick and fast, the blood of Jesus is our only sanctuary.* Of this only can we say, "See, O God, our shield: we are indebted to Thy atoning blood for blessings that far transcend deliverance from Egyptian bondage or from temporal death. By Thy blood we are delivered from the wrath that is to come. Thou art our hiding place" (see Ps. 32:7; 119:114). Under this covert of Thy blood, we shall not be afraid of sudden fear, nor of the desolation of the wicked, but shall dwell in peaceable habitations, sure dwellings, and quiet resting places, nigh which no plague shall come.

Many a time the haughty tyrant of Egypt was frightened by the awful prodigies wrought by Moses, but never was he thoroughly subdued till the blood was sprinkled. Then the prey was taken from the mighty (Isa. 49:24–25). In vain he pursues after them, for nevermore shall they wear his chain. So many a time the prophecies of Christ might frighten the black prince of hell, but never was he thoroughly subdued till on the cross He spoiled principalities and powers and made a show of them openly, triumphing over them in it. Even so His elect people are said to overcome, by the blood of the Lamb, the enemy of their salvation (Rev. 12:11). By this same blood the idols are utterly abolished. As in that night of desolation the temples of Egypt were not spared more than the palaces, so in the days of the Messiah shall a man cast away his "idols of silver and...of gold" which he "made...for himself to worship" to "the moles and to the bats; to go into the clefts of the rocks, and into the tops of the ragged rocks, for fear of the LORD, and for the glory of his majesty, when he ariseth to shake terribly the earth" (Isa. 2:20–21). Well may this happy period be unto us the beginning of months (Ex. 12:2). If the beginning of the year was changed to the Israelites, and the seventh became the first month, much more may the beginning of the week be altered to the Christians, and the seventh day be changed for the first, for a Sabbath unto the Lord, for on that day a much more glorious work was finished than when He brought Israel out of Egypt or even when He finished the heavens and all their host and laid the foundation of the earth.

Christ Our Passover Lamb
We have seen how the blood of the Lamb was sprinkled and the happy consequences of this symbolic action; let us now attend how its flesh was to be eaten and how we are made partakers of Christ, who is at once our shield to protect us from danger and our food to preserve our soul in life. It was eaten roasted, for Christ is savory to faith. A bone must not be broken, and mysteries must not be too curiously pried into. A whole lamb must be eaten in every house, and a whole Christ received by every believing soul. It must be eaten in haste, and whatsoever our hands findeth should be done with all our might. The bitter herb signified the bitterness of contrition for sin and of the tribulation we shall have in this world. Unleavened bread is sincerity and truth (1 Cor. 5:8). The loins girt and feet shod signifies the girding up the loins of the mind and the preparation of the gospel of peace, or a readiness to every good work. The staff in the hand might signify that here we have no continuing city. The Passover was only to be eaten by the circumcised and the clean, but if a man was unclean by reason of a dead body, or in a journey afar off, he was permitted to keep a second Passover on the fourteenth day of the second month. Here let us end adoring that condescending love that has appeared toward us, the sinners of the Gentiles. At the first

Passover we were uncircumcised and unclean by reason of death; we were afar off and without God in the world. But us hath He quickened who were dead in trespasses and sins, and in Jesus Christ we who sometimes were afar off are made nigh by the blood of Christ. "Therefore let us keep the feast"; for even Christ our second, Christ our best Passover, is sacrificed for us (1 Cor. 5:7–8).

10

The Ordinance of the Scapegoat
Leviticus 16

Of all the ceremonies enjoined in the book of Leviticus—that gospel of Moses—none were more significant and expressive of evangelical mysteries than those prescribed on the solemn anniversary of general atonement. The rites of this solemn day, though in themselves but carnal ordinances, were, in their use, shadows of good things to come and without all doubt expounded in this view unto the people by the godly priests, whose lips kept knowledge (Mal. 2:7). To what other purpose had been the multitude of their sacrifices unto Him who delights not "in the blood of bullocks,...or of he goats" (Isa. 1:11)? On this day the Jewish high priest was not first to array himself with his most costly attire, but with his linen garments (Lev. 16:4, 23, 32; Ezek. 44:17). These are an emblem of the Christian High Priest's incarnation, who, when He came to expiate our sin did not array Himself with light as with a garment but with the robe of our human nature, which, though clean and white, was without splendor or magnificence. On this day he offered expiatory sacrifices both for himself and all the people. Jesus, in all things Thou must have the preeminence (Col. 1:18)! "For such an high priest became us...who needeth not daily, as those high priests, to offer up sacrifice, first for his own sins, and then for the people's: for this he did once, when he offered up himself. For the law maketh men high priests which have infirmity; but the word of the oath, which was since the law, maketh the Son, who is consecrated for evermore" (Heb. 7:26-28). On this day he made his solemn entrance into the holy places made with hands, with the blood of bulls and goats, the meaning of which the great apostle declares is the entrance of Jesus Christ, the high priest of good things to come, by a greater and more perfect tabernacle, into the Holy Place not made with hands—that is, into heaven itself, having obtained eternal redemption for us.

Two Kids of the Goats (Lev. 16:5–9)
But what we shall chiefly confine our attention to, for the present, is another ceremony peculiar to this day of atonement. Besides the bullock and the ram which Aaron was to offer, the first for himself and the second for the people, he was also to take for all the congregation of Israel two kids of the goats for a sin offering. They were to be brought, as usual, to the door of the tabernacle of the congregation. But both were not killed as was usually done, for by an uncommon rite the two victims were pitched upon by lot, the one to be offered up in the accustomed manner unto the Lord (and its skin, its flesh, and dung to be burned with fire without the camp), the other to be presented alive before the Lord, where Aaron, laying both his hands upon its head, confessed over him all the iniquities of the children of Israel and all their transgressions in all their sins (v. 9). And lastly, it was to be conducted into the wilderness by the hand of a proper person (who they say might be either a Gentile or an Israelite), and probably it was never more inquired after, wherefore it might be called *Azazel* or the *scapegoat* (v. 8). We shall, for the present, leave to others the discussion of some curious inquiries about the name and fate of this devoted creature and proceed to notice how in both these victims Christ was set forth as the propitiation for our sins (cf. Rom. 3:25; 1 John 2:2; 4:10).

It is true indeed that the goat is not one of these creatures that are supposed to have the most amiable properties. And it may seem odd that the Lamb of God should be prefigured by these beasts, which, for their uncleanly and unruly temper, are emblems of the wicked, who in the last day shall be separated from the godly by the Judge of all the earth. But perhaps even this circumstance in the type might signify that Christ was to appear in the likeness of sinful flesh. The goat, though commonly held an unclean creature, was notwithstanding of the number of clean beasts in the law of Moses; and Jesus Christ, though reputed a sinner among men, was pure and righteous in the eye of God. And if it be true what is commonly reported of the medicinal qualities of this creature's flesh and of its blood softening the rigid adamant, what hinders us to think of Christ healing our diseases, taking away our hard and stony hearts, and giving us hearts of flesh?

But why two goats? Or if two, why not both used in the same manner? Why was one of them put to death and the other saved alive? Doubtless they are both to be viewed as types of the great propitiation. The first goat may signify that complete satisfaction which Christ made to vindictive justice by the offering up of Himself, and the second goat may signify the happy consequence of this propitiatory sacrifice in finishing transgression, making an end of sin, and carrying it, as it were, into the land of forgetfulness, that, to use the elegant words of Jeremiah, when "the iniquity of Israel shall be sought for, and there should be none; and the sins of Judah, and they shall not be found" (Jer. 50:20). Nor ought it to seem strange that such a momentous truth should be inculcated so many various ways on the same occasion, for it is a singular effect of the goodness of God to exhibit such interesting truths in different views, that we may have strong consolation. Besides that, all similitudes and types fall infinitely short of the great mysteries they point at; therefore, they are multiplied, that they may mutually supply the deficiencies of one another, for here the saying is made good, "Two are better than one;... For if they fall, the one will lift up his fellow" (Eccl. 4:9–10).

That the first goat was an emblem of Christ sacrificed for us, as much as any other sacrifices, is not difficult to persuade. For like other sacrifices, it was killed because Christ was to die. Its blood was carried "within the vail" (Lev. 16:15), for Christ was to appear in the presence of God for us with His own blood (Heb. 6:19–20). Its body was burned without the camp, and Christ suffered "without the gate"

(Heb. 13:12). But let us more particularly attend the mystery of the scapegoat and its likeness to Jesus Christ.

The Scapegoat (Lev. 16:10)
It was, like the other, to be taken from the congregation of Israel and doubtless purchased with the public money. So Christ was taken from among His brethren and bought, in some sense, for thirty pieces of silver out of the public treasury, that He might be numbered with transgressors and bear the sins of many (Isa. 53:12; Mark 15:28).

It was, like the other, presented at the door of the tabernacle of the congregation before the Lord and all the people. So Christ presented Himself to do His heavenly Father's will before both God and the people when at the Passover solemnity He went up to Jerusalem, not ignorant of what was to be done unto Him by Jews and Gentiles.

It was, as the other, chosen by lot, which, though "cast into the lap," is not fortuitous or accidental, for the "disposing…is of the LORD" (Prov. 16:33). So Jesus Christ was destined in the eternal counsels to bear the iniquities of His people. He was delivered into His enemies' hands by "the determinate counsel and foreknowledge of God" (Acts 2:23), and by this same counsel was determined before to be done whatever happened unto Him. Hence it was that Pilate was deaf to the remonstrances of his own conscience in condemning Him that was most just. And hence the people of the Jews preferred a murderer to the Lord of life when they desired that Barabbas should be released and Christ should be crucified (Matt. 27:17, 20).

The sacred animal being thus presented and chosen of God, the high priest was to lay both his hands on its head, devoting it by this action to the service of God and translating the sins of Israel upon it in a typical manner. Perhaps it might signify that the hand of vindictive justice was to lie heavy on the Surety of sinners (Heb. 7:22), and it is expressly affirmed by the prophet, "The LORD hath laid on him the iniquity of us all" (Isa. 53:6).

That this was the meaning of the rite appears more evidently from the following one. For in this posture did the high priest confess all the sins of his people, from whom the goat was taken. Why should their sins be confessed in this manner if it was not to signify that they were in some sort laid upon the head of the innocent victim? It was thus the great Doer of God's will was made sin for us, who knew no sin. The goat could not be guilty for these sins, for it was a brute beast. Nor could its antitype be Himself a transgressor of the law, for He was a divine person. Yet both the one and the other did bear the sins of many, to which it was, in the nature of things, impossible they could be accessory in the smallest degree. It was not Thy sin, O spotless victim! but the sins of Thy elect people that consigned Thee over to the bloody and shameful cross! These were the sins that took hold upon Thee and justified Thy death. Surely, surely, He bore our griefs, He carried our sorrows, and the chastisement of our peace was upon Him (Isa. 53:4–5). How else could His heavenly Father have been pleased to bruise Him, for whom it is no more good to punish the just than to clear the guilty?

The devoted creature, thus laden with sin, is by the hand of a proper person conducted into the wilderness. Why should not this wilderness be viewed as an emblem of these afflictions to which the Surety was exposed by the sins He was charged with? Or shall we say it might be a faint intimation that the blessings of atonement should be extended to the world of Gentile sinners, which, in the style of the prophet, is called "the wilderness of the people" (Ezek. 20:35)? Or rather the meaning may be that as the mystic goat was never more looked after or heard of—for probably it would soon perish, if not by hunger, at least by wild beasts—so Jesus Christ, by His atoning blood, would take away the sin of the world and remove from them all the iniquities of the elect people, as far as the east is distant from the west (Ps. 103:12). O condemning law, you have nothing to lay to their charge, for Christ is dead! Therefore, "it is God that justifieth" (Rom. 8:33), and their sins and iniquities will He remember no more (Heb. 8:12; 10:17).

Draw Near to Christ, the New Testament Scapegoat
What thanks shall be rendered to that gracious Redeemer, who was manifested to restore that glory to God which He took not away and

to take away that sin of man which He did not introduce? Be it so, there are, alas! too many to whom this all-important truth is of small account (for some deride, and more despise it), yet to the weary soul, to the conscience burdened with guilt, it is grateful and delicious as the full-flowing stream to the hunted hart (Ps. 42:1). The happy soul to whom the doctrine of atonement is manifested, he hears upon the matter the voice of the great Jehovah speaking to him in such ravishing accents, "Behold, I have caused thine iniquity to pass from thee, and I will clothe thee with change of raiment" (Zech. 3:4), or, in the words of Nathan to the penitent king David, "The LORD also hath put away thy sin; thou shalt not die" (2 Sam. 12:13). Who would not be constrained by this love to put away the evil of their doings from before His eyes who hath put away the guilt of them from before His face?

Draw near all ye whose consciences are burdened with the intolerable pressure of a thousand aggravated iniquities, who are ready to cry, "Mine iniquities are gone over mine head: as an heavy burden they are too heavy for me" (Ps. 38:4). While some, with Cain, go from the presence of the Lord and drown their dismal thoughts in the delights of sense or else in the whirl of business, while others have no ground of comfort but the general and unatoned mercy of God, while a third sort derive comfort to their troubled hearts from their own imperfect righteousness, their tears of repentance, their sorrow for what is past, and their resolutions to do better for the future, confess your iniquities over the head of the New Testament scapegoat, for "whoso confesseth and forsaketh them shall have mercy" (Prov. 28:13). Thus runs the gracious promise of the Holy One of Israel. "By his knowledge shall my righteous servant justify many; for he shall bear their iniquities" (Isa. 53:11). But he that despises this way of peace shall bear his own burden, whosoever he be (Isa. 59:8ff.).

11

The Ordinance of the Red Heifer
Numbers 19

Having seen the mystery of the lamb that was slain and the goat that was sent away, we come next to the red heifer, whose ashes sprinkling the unclean did sanctify to the purifying of the flesh when defiled by touching corpses, graves, and dead men's bones; and we shall see how it signified the sprinkling of Christ's blood upon our souls, to purge our conscience from dead works, to serve the living God (Heb. 9:14).

It was an ordinance which God was pleased to enjoin in a very direct manner, for "the LORD spake unto Moses and unto Aaron, saying, This is the ordinance of the law which the LORD hath commanded" (Num. 19:1–2). Indeed, what but the authority of God could have reconciled the minds of the ancient church to such a burdensome yoke of ceremonies? Therefore, the Hebrew lawgiver takes such particular care to inculcate everywhere that he delivered no laws unto them which he received not from the Lord. No wonder that the whole system of ceremonial worship was purely founded on the sovereign pleasure of God, when it was intended to shadow forth that adorable plan of redemption which arises from the same source and is styled in the New Testament "the mystery of his will" (Eph. 1:9). It is this that imparts a venerable air to all those rites which, had they been of human institution alone, would have merited contempt and ridicule. Let us, for one proof of this, observe the qualities, the sufferings, and the use of this heifer. We shall see that these are capable of being fairly applied to Jesus Christ, who "gave himself for us, that he might…purify unto himself a peculiar people, zealous of good works" (Titus 2:14).

The Qualities of a Sacrificial Victim (Num. 19:1–2)

What, then, were the qualities required in this victim? It was a heifer,[1] perhaps to intimate that in Christ Jesus there is neither male nor female, or to signify that He would assume our nature, not in its strongest state of innocence but in its enfeebled state of sin and misery, for He was made "in the likeness of sinful flesh" (Rom. 8:3) and "compassed with infirmity" (Heb. 5:2).

It was a *red* heifer. The reason of this (say the Jews) was hidden from Solomon himself but is not perhaps altogether concealed from the simplest believer, who knows that his Savior came from Eden "with dyed garments from Bozrah" (Isa. 63:1) or that He is "clothed with a vesture dipped in blood" (Rev. 19:13). Red is a color of beauty, and He is "fairer than the children of men" (Ps. 45:2). Red is a color of strength, and He is the "one that is mighty" (Ps. 89:19). Red is the color of guilt, and He took the scarlet and crimson-colored robes of our imputed sin, that He might clothe us with the robes of His imputed righteousness, whiter than wool, purer than snow.

It was a heifer *without spot or blemish*. Indeed, this was required in every victim, and in Christ the Holy One of God it was fulfilled. An unatoned God accepts nothing less than the most absolute perfection; an unatoned God was He with whom our Savior had to do. It is therefore easy to see that any the smallest spot would have entirely disqualified Him from approaching unto God in an acceptable manner.

It was a heifer on which a *yoke* never came. As man, Christ never came under the yoke of sin, and as God He was not under the yoke of duty; that is, He was not obliged to obey the law. If He paid tribute to the temple, He was not obliged to do so. (For even the kings of the earth hold their own children free from paying taxes.) But lest He should offend them who were ignorant of His true character, He

---

1. Editor's note: A heifer is a young female cow that has not borne a calf.

pays the tribute, not with money out of His private pocket but, to show that He was Lord of all, with money He commanded a fish to bring from the bottom of the sea (cf. Num. 19:3, 9; Matt. 17:24–27). If He appeared in the form of a servant, it was wholly owing to His voluntary condescension. If He expires in agonies on a cross, it is not because His life is violently taken away by the hands of sinful men, but because He laid it down of Himself (John 10:17–18). Therefore does His Father love Him; therefore is His obedience and death strictly meritorious; and because He has done more than was His duty to do, He is not an unprofitable servant (cf. Luke 17:10).

What Was Done with the Red Heifer? (Num. 19:3–5)
When a heifer was found in which these qualities did meet, what was to be done unto her? First of all, she is brought to Eleazar the priest. Here indeed the type is defective, for our high priest and sacrifice are one and the same. Next she is brought without the camp, for Christ suffered without the gate (Heb. 13:12). She was killed before his eyes. So Christ was crucified and slain in the most public manner. Her flesh and skin and blood were burned in fire, together with her dung. So Christ suffered in the whole man, and when He endured the wrath of God, which is often compared to fire, they cast upon Him the dung of the most virulent reproaches.

The Cedar Wood, the Scarlet Cloth, and the Hyssop (Num. 19:6)
But what shall we say to the cedar wood, the scarlet cloth, and the hyssop[2] that were thrown also into the burning? Perhaps it never was intended by the Holy Spirit that every minute circumstance in that ritual worship should have a separate meaning affixed to it. Many usages were doubtless to be practiced in the ancient dispensation with no other view than to testify their absolute submission to the divine will. What if we should say that the cedar wood, the scarlet,

---

2. Editor's note: Hyssop is a medicinal herb used for its aromatic properties in cooking and its antiseptic and expectorant properties in medicine. In Bible times dried bunches of hyssop were used for ceremonial sprinkling symbolic of spiritual cleansing (Ex. 12:22; Lev. 14:1–7, 33–53; Ps. 51:7).

and the hyssop were the materials of which they made the sprinkler, but first these very things must be thrown into the fire, so the means and ordinances by which the clean water of Christ's blood is sprinkled on our souls are themselves first sanctified by His sufferings? Or the scarlet cloth might denote the guilt of sin, which was the cause of His death. The hyssop might signify the necessity of its being applied unto the conscience or of the sprinkling the blood of Jesus upon our hearts. And the cedar wood, which is durable and fragrant, might adumbrate the sweet savor of His sufferings and the perpetual efficacy of His atoning blood.

The Purpose of the Ashes (Num. 19:7–10)
But when the heifer was thus reduced to ashes, are these ashes left to lie and rot with the common earth or to be scattered by the winds? No, they were carefully to be gathered up by a clean person and deposited in a clean place without the camp, where they are to be kept, in order to make with them a purifying water to sprinkle the unclean. Who would have thought the ashes of a burned heifer worthy of such regard, had he judged only by outward appearance? But though seemingly vile, they were really precious by the divine ordinance. Even so the death and crucifixion of the dying Redeemer, though in appearance an event worthy of small regard, was in reality the most memorable transaction that ever the sun beheld. "Precious in the sight of the LORD is the death of his saints" (Ps. 116:15). How much more the death of His beloved Son? His blood, though trodden under foot by many, and by many esteemed as water spilt on the ground, is notwithstanding the price of our redemption and infinitely more valuable than gold and silver and all corruptible things.

The clean place where the ashes were deposited, was it an emblem of the church, where alone the sacred treasure of His blood is dispensed? It was outside the camp, perhaps to intimate that those who were without the commonwealth of Israel should partake of the cleansing efficacy of Christ's blood and that God would put no difference between the Gentiles and His ancient people, purifying their hearts by faith. Or shall we say that as the precious relics were to be laid in a clean place, so the mystery of faith in His blood can only be held in a pure conscience? The ashes thus preserved were fit for use upon every occasion, as long as they lasted, whereas the blood of common sacrifices soon congealed and was unfit to be sprinkled when it grew cold.

Was not this a significant emblem of the everlasting fitness of Christ's blood to purge the guilty conscience? For it is no less capable of being sprinkled now than the moment it was shed, being always warm, always new and living blood. Let us consider, in a few words, the occasion for keeping these purifying ashes, the manner of preparing them, the rite by which they were sprinkled, and the danger of neglecting it.

The Occasion for the Ashes (Num. 19:11–16)

The occasion for the ashes was the uncleanness of the Israelites, or strangers that sojourned among them, by reason of the necessary and voluntary or involuntary and accidental touch of dead corpses, bones, and graves. The touch of these defiled them legally and debarred them from access to the sanctuary of God. But our defilements now arise not from dead corpses but from dead works, the sins we daily commit. Well might each one of us say with Paul, "O wretched man that I am! who shall deliver me from the body of this death?" (Rom. 7:24). Yea, what else are the best duties we can perform but dead works if God should enter into judgment? Even these need to be buried out of our sight and covered from the view of impartial justice with the covering of Immanuel's righteousness, and till we are purged from these we cannot serve the living God.

The Proper Use of the Ashes (Num. 19:17–19)

The manner of preparing these holy ashes was to mix them with running water in a vessel, an emblem of that divine Spirit which they that believe on Christ shall infallibly receive, by whose invisible but powerful operation the blood of Christ is made effectual to purify our hearts. As the ashes were mixed with the water in this typical ordinance, so the blood and Spirit of Christ are undivided in their working, for they that are justified in the name of the Lord Jesus are washed in the same name by the Spirit of our God, and from them whom He sprinkles with clean water He takes away the hard and stony heart.

The rite of sprinkling was in this manner. On the third day, and on the seventh day, after the pollution was contracted, a clean person, dipping a bunch of hyssop in the purifying liquor, was to sprinkle the unclean; and on the evening of the seventh day, but not before, he was perfectly cleansed. Let the clean person be an emblem of the ministers of the gospel, who have the precious treasure of Christ's purifying blood and Spirit, as it were, in earthen vessels. These ought (at least) to be clean persons and an example in purity to the believers among whom they minister. Let the bunch of hyssop represent the ordinances of the gospel, or faith, both which are the applying means. The third day was the time of the first sprinkling. We may here take occasion to think that on the third day Christ rose again from the dead: and here indeed began our purging from guilt, for He was raised for our justification. On the seventh day, the last of a weekly revolution, the purification was complete on the evening. Nor will we be perfectly cleansed from the inheritance of moral stains till the evening of death and the commencement of the eternal Sabbath. Thus shall He sprinkle not a small number of Israelites but many nations, not merely from the impurities of the flesh but from the pollutions of the conscience. Though we are defiled not only with smaller transgressions but with the most deadly and abominable iniquities—or, to use the Old Testament phrases, though we have not only touched but remained among the graves and lodged in the monuments—yet if we come to Jesus, the mediator of the new covenant, and to the blood of sprinkling, we shall be clean through the word that He has spoken unto us.

The Danger of Neglecting This Ordinance (Num. 19:20–22)

The danger of neglecting this ordinance was no less than excision from the congregation of the Lord. So shall they perish as the vilest part of the creation, who say they are not polluted, when the judgment of unerring wisdom about all the children of men is, "They are altogether become filthy"; or who turning away disdainfully from the fountain opened for sin and for uncleanness think to wash out their stains by the nitre[3] and soap of their own endeavors (Jer. 2:22), for God shall plunge them into the ditch, and their own clothes shall abhor them (Job 9:31).

One other circumstance deserves to be noticed before we leave this subject. The very same water that sanctified the unclean defiled the man who touched or sprinkled it, though he was clean before (Num. 19:19). Perhaps this might denote the imperfection of these shadows, which never could make them perfect by whom they were used, or it might intimate that the virtue of divine institutions depends not on the person that ministers about them. Or shall we say that faith in Christ's blood, like this consecrated water, defiles them that are clean, by discovering more of their natural pollution, and cleanses them that are defiled, by sprinkling their hearts from an evil conscience? But it is certain the effects of this water were not more contrary than these of Christ Himself, as preached in the gospel, who is to some "the savour of life unto life" and to others "the savour of death unto death" (2 Cor. 2:16).

---

3. Editor's note: "Nitre" in Jeremiah 2:22 is a transliteration of the Hebrew נֶתֶר, which probably was sodium carbonate. What we today call nitre is potassium nitrate (or saltpeter), a component of gunpowder. Modern English Bible versions translate it as "lye," which is a caustic solution of sodium hydroxide found, for example, in drain cleaners.

12

The Ordinance of the Year of Jubilee
Leviticus 25:8–17

The institution of the Jubilee was one of the most remarkable regulations in the commonwealth of Israel and deserves our special attention. Besides the rest which the land enjoyed every seventh, it was ordained to rest also every fiftieth year. The husbandman was forbidden to subdue his field with the plough or to scatter seed in the furrows. What the earth spontaneously produced, whether corn or vines, might be indifferently used by all and was the special property of the poor inhabitants of the land. The God who commanded this was fully able to compensate the want of harvest and vintage by crowning the year preceding with uncommon plenty. But besides the intermission of servile labor in this extraordinary year, it was the will of God that, by its welcome approach, the poor Israelite should reap great advantages and enjoy very valuable immunities. The insolvent debtor was delivered from his creditor. The hired servant regained his former liberty, and inheritances reverted to the families to which they originally belonged. The joyful sound of trumpets announced the commencement of this year of liberty, and they were blown on the Day of Atonement, when they were fasting for their sins and afflicting their souls. This was the fast which the Lord did choose to undo heavy burdens and let the oppressed go free. In short, it was a time of the restitution of all things in the commonwealth and a remedy against the caprice of fortune, or rather the inequalities which sovereign providence introduces among men as to their outward state.

Several things might be suggested to evince the propriety of this regulation, viewed in a civil as well as a religious light. It was admirably well calculated to promote brotherly love; to prevent the ruin of families, whether by avarice or prodigality; to preserve the distinction of tribes till the Messiah should come; and to impress upon their hearts a sense of their absolute dependence upon God as their great landlord, whose property the land was and with whom they were strangers and sojourners. Therefore, it was to be sold only for a time and not forever.

The Future Day of Salvation

But let us raise our thoughts still higher to the year of grace and day of salvation, wherein far greater immunities are proclaimed to the human race than were announced to the Israelites by the trumpet of the jubilee. Detesting the impious imitation of this sacred ordinance in the pretended jubilee of Rome,[1] let us take occasion to meditate on that happy season, which, in allusion to this very thing, is styled by the prophet the "year of my [God's] redeemed" and "the acceptable year of the LORD" (Isa. 63:4; 61:2). Joyful was the sound of liberty to the poor Israelite who was drowned in debt, for which he was obliged to part with his beloved freedom and to sell the inheritance of his fathers. But more joyful is the sound of liberty to the wretched sinner, who is deep in arrears to the divine justice, a miserable captive of sin and wrath, and utterly deprived of all inheritance in the heavenly kingdom. "Blessed is the people that know the joyful sound: they shall walk, O LORD, in the light of thy countenance. In thy name shall they rejoice all the day: and in thy righteousness shall they be exalted" (Ps. 89:15–16). But a more particular attention to what Moses informs us about this grand festival will discover the resemblance between the trumpet of the jubilee and the trumpet of

---

1. Editor's note: The first so-called Christian Jubilee was apparently instituted in February 22, 1300, by Pope Boniface VIII, offering indulgences and remission of sins to penitents who visited the basilicas of St. Peter and St. Paul in Rome. The Roman Catholic Church has announced similar observances over the centuries, with the thirtieth occurring in 2016.

the gospel, whose sound, far from being confined to Judea alone, is gone through all the earth—of which the prophet Isaiah, rapt into future times, utters that glorious prophecy which has received its accomplishment in the days of the Messiah: "And it shall come to pass…that the great trumpet shall be blown, and they shall come which were ready to perish in the land of Assyria, and the outcasts in the land of Egypt, and shall worship the LORD in the holy mount at Jerusalem" (Isa. 27:13).

The time when this glad signal was given by the solemn sound of trumpets was the tenth day of the seventh month, or the Day of Atonement—a day wherein the future expiation of the Messiah was clearly exhibited in the goat that was slain, and in the goat that was sent away, and in other ceremonies truly significant and expressive. This is a circumstance greatly to be observed. Who sees not here that our jubilee begins in the atonement of Jesus Christ as theirs began on the day in which it was prefigured? The trumpet that was not sounded on this day was some other than the jubilee trumpet, and the sermon that is not built on the doctrine of atonement is something different from the gospel. O Jesus, were it not for Thy bloody death, Thy glorious resurrection, and still more glorious ascension, our ears had never heard the gospel trumpet's joyful sound, nor of the gifts which Thou received for men, far surpassing the gifts and immunities of this gladsome year.

The Sabbatical Year an Emblem of Our Rest in Christ

The intermission of toil and labor in this sabbatical year in which the land was not tilled, and the common property which everyone had in the spontaneous productions of the earth, may be considered as an emblem of that blessed rest which is proclaimed in the gospel of Jesus Christ from the works of the law and of the flesh and from anxious, carking[2] cares about the good things of this present life. He that feeds the ravens without their labor and clothes the lilies

---

2. Editor's note: *Carking* is an archaic adjective denoting things burdensome or vexatious, and it principally survives in the expression "carking cares," as in this case.

without their toil will certainly withhold no necessary thing from the objects of His choice regard. The joyful sound forbids you to ask with painful anxiety, "What shall we eat? or, What shall we drink? or, Wherewithal shall we be clothed?" (Matt. 6:31). Leave Him who knows your wants to answer these perplexing questions. "Be careful for nothing" is a cheerful note sent from the gospel trumpet (Phil. 4:6). Hear it, ye happy people who know the joyful sound, and turn your timorous cares into believing confidence (Ps. 89:15).

The Canceling of Debts
The canceling of debts at this happy season may well be viewed as an emblem of the forgiveness of sin, or that dreadful debt of punishment, which all the human race owe to eternal justice, the most inexorable of all creditors. This debt we are born under, and are every day contracting more, is marked—every farthing[3]—in the book of God's remembrance, and the time of final reckoning is hasting apace (Matt. 5:26). Miserable they whom that awful day shall find without a Surety! How can we discharge it who are not even able to so much as number it? But listen to the charming accents of the gospel jubilee: "I, even I, am he that blotteth out thy transgressions for mine own sake, and will not remember thy sins" (Isa. 43:25). Dismiss your fears, you poor insolvent debtors, for there is forgiveness with your great Creditor, and for the sake of His dear Son, He will not enter into judgment with you.

The Release of Servants
The release of servants and delivering from bondage is another joyful sound of "the acceptable year of the LORD" (Isa. 61:2): a privilege so much more glorious than the liberty of the Israelites as the slavery from which we are redeemed is more miserable than the service to which they bound themselves. The gospel is a joyful sound of liberty

---

3. Editor's note: The word *farthing* translates the Greek κοδράντεσ and/or Roman *quadrans*. It literally means "quarter" and describes the lowest-value coin of its time. The British farthing from Victorian times until its withdrawal in 1961 was one-fourth of the predecimal penny before 1971.

from the bondage of *God's wrath*, which we are taught to dread no more with servile fear but with a filial reverence; from the bondage of *Satan's tyranny*, that we may no more be led captive at the will and pleasure of that wicked spirit; and from the *fear of death*, which has subjected many to bondage all the days of their life. It is a sound of freedom from the law, not indeed as it is a rule of life (for the obligation to all sorts of religious and civil duties is strongly confirmed by the gospel) but as it is a covenant of works. The law is a severe and rigorous master indeed! It accepts no work if it is not absolutely perfect! It never readmits into favor those who in the smallest instance have incurred its displeasure, though they should be ever so solicitous to do all in their power to please it! Eternal death is the smallest punishment the law will be satisfied to inflict, and obedience absolutely perfect the only condition of acceptance. They who are under the dominion of this rigid lord—and such are all the race of Adam before the gospel comes—can never hope to attain everlasting life or escape everlasting death; for one sin, though ever so small, will do them more harm than all their duties, however many, can do them good. But we must not forget to mention how the gospel is a joyful sound of liberty and freedom from the domineering power of sin and the lusts of our hearts, which, though divers, and often contrary, demand all homage and perfect gratification.

Between the bondage of the law and the bondage of sin, there is a most indissoluble relation, though one would not think so at first view. But the great apostle expressly affirms that "the strength of sin is the law" (1 Cor. 15:56) and makes our not being "under the law, but under grace" a reason why sin "shall not have dominion" over us (Rom. 6:14–15). Alas, it is the case that "serving divers lusts and pleasures" (Titus 3:3) is not esteemed by many as an intolerable thraldom, but, on the contrary, they think it a state of liberty to be the servants of corruption (2 Peter 2:19). They are not the only madmen who glory in their chains, mistaking them for regal ornaments. A most unquestionable judge of human nature has taught us that he who commits sin is the servant of sin (John 8:34). A saint of the first magnitude affirms that to "seek [God's] precepts" is to "walk at liberty" (Ps. 119:45). And who has not heard the dismal groans of the blessed apostle, which the body of sin and death extorted from the bottom of his heart (Rom. 7:24)? O sin, what an imperious lord art thou! and thy service of all others the most ignominious, the most laborious, and the most unprofitable, for "the wages of sin is death" (Rom. 6:23). But the gospel trumpet says to "the prisoners, Go forth; [and] to them that are in darkness, Shew yourselves" (Isa. 49:9), and when they "know the truth…the truth shall make [them] free" (John 8:32).

The Reversion of Inheritances
The reversion of inheritances is the last thing we shall notice. We lost our inheritance by the first mortal transgression in Adam and were every day resigning more and more our claim to the divine favor for the transitory pleasures of sin. We have sold for nothing the invaluable treasures of eternity and are by no means able to redeem what we have so foolishly foregone. But these are the glad tidings of the everlasting gospel: in Jesus Christ, O ye children of men, you may obtain an inheritance infinitely more valuable than what returned to any Israelite at the year of liberty—an inheritance of exceeding glorious riches, "incorruptible, and undefiled, and that fadeth not away, reserved in heaven for you" (1 Peter 1:4). The blood of Christ is the price that bought it; the Spirit is the earnest that secures it. And when the Redeemer comes again, they shall perfectly enjoy the purchased possession, for "the LORD knoweth the days of the upright: and their inheritance shall be for ever" (Ps. 37:18).

Happy they who hear by faith the trumpet of the gospel jubilee in this accepted time, who look into the perfect law of liberty and continue therein (James 1:25). In the decisive hour of judgment, the trump of God itself shall not affright; and even in this present state, they shall be brought into the glorious liberty of the sons of God (Rom. 8:21). They shall take them captives, whose captives they were, and rule over their oppressors (Isa. 14:2).

13

The Law of the Leper
Leviticus 13–14

The law of the leper, which is delivered by the Hebrew lawgiver with considerable prolixity, is indeed a portion of sacred writ we are apt to skim over with a heedless glance, supposing that very little instruction can be derived from such antiquated usages as were to be observed about the discovery, the separation, and the cleansing of the infected Israelite. One is apt to wonder at the distemper itself, which infected not only the bodies of men but their garments and houses, and to be no less surprised that the heavenly Majesty should condescend to give such minute directions about the symptoms of the leprosy and the manner of its cleansing (Lev. 14:54–56). But when we consider that everything almost about the typical nation was figurative—their diseases not excepted—perhaps we may cease to wonder and willingly acknowledge that here, as in other ancient rites, the body is of Christ.

It was a skin disease well known to the Jews and to other nations in those parts of the world.[1] Though in itself it was only a natural evil, it was, however, inflicted oftentimes by the immediate hand of the Lord as the punishment of sin, as in the case of Miriam, Gehazi,

---

1. Editor's note: The "leprosy" mentioned in the Bible (sixty-eight times, no less) is probably not the same as modern leprosy—called Hansen's disease since 1873—but encompasses a range of skin diseases that exhibit one or other of the symptoms described in various Scripture passages. However, the man with the withered hand in Matthew 12:13, and parallel gospel passages, may be a case of our leprosy (Hansen's).

and King Uzziah (Num. 12:10; 2 Kings 5:27; 2 Chron. 26:19ff.). That it was always an indication of any flagrant guilt, we will not presume to say. But the unhappy patient who was seized with that hateful malady was by the divine law excluded from the cheerful society of men, and from access to the tabernacle of God, till it should please God to recover him or at least till the symptoms of recovery were perceived by the priest by whom the sentence was pronounced. But let us take a more exact view both of the disease and the manner of its purgation.

Leprosy as a Figure of Sin
Was the Almighty displeased with the leprosy? Was His indignation against the poor leper? No! He despises no man for the affliction of his body, however loathsome. A Lazarus covered with sores, and a Job with boils, are the objects of His special love, while the most healthy and wealthy sinner that wears the finest purple is a vile person in His eyes. *Sin is that loathsome disease, and the sinner that abominable leper, here described.* "Behold, I am vile," "I am a man of unclean lips," "I abhor myself," is the language of the convinced soul (Job 40:4; Isa. 6:5; Job 42:6). An infant wallowing in the blood of its nativity, a dog returning to his vomit, a sow wallowing in the mire (2 Peter 2:22), and a sepulcher exhaling the stench of a putrefying carcass are not greater offenses to the senses than the soul that lies in sin is to the pure eyes of God (Hab. 1:13). *Sin* is that abhorred leprosy which spreads its dire contagion far and wide, infecting all the duties which the sinner can perform and all the comforts that he tastes, for to him that is "defiled and unbelieving is nothing pure" (Titus 1:15).

Beware how you approach the society of the wicked, which is a thousand times more infectious than the company of the filthiest leper. O my soul, be not united to their assembly that are the workers of iniquity, if thou wouldst keep the commandment of thy God. He that was infected with the typical leprosy was not only in danger of defiling those with whom he conversed but the very garments he wore and the house in which he dwelt. But sin has subjected all creatures to the bondage of corruption. Therefore, as the infected garment was burned with fire and the infected house demolished from its very foundation, it is revealed that "the heavens being on fire shall be dissolved, and the elements shall melt with fervent heat" (2 Peter 3:12). The leper under the law was excluded from the society of men, and when the distemper came to a great height or infected the head, he was to use the signals of deepest mourning—his clothes were to be rent, his head bare, and a covering upon his upper lip—and as he went, he was to cry, "Unclean, unclean" (Lev. 13:45).

Leprosy Is a Figure of Separation from God

But the leprosy of sin excludes the miserable soul from all intercourse with God, communion with angels, fellowship with Jesus, society with the spirits of just men, and access to the heavenly Jerusalem, where nothing that is defiled can enter. O dismal solitude! O terrible separation! With what tears shall it be deplored! What tokens of mourning are deep enough to express the melancholy state! And, alas, we speak not of a malady that is rarely found. It is hereditary to all the sons of Adam without exception, for "they are all together become filthy: there is none that doeth good, no, not one"; "How can he be clean that is born of a woman?" (Ps. 14:3; Job 25:4).

Leprosy as a Figure of How Sin Is to Be Dealt With

No wonder the priest was enjoined to proceed with extraordinary caution in inspecting the symptoms of this hateful distemper, when so much depended upon the sentence he should pronounce. A person was not to be pronounced unclean on a sudden, nor upon every slight symptom of leprosy that might have appeared in his flesh, for the suspected Israelite was to be shut up seven days, and on the seventh day to be judged according as the symptoms were favorable or malignant (Lev. 13:1–8). This surely was designed to inculcate the extraordinary caution wherewith the office-bearers in the church, as well as others, ought to try the spirits and separate the precious from the vile, and that no man's state should be deemed bad unless there are most evident tokens of sin having the dominion over him. Every man who had in his skin a spot, freckle, or blister was not to be judged a leper, nor must we say of every sin of infirmity. It is "not the spot of his children" (Deut. 32:5), for in many things we offend all (James 3:2). Again, a man whose hair fell off his head or forehead, through the decay of nature, or otherwise, though he was bald, yet he was not a leper.

Nor are they all in a state of sin, the vigor of whose spiritual life is much abated and who, alas, have left their first love (Rev. 2:4). Yea, though an Israelite was actually seized with a leprosy, if there were tokens that it was not gaining upon nature but that nature was expelling it—as suppose the plague was not in sight deeper than the skin, or if it spread not in the skin, or if the plague was somewhat dark and there were black hairs in the rising, or if it covered all the skin from head to foot wheresoever the priest looked—in any of these cases he was not pronounced unclean. For these were favorable symptoms that the distemper had not infected the vitals, that the whole mass of blood was not corrupted, and that nature was still strong and working out the contagion (Lev. 13:12–13, 16, 23, 26–28, 31–34, 37, 38). No more must we conclude that they are all in a bad state who may take up the pitiful complaint of David, "My loins are filled with a loathsome disease: and there is no soundness in my flesh" (Ps. 38:7).

The leper whose plague is not in sight deeper than the skin is he whose life may indeed be stained with some external blemishes, but he sins not with all his heart, which is still sound in God's statutes. The leper whose plague spreads not in the skin, but was at a stay, is he who emerges from his fall, like David or Peter, by a speedy repentance. Their sin was but a scab; they washed their clothes in the blood of Christ and were clean.

The leper whose plague was somewhat dark, and the hairs not turned white (a sure sign of the strength of nature), is he who has a principle of life and strength within him that never can be subdued by the strongest efforts of sin but shall prevail at the last. The leper who was all turned white in every part from head to foot (a sign that the distemper was expelled from the vitals to the external parts, and that the cure was as good as wrought) is he who has obtained an evangelical conviction of his natural pollution in heart and life, that he is altogether become filthy, and that in him (that is, in his flesh) there dwells no good thing (Rom. 7:18).

But, on the other hand, the bad symptoms were such as these: if the hair in the plague was turned white; if the plague was in sight deeper than the skin of his flesh; if there was quick, raw flesh in the rising; and if it spread itself further and further in the skin. And the worst of all kinds was the leprosy in the head: the priest shall pronounce him utterly unclean; his plague is in his head (Lev. 13:44). He that had white and yellow hair in the sore of his leprosy is the sinner who has no strength to oppose any temptation and can make no resistance at all to the lusts of his own heart: for white hairs are signs of the debility of nature, and that death is fast approaching. "Gray hairs," saith the prophet Hosea, "are here and there upon him, yet he knoweth not" (Hos. 7:9). And saith the Lord God in Ezekiel, "how weak is thine heart,…seeing thou doest all these things" (Ezek. 16:30).

He whose leprosy was in sight deeper than the skin is an emblem of the sinner who works wickedness with full consent and from the very bottom of his soul, whose transgression proclaims that his heart is not right in the sight of God, and to whom the words of the prophet may be addressed: "This…thy wickedness…is bitter, because it reacheth unto thine heart" (Jer. 4:18). He that had quick, raw flesh in the rising of his plague may perhaps denote the sinner who cannot endure to be touched or reprimanded for his fault, though in the most gentle manner. This is a dangerous symptom indeed! David, this was not thy spot: "Let the righteous smite me, it shall be a kindness; and let him reprove me; it shall be an excellent oil, which shall not break my head" (Ps. 141:5). He whose plague did spread in the skin is the sinner who waxes worse and worse and increases unto more ungodliness. And, lastly, the man whose plague was in the head is the sinner, the faults of whose life proceed from the errors of his mind, whose understanding is debauched by his will, and he is arrived at such a pitch of wickedness as to vindicate himself in the gratification of his lusts and even to glory in his shame. He is utterly unclean, and hardly, very hardly, shall his cure be ever effected. But the rites of cleansing demand our next attention.

The Rites of Cleansing

When it pleased God, who sent this doleful plague, to remove it again, the leper was fetched to the priest, or rather the priest unto the leper; and when upon a narrow scrutiny it appeared the cure was really wrought, he was pronounced clean, but not without practicing various purging ceremonies on the first, the seventh, and the eighth day. Jesus Christ is that priest to whom the leprous soul is brought, or rather who hath condescended to come to us, who could not go to Him because we were polluted in our blood without the camp, aliens from the commonwealth of Israel. He is come not merely to cleanse them who are already healed, like the legal priest, but to heal them who without His helping hand were absolutely incurable. The Israelite who was brought for cleansing to the priest was himself to provide the necessary oblations, not without some cost and toil. But the High Priest of good things to come demands no such conditions from those who come for healing to their souls: He Himself has laid out the necessary charges and has by the one offering of Himself for us forever perfected all them who are sanctified. But let us more narrowly attend to the ceremonies of cleansing, in the order wherein they were performed.

Cleansing Ceremonies of the First and Seventh Day

On the first day of the leper's appearance before the priest, the priest was to take for him two birds alive and clean, and cedar wood, and scarlet, and hyssop, to make with them a sprinkling instrument (Lev. 14:1–4).

An earthen vessel was filled with running water, over which one of the birds was to be killed; and the other bird together with the sprinkling instrument, being dipped in the bloody water, the leper was to be sprinkled with it seven times, and the bird let loose into the open field (Lev. 14:5–7).

And the leper, though pronounced clean by the priest, was notwithstanding to cleanse himself still more by washing his clothes, shaving his hair, and bathing his whole body. And after that, he was permitted to come into the camp; but he was to tarry abroad, out of his tent seven days (Lev. 14:8–9).

Some have thought, and perhaps not without some reason, that the materials which were to be procured on this occasion might be expressive of that wholesome state on which the leper was now to enter. Before he was in a manner dead, but now restored to life, which might be signified by the living birds. Before he was putrefying and in a state of corruption, but now vigorous and robust, signified by the cedar. Before he was pale and wan, but now of a lively brisk complexion, signified by the scarlet. Before he was nauseous to the smell, but now cured of his ill scent, signified by the hyssop. But what hinders us to think of still greater mysteries and to lift our thoughts to the purging of our sins by our Great High Priest?

The *two birds alive and clean* may denote the two natures of Jesus Christ. The human nature was put to death, but the divine nature was incapable of suffering. By the human nature He died for our offenses, and by the divine nature He rose again for our justification.

The *sprinkling instrument of cedar, scarlet, and hyssop* may signify the ordinances of the gospel, by which the blessings of Christ's death are communicated; the running water is the Spirit of Christ, who is always imparted to the heart when the blood is sprinkled on the conscience (Jer. 2:13; John 4:10–11; 7:38; Heb. 10:22).

The *earthen vessel* is an emblem of the ministers of Christ, who, though frail and brittle creatures, and despicable in the eye of the world, and some but of small capacity and size, are entrusted with this invaluable treasure of gospel grace, to be dispensed unto others (2 Cor. 4:7).

And whereas the priest was to *kill one of the birds*, this intimates that without shedding of blood is no remission (Heb. 9:22). That he was to dip the living bird in the blood of the dead one imports that the blood of Christ's humanity is, by the hypostatical union, the blood of His divinity, or the blood of God which is the very thing that renders it the blood of atonement. The sprinkling instrument of cedar, scarlet, and hyssop was to be dipped in the same blood: for *all the ordinances, and all the means of salvation, are sanctified by the blood of Christ alone*. In this blood, if we may be allowed the expression, must ministers dip their sermons if they would be profitable to men; and in this blood must Christians dip their good works if they expect them to be acceptable to God.

The *sprinkling the leper seven times* signifies that perfect cleanness which is by the blood of sprinkling introduced into the conscience and which the royal penitent so pathetically breathes after, "Purge me with hyssop, and I shall be clean: wash me, and I shall be whiter than snow" (Ps. 51:7).

The *dismissing of the other bird into the open field* may perhaps denote the resurrection of the Son of God or that His divine nature was untouched by death. Or as the living bird received its liberty when dipped in the blood of the dead one, so we are made to know "the power of his resurrection" by "the fellowship of his sufferings" (Phil. 3:10) and may truly say, "Our soul is escaped as a bird out of the snare of the fowlers" (Ps. 124:7).

The leper thus sprinkled according to the ordinance, though pronounced clean by the priest, was required to shave his hair and wash himself and his clothes in water, that he might be clean (Lev. 14:9), which was not only a precaution to prevent relapse, through any relics of the distemper lurking in his hair or garments, but may also point forth to us this momentous truth, that our being sprinkled by our High Priest with the clean water of His blood does not at all supersede the cleansing ourselves from all filthiness of the flesh and spirit. There is no person who partakes this glorious privilege who endeavors not as his duty to purify himself to lay aside all "superfluity of naughtiness" (James 1:21), to "put off the old man" (Col. 3:9), and to hate "even the garment spotted by the flesh" (Jude 23) by having "no fellowship with the unfruitful works of darkness" (Eph. 5:11). Nor are his purifying endeavors to be intermitted, but persisted in all the days of his life, as the leper was to repeat on the seventh day the ceremonies of shaving and washing:

for sanctification is a gradual and progressive work that shall not be completed till the week of this mortal life is fulfilled. Such were the ceremonies of the first and of the seventh day.

Cleansing Ceremonies of the Eighth Day
On the eighth day, three lambs were to be fetched for a trespass offering, a sin offering, and a burnt offering, a quantity of fine flour for a meat offering, and one log of oil (Lev. 14:10–13). If he was not able to afford such costly offerings, the Lord accepted such as he was able to get, which are also condescended upon in the law (Lev. 14:21–22). These sacrifices being presented, together with the leper, before the Lord, were to be offered in the usual manner. But the blood of the trespass offering was by a peculiar ceremony to be applied to the extreme parts of the leper's body, the tip of his right ear, the thumb of his right hand, and the great toe of his right foot (Lev. 14:14–17, 23–28). Above the blood, the oil was to be applied in the same manner and the overplus poured upon his head who was to be cleansed (Lev. 14:18, 29).

These sacrifices, without all doubt, had the same general meaning as other sacrifices; and the peculiar ceremonies were doubtless very significant, as if the priest had said to the leper, "I put this blood and this oil on your ear, now you are free to hear the Word of God in any synagogue; I put it on your thumb, now you may handle anything and not defile it; I put them on your toe, now you may go where you please, and men will not avoid your society."

But what forbids us to think of still higher mysteries? "These particular parts of the body may signify the perceptive and executive faculties, in both of which we offend, and for both of which we need the great propitiation."[2] Was not this the language of that solemn rite? "Now you are made clean; let all of your faculties and powers be devoted to the service of God. Let your ears be open to the commands

---

2. Editor's note: James Hervey, *Theron and Aspasio: or, A Series of Dialogues and Letters, upon the Most Important and Interesting Subjects* (London: Rivington, 1755), vol. 1, dialogue 3, p. 115.

of God. Let the works of your hands be established and accepted by Him. Let your footsteps be ordered in His Word."

The oil that was put upon the blood most certainly signifies the Holy Spirit as a Spirit of sanctification. By the blood of His merit, He forgives all our iniquities; and by the oil of His Spirit, He heals all our diseases. By the first we are justified. By the second we are sanctified (Rom. 4:25). By the one, sin shall not condemn to suffer the punishment it deserves, and by the other it shall not command to obey the orders it gives (Rom. 6:14). And whereas the remnant of the oil in the priest's hand was to be poured on his head that was cleansed, this most undoubtedly prefigured the shedding of the Holy Spirit on us abundantly through Jesus Christ our Savior. It is said in one place, "Ye have an unction from the Holy One" (1 John 2:20), and in another, "Now he which stablisheth us with you in Christ, and hath anointed us, is God; who hath also sealed us, and given the earnest of the Spirit in our hearts (2 Cor. 1:21–22).

How foolish a part had the Israelite acted who had contented himself with making application to the physician without having recourse to the priest for the cleansing of his leprosy! Alas! The balm in Gilead could not supply the place of the sacrificial blood (Jer. 8:22; 46:11). Nor do they act a wiser part who seek the physicians of their own legal endeavors for the cure of their leprosy, but not unto Jesus Christ, the high priest who stands ready with His hyssop and blood. Can the rivers of Damascus compare with the waters of Israel (2 Kings 5:12)? Bring us, O Lord, to the Jordan of Thy grace for cleansing our leprous souls: "Lord, if thou wilt, thou canst make [us] clean" (Matt. 8:2); "Purge [us] with hyssop, and [we]...shall be whiter than snow" (Ps. 51:7).

14

The Law of the Near Kinsman

Deuteronomy 25:5–10; Ruth 4

It is not for nothing that the near kinsman among the Jews, and the Lord Himself, are alike denominated in the original language of the Hebrews. Why should the name *Goël*[1] be common to him that acted the kinsman's part among the Jews, and to the God of Israel, if there were not a great resemblance between the kindly offices of the one and the gracious benefits of the other? And the propriety of this observation will more evidently appear from an induction of particulars. For what the earthly *Goël*, or nearest blood relation, was enjoined to do for his brother under the law, the heavenly *Goël*—that is, the all-gracious Redeemer—hath done in the most eminent manner for sinners of the human race under the gospel. If an Israelite died without children, the *Goël* was to marry his widow to raise up seed unto his brother so that his name might not perish (Deut. 25:5–7). If through poverty he had sold away his possession, the *Goël* was to buy back his inheritance (Lev. 25:25–28). If for the same reason he had sold himself for a servant to another man, the *Goël* was to redeem

---

1. Editor's note: The Hebrew *gōʾēl* is best rendered "kinsman-redeemer" (NIV). This more accurately conveys the significance of the relationship required to fulfill the terms of the "levirate marriage" provision of the Mosaic law (Deut. 25:5–10) and therefore its antitype in Jesus, the Redeemer who "sticketh closer than a brother" (Prov. 18:24). The terms *near kinsman* (AV), and *close relative* (NASB, NKJV) are not quite specific enough to convey the element of redemption that is involved in this transaction, which in the end points to Christ as the Redeemer of His people.

him from his master (Lev. 25:47–48). And, lastly, if an Israelite was murdered, his *Go'el* was to avenge his blood by bringing the willful murderer to suffer condign punishment (Deut. 19:1–13). Waiving the political reason of these laws, we shall confine ourselves to their allegorical interpretation: for on all these accounts the believer in the promised Messiah may say of Him with Job, "I know my [*GO'EL*] liveth" (Job 19:25).

A Kinsman Who Marries and Saves His Bride

Blessed be the Lord who hath not left us this day without a Kinsman, to marry and raise up the seed of good works unto our barren nature. Once she was fruitful unto God, before the breach of the first covenant. But now, alas, the image of God she wore at first is miserably defaced, her husband the law is become dead and "weak through the flesh" (Rom. 8:3), and she can bring forth no children unto God— that is, can produce no action that bears resemblance unto Him or corresponds to the demands of the law. "Sin and death" (Rom. 8:2), these are the only births of corrupt nature, and we may truly say of all men in their unrenewed state, "They conceive mischief, and bring forth vanity, and their belly prepareth deceit" (Job 15:35). At best they can only say, "We have been with child, we have been in pain, we have…brought forth wind" (Isa. 26:18). But the loving Kinsman consented to marry this barren nature by assuming a true body and a reasonable soul, its two essential parts, into a personal union with Himself, and by uniting with Himself, in a mystical union, a great number of individuals of our race.

It is true, the match was most unequal, and huge difficulties were to be surmounted before the marriage could be solemnized and the bride prepared for her husband. But His love was stronger than death itself, and we are become dead to the law by the body of Christ, that we might be married to another husband, even to Him that was raised from the dead, that the barren woman might keep house and become a joyful mother of children (Ps. 113:9). Now that our Maker is our husband (Isa. 54:5), she that was "barren hath born seven" (1 Sam. 2:5), and the promise is accomplished, "Thy wife shall be as a fruitful vine by the sides of thine house: thy children like olive plants round about thy table" (Ps. 128:3). We may truly affirm of all the happy souls that are espoused to the one husband, "Every one beareth twins," the love of God and his neighbor, "and none is barren among them" (Song 6:6; 4:2). These children are indeed the heritage of the Lord, and this fruit of the womb his reward: "happy is the man that hath his quiver full of them" (Ps. 127:5). "Behold I," will he say in the great day of the Lord, "and the children whom God hath given me" (Heb. 2:13).

A Kinsman Who Gives Everlasting Life to the Dead

Blessed be the Lord who hath not left us without a Kinsman to redeem the mortgaged inheritance of everlasting life, which, alas, we sold away for one morsel of forbidden fruit but are not able to buy back again by all the money of our obedience or sufferings. None of our kin was able to pay the price. For all men being equally involved in the same ruin, none of them could redeem his brother, and angels, though glorious and perfect creatures, yet needed all their holiness for themselves; and had they undertaken to pay our debt, they would have, like the kinsman in Ruth, but marred their own inheritance. But lo! What men and angels could not have done, the Son of God clothed in flesh and blood hath completely effected. The ransom was paid down in the liquid gold of His precious blood, to the uttermost farthing of the legal demand (Matt. 5:26). Now heaven is a purchased possession, and by Thy poverty we are become rich, O gracious Redeemer, who for our sakes became poor (2 Cor. 8:9), though the silver and the gold is Thine.

A Kinsman Who Secures an Eternal Inheritance for His Poor

Blessed be the Lord, who hath not left us without a Kinsman to redeem not only the inheritance to us, but us to the inheritance: for being reduced to the most abject poverty by the loss of original righteousness and communion with God, we sold ourselves, like the prodigal son in the parable, to the most sordid slavery of the devil, sold ourselves for a wretched sustenance, even "the husks that the swine did eat" (Luke 15:16). From this inglorious servitude we could not by any means have extricated ourselves except the Kinsman, the Redeemer, had come to Zion (Isa. 59:20), had taken upon Him "the form of a servant" (Phil. 2:7), and given Himself a "ransom for all" (1 Tim. 2:6). Such was the hard condition of our rescue; but in His love and in His pity He redeemed us, who had sold ourselves for naught: "For with the LORD…is plenteous redemption. And he shall redeem Israel from all his iniquities" (Ps. 130:7–8).

A Kinsman Who Avenges the Blood of His Redeemed People
Blessed be the Lord who hath not left us without a Kinsman to be the avenger of our blood when the prince of the rebellious angels had massacred the human race in the loins of their great progenitor. That wicked spirit, stung with fierce resentment against the avenging God and stimulated with envy against innocent and happy men, seduced him to fall off from his Creator and to partake of his revolt. Thus, Satan was "a murderer from the beginning" (John 8:44), not only of our bodies, which are by his means subjected unto the first death, but of our souls, that are naturally "dead in trespasses and sins" (Eph. 2:1) and liable to everlasting vengeance, which is "the second death" (Rev. 20:14). The holy and righteous law of God was, shall we say, the city of refuge to which he fled. He boasted, "Shall the prey be taken from the mighty, or the lawful captive delivered?" (Isa. 49:24). For having in some sense the power of death, the sting of which was sin, and the strength of sin was the law (1 Cor. 15:56), what mere creature was able to enter into the palace of this strong-armed Apollyon (Rev. 9:11) and spoil him of his armor? Whoever enters on this arduous enterprise, he must be able to unsting death by satisfying the law.

Here then let us adopt the sublime rapture of the prophet: "The LORD saw it, and it displeased him that there was no judgment. And he saw that there was no man, and wondered that there was no intercessor: therefore his arm brought salvation unto him; and his righteousness, it sustained him. For he put on righteousness as a breastplate, and an helmet of salvation upon his head; and he put on the garments of vengeance for clothing, and was clad with zeal as a cloak" (Isa. 59:15–17).

Or shall we use the style of the New Testament apostle when speaking of this very thing? "Forasmuch then as the children are partakers of flesh and blood, he also himself likewise took part of the same, that through death he might destroy him that had the power of death, that is, the devil" (Heb. 2:14). The Redeemer has died; the Redeemer has risen again. O Satan, where is thy power? O death, where is thy sting? For though "the sting of death is sin; and the strength of sin is the law. But thanks be to God, which giveth us the victory through our Lord Jesus Christ" (1 Cor. 15:56–57). The glorious Avenger of our blood has not only punished the murderer (which is all that man can do for his slaughtered brother) but has restored life to the murdered, that in their own persons they may overcome the wicked one. Thus has Christ our Kinsman redeemed their soul from deceit and violence, and precious has their blood been in His sight.

15

The Holy Nation of Israel
Genesis 12:1–9

When the knowledge of the true God was lost among the nations of the ancient world, the family of Abraham was chosen to be the repository of that most invaluable treasure. It was promised in a solemn manner to this venerable patriarch that he should have a numerous progeny and a peculiar seed that should become a universal blessing to the world. In process of time he was the progenitor of a mighty nation, divided into twelve tribes, who being for a long time the only visible society where God was worshipped, were distinguished from other people with very high appellations and valuable privileges. They are styled in the Old Testament "a peculiar treasure...a kingdom of priests, and an holy nation" (Ex. 19:5–6), the "inheritance" (Jer. 10:16), the "vineyard" (Isa. 5:7), the "congregation" (Num. 16:3), the "tribes of the LORD" (Ps. 122:4), and his firstborn son (Ex. 4:22). To them "pertaineth the adoption, and the glory, and the covenants, and the giving of the law, and the service of God, and the promises; whose are the fathers, and of whom as concerning the flesh Christ came" (Rom. 9:4–5). This famous nation, after many vicissitudes of fortune, were at last, for the horrid crime of rejecting and murdering the Messiah, disinherited by the offended God of their fathers, divested of all their glorious privileges, ejected from the land of promise, and are become miserable wanderers among the nations.

What shall we say then to these things? Has God cast away His people (Rom. 11:1–2)? Is there no Israel now to be found, among whom His name is great? Yes, though Israel according to the flesh is no more the people of God, still there is a holy nation, a royal priesthood, a peculiar people, a true circumcision that worship God in the spirit and have no confidence in the flesh (1 Peter 2:9–10; Phil. 3:3). The "sinners of the Gentiles" (Gal. 2:15), who were once polluted as "dogs" (Mark 7:26–28), stupid as stones, are now by the power of divine grace become the children of Abraham and the true "Israel of God" (Gal. 6:16). John saw the Christian Israel sealed in his mysterious vision, of every tribe a select number (Rev. 7:4–8). And the twelve apostles of the Lamb are said, in a prophetic style, to sit on twelve thrones and judge the twelve apostate tribes of Israel (Matt. 19:28) when they became the spiritual fathers of the holy Christian nation, of which the Israel according to the flesh was a figure. Let us see where the resemblance lies.

The Smallness of Israel's Beginning
And, first, we might observe the smallness of their beginning. They were once but few in number, the fewest of all people, as their lawgiver told them. Though afterward they received a prodigious increase, they descended from twelve men, who sprung from one as good as dead, that was called being alone. Exactly so, the Gentile church, though a great multitude that no man can number, are the spiritual children of the twelve apostles, who sprung from One that was actually dead, though He lives forevermore. Though the beginning of the gospel church was small, like a grain of seed, or a little leaven, yet its latter end did greatly increase.

The Number of Israel's Enemies
Second, the number of their enemies deserves our attention. This ancient people were never without enemies of one sort or other—in Egypt, in the wilderness, and even in Canaan itself. The church of Christ has always in this state of warfare her Egypt, her Amalek, her Edom, her Moab, her Philistines, and her Babylon. This last being the most eminent foe of the ancient race of Israel is viewed, in the prophetic book of the New Testament, as a figure of the malignant

church, or anti-Christian state, the most formidable adversary of the true church since the ascension of our Lord. And truly, the prophetic descriptions of ancient Babylon, by whose rivers the melancholy captives of Israel sat down and wept, are, with the most evident propriety, applied by the New Testament prophet to that powerful, that wealthy, that idolatrous, that persecuting church of Rome, that sits on the "many waters" of "kindreds, and tongues, and nations" (Rev. 17:1; 13:7). Though, like the ancient Babylon, her predecessor and type, she should defy all danger, live deliciously, and boast, "I sit a queen, and am no widow, and shall see no sorrow" (Rev. 18:7) and "neither shall I know the loss of children" (Isa. 47:8), yet at the appointed time, the cry of her destruction—her final, her total destruction—shall be heard, "O daughter of Babylon, who art to be destroyed; happy shall he be, that rewardeth thee as thou hast served us" (Ps. 137:8).

The Eminent Deliverances of Israel

The eminent deliverances of Israel is the next thing we shall notice. Though they were an afflicted nation from the beginning, lying among the pots, traveling through the floods, traversing the wilderness, weeping by Babel's stream (Ps. 68:13; 66:6; 107:4; 137:1), yet "Happy art thou, O Israel: who is like unto thee, O people saved by the LORD, the shield of thy help, and who is the sword of thy excellency! and thine enemies shall be found liars unto thee; and thou shalt tread upon their high places" (Deut. 33:29). The house of bondage could not detain them, the waters of the sea could not overflow them, the wilderness could not famish them, and Babylon could not hold them in captivity. Who knows not that these illustrious works of God in behalf of the chosen seed are sung in lofty numbers by the inspired penman, in phrases that describe the common salvation and the redemption of the world from still more dreadful foes (e.g., Pss. 105–107)? And the illustrious persons who, under God, achieved the several rescues of ancient Israel are spoke of in the prophets in phrases that may be well adapted to the Messiah Himself.

The Distinguishing Sanctity of Israel
The singularity of their laws and customs, which were by heaven's appointment, diverse from all people, was no doubt intended to adumbrate the distinguishing sanctity, so different from the fashions of this world, which ought to adorn the holy Christian nation. The Jews of old were not more ridiculed by their scornful neighbors for the seeming oddity of their national usages than the peculiar people of Christ have been in every age for their zealous attachment to the divine law and because they were not conformed to this world.

The National Privileges of Israel
But a principal thing for which the Jewish nation was a typical people is the glorious national privileges they possessed, the chief of which we shall mention. To them belonged the adoption to be God's firstborn son, or the election to be His peculiar people (Rom. 9:4; 11:5; Deut. 14:2): a privilege that exalted them high above all nations and yet was not conferred upon them because of their own worthiness or excellency, of whatever kind, but solely because it was the good pleasure of God to bestow this glorious dignity upon them. Even so, the election and adoption of the general assembly and church of the firstborn, whose names are written in heaven (Heb. 12:23), arises from the same source, the good pleasure of His will, and purpose in grace, not of works, lest any man should boast (Eph. 1:5; 2:9). To them belonged the glorious symbols of the divine presence, as the holy temple, the sacred fire, and the bright cloud of the sanctuary, though by degrees these shadows vanished as the substance approached.

What nation was so great to have the Lord so near them in the visible tokens of His presence? None but that holy nation, whose prerogative it is to behold the glory of the incarnate Word, God manifested in the flesh (1 Tim. 3:16). To Israel belonged the law or covenant of works, ordained in the hand of Moses as a mediator between God and them. So to the Christian church belongs the law or covenant of works, ordained in the hand of Jesus Christ, the mediator between God and man (1 Tim. 2:5). Their mediator could not fulfill the law for them; they brake the covenant, and God regarded them not (Heb. 8:9). But Christ has magnified the law and made it honorable (Isa. 42:21) by a most complete satisfaction and meritorious obedience. To Israel belonged a civil government, modeled by God Himself; for their state was a theocracy, and the Lord said unto them, "I will be thy king" (Hos. 13:10). Exactly so, the laws of the New Testament kingdom are all enacted by Him that sits upon the throne, nor must the ordinances of men claim homage from the subjects of Jesus Christ, except insofar as they comport with His positive institutions. To Israel belonged the service of God, according to these rites which Himself prescribed—an emblem of that reasonable and acceptable service which appertains to the true church (Rom. 12:1) and which is found nowhere but among the societies of Christian worshipers. To Israel pertained the promises of rest in Canaan, the pleasant land, and of victory over the nations of the land. So to the Christian church belongs the promise of everlasting life and final rest in the better heavenly country (Heb. 11:16), to recompense their wanderings through the mazy wilderness of this world, and the promise of complete victory over the nations of spiritual foes, the lusts that war in their earthly members (James 4:1). A more glorious honor this than to storm a city: as he that ruleth over his own spirit is better than the mighty (Prov. 16:32). "This honour have all his saints" (Ps. 149:9).

Heirs According to the Promise
Here let us end—adoring the riches of that divine goodness in bringing nigh, by the blood of His dear Son, those that were far off, Gentiles in the uncircumcision of their flesh, aliens from the commonwealth of Israel (Eph. 2:11–13). And trembling at the severity of divine justice toward that sinful nation (Isa. 1:4ff.), who are now as much depressed below all other people as once they were exalted above them. Let us recollect the apostle's necessary admonition: "because of unbelief they were broken off, and thou standest by faith. Be not highminded, but fear" (Rom. 11:20). Happy they who are endowed with this noble grace. Such are Israelites indeed,

though Abraham be ignorant of them and Israel according to the flesh acknowledge them not (Isa. 63:16). For if we are Christ's, then are we "Abraham's seed, and heirs according to the promise" (Gal. 3:29).

16

The Victory over the Nations of Canaan
Joshua 1:1–9

Before the tribes of the Lord could possess their goodly heritage, the numerous and mighty nations that dwell in Canaan were first to be expelled. What if for once the eternal Sovereign and just governor of the world shall transfer to a chosen seed the property of a land inhabited by guilty wretches and put "a two-edged swords in their hand; to execute vengeance upon the heathen, and punishments upon the people; to bind their kings with chains, and their nobles with fetters of iron; to execute upon them the judgment written" (Ps. 149:6–9)? Shall we therefore presume to censure the Majesty of heaven as cruel and unjust? No: the horrid wickedness of these nations fully justified the severity of their doom, and the peremptory command of God absolves the Israelites from the charge of barbarity in becoming the executioners of the sentence. Some in later ages have, with equal cruelty and injustice, for heaven's cause (a horrid pretense!) made desolate the earth. Let them not plead this precedent: for as such a mandate was never given before, so shall it never be repeated again. But leaving it to God Himself to vindicate His ways to man, as He is well able to do, we shall proceed to notice that spiritual privilege of the true Israel, signified by this victory over the nations.

The Growth of the Gospel Church
Perhaps it was not improper to view it as an emblem of the conquest over the world obtained by the first preachers and possessors

of Christianity, under the banner of the cross, though not with carnal weapons. Though it is very fit that the anti-Christian kingdom shall be promoted by the horrid methods of torture, massacre, fire, and faggot, "the Son of man is not come to destroy men's lives, but to save them" (Luke 9:56). If the apostles of the Lamb had a two-edged sword in their hand, it was the sword of the Spirit, which is the Word of God (Eph. 6:17; Heb. 4:12): faith was their shield (Eph. 6:16), righteousness their breastplate (Isa. 59:17), and their helmet was the hope of salvation (1 Thess. 5:8). Equipped with this armor of light, they subdued the nations to the obedience of faith; nor could the persecutor's sword, the philosopher's wisdom, nor the inveterate customs of the populace, received by tradition from their fathers, retard the progress of their victorious arms, though, to the outward eye, they seemed but as grasshoppers before these formidable sons of Anak (Num. 13:33).

The Morning of the Resurrection

We might also here take occasion to think of that dominion which the upright shall have in the morning of the resurrection, when the saints of the Most High shall sit with Christ upon His throne and, in such manner as is competent unto them, shall judge the world of wicked men and angels (Dan. 7:18; 1 Cor. 6:2). Even in our present imperfect state, the luster of divine graces and beauties of holiness have commanded respect and veneration in the minds of proud and wicked men. A judge has trembled before a prisoner, and a fox has feared a lamb. These are preludes of that final superiority of the righteous in the decisive hour of judgment, when the evil shall bow before the good and be ashamed for their envy at the people they despised: "Then cometh the end, when he shall have delivered up the kingdom to God, even the Father; when he shall have put down all rule and all authority and power" (1 Cor. 15:24).

The Good Fight of Faith

But chiefly the Canaanites we must endeavor to extirpate are the lusts that war in our members that war against the soul. Against these inward foes must we lift the hand of violence if we mean to take the kingdom of heaven. Israelites indeed, here point your revenge, here bend your indignation! To pity these is the highest cruelty to yourselves, and to make any league with them is to be overcome. To mingle with these nations was fatal to Israel of old; they were forbidden to seek their peace or their wealth forever, but if they should cleave to the remnant of these nations, on whatever pretense, "know for a certainty that the LORD your God will no more drive out any of these nations…but they shall be snares and traps unto you, and scourges in your sides, and thorns in your eyes" and "shall vex you in the land wherein ye dwell" (Josh. 23:13; Num. 33:55). Such grieving thorns are unmortified corruptions in our hearts, and if we consult our peace and safety, it will be our constant work to weaken their power by all possible means. But to attempt a reconciliation of holiness and sin, to mediate peace between these contrary principles, is to entail upon ourselves a source of perpetual disquietude.

The Canaanite nations were not only the first inhabitants of the country but greater in number and mightier in power than Israel their conqueror. So also in the holy war, the sin that dwells in the soul is the first possessor and mightier than the principle of grace received. Thanks to its omnipotent Ally that iniquity prevails not against it, even to a total victory. Let none be deterred from fighting "the good fight of faith" against these inward enemies (1 Tim. 6:12), though perhaps some branches of the body of sin may seem so vivacious as even to gather new life by their foils. They may seem to have entrenched themselves so deeply in the constitution of the soul, and to derive so many advantages from outward circumstances in life, that to expel them is equally impossible as for the Israelites to drive out those Canaanites who had chariots of iron.

Victory Promised in Christ
Under the divine conduct of Jesus Christ, our true Joshua, we shall set our feet upon the necks of these dreaded foes. Take unto you the whole armor of God and remove every accursed thing from the midst of thee, O Israel, and the Lord thy God will drive out

these nations before thee by little and little. Their defense is already departed from them since the law, the strength of sin, is perfectly fulfilled and stripped of its condemning power. A time, a happy time will come when no Jebusite shall dwell in the land, when no latent corruption shall infest thy soul, and "there shall be no more a pricking brier unto the house of Israel, nor any grieving thorn of all that are round about them" (Ezek. 28:24). It is the gracious promise of the Captain of our salvation, "He that overcometh, and keepeth my works unto the end, to him will I give power over the nations: and he shall rule them with a rod of iron; as the vessels of a potter shall they be broken to shivers" (Rev. 2:26–27).

17

The Allegory of Hagar and Sarah
Genesis 16

As we are informed by the great apostle of the Gentiles that the private history of Abraham's family was a presage of the events that happened to his posterity, we shall glance at it a little. This faithful patriarch had received the promise of a seed, in whom all nations should be blessed (Gen. 12:1–3; 22:18; Gal. 3:8). But the accomplishment was long delayed, his wife proved barren, old age was stealing on apace, and there seemed no human probability that Sarah should have a son. She ought, however, to have believed Him faithful who had promised and fully able to perform what He had said. She should not have devised unlawful means of helping the promise to bring forth, but patiently expected God's time of visitation, which is always the best.

Sarah's Impatience and Its Sad Fruit (Gen. 16:1–6)

But it was otherwise: for in the ardor of impatience she urges Abraham her husband to marry her bondmaid, fondly imagining that this stratagem might compensate her own barrenness and forward the birth of the promised seed. Whatever humility and self-denial this good woman may be supposed to have acted in making such a proposal, it cannot certainly be vindicated from the charge of being in itself immoral and contrary to the original dictates of the law of nature: for though polygamy was ordinarily practiced in the primitive ages of the world, and even in the patriarchal families who professed the true religion, it is neither to be excused nor imitated. There is no ground to think that God approved, though He tolerated the custom of having more wives than one. From the beginning it was not so. And indeed the family broils, which the Scripture frequently mentions, as occasioned by this practice is a sufficient confirmation of its manifest inconvenience. Of this we have a little instance in the present case, for no sooner is this unlawful overture of Sarah complied with by her husband, by taking Hagar into his bed, than the insolent and disrespectful carriage of the bondmaid, when she saw that she had conceived, raised such variance in the family that at last she is obliged to run away from the resentment of her injured mistress.

Ishmael Is Born to Hagar (Gen. 16:7–16)
But returning and humbling herself, a peace was again patched up for a time. She bears Ishmael, Abraham's firstborn son. But this was not the child of the promise. There was nothing extraordinary about his birth, which was, to use the phrase of the apostle, after the flesh. The happy seed that should become a blessing to the world must be born in lawful wedlock, not of a bondmaid but of a free woman.

Isaac Is Born to Sarah (Gen. 21:1–8)
And, Sarah, why did you doubt if the power of God was able to make the barren woman a joyful mother? How absurd is it for any to hasten providence? Give it time, and it will do all things well. For when, in process of time, Abraham's body is dead as Sarah's womb, lo, Isaac is conceived and born; Isaac the promised seed, Isaac the long-expected child, is brought forth to the great joy of his parents, a son of their old age.

Hagar and Ishmael Cast Out (Gen. 21:9–21)
By this time Ishmael is become a youth and arrived at years of some discretion, but he walks rather in the steps of his mother than of his father and is so daring as to mock at his younger brother, at his weaning feast. Though one would be willing to excuse this behavior as proceeding only from puerile levity, the severity of the punishment

inflicted for this fault seems to evince that there was a great mixture of impiety in this insulting carriage and that the promise itself was the chief thing he derided. It could not fail to be very irritating to Sarah to observe how ill her kindness to Hagar was requited by the undutiful deportment of her son, and when she urged their present dismissal from the family, Abraham was not overready to comply with this request, because of the affection he bore to Ishmael, and he hoped that the passion of his wife, though just, would soon subside. But the motion of Sarah, "Cast out this bondwoman and her son: for the son of this bondwoman shall not be heir with my son, even with Isaac" (Gen. 21:10), is backed with a mandate from God Himself. And accordingly the father of the Jewish nation, which is very remarkable, discards from his family his eldest son, who was equally circumcised with Isaac, never, as would seem, to return again. And this was done by the positive command of God Himself, with a special view to prefigure the future rejection of a great part of Abraham's natural posterity that were only descended from him according to the flesh.

An Allegory of Two Covenants (Gal. 4:21–31)

That this was the secret design of Providence in this memorable story might be conjectured from the narrative of Moses. But we are not allowed so much as to doubt of it by that infallible expositor of the law, Paul the apostle of Jesus Christ, who discoursing on this very subject to the revolted Galatian churches expressly says, "Which things are an allegory: for these [women] are the two covenants" (Gal. 4:24).

According to this apostle, Hagar, with her son, was secretly designed to represent the covenant that prescribes our own obedience as the representation of which covenant was exhibited at Mount Sinai in Arabia, and it also answers to Jerusalem that now is, and is in bondage with her children—that is, to the present apostate church of the Jews, who expect to be justified by the works of the law, and all who imitate their example.

Upon the other hand, Sarah the free woman, with Isaac her son, is an emblem of the covenant that directs to look for salvation only by the righteousness of a middle person, without the works of the law, which covenant was published from Mount Zion and answers to "Jerusalem above," or the true church, whether of Jews or Gentiles, that is free from the legal yoke and is "the mother of us all" if we believe (Gal. 4:26). Let us pursue this beautiful allegory a little in the track which the apostle has marked out.

The Freewoman: Grace before Law Brings Freedom

And, first, it may be said that as Sarah the free woman was before Hagar, so the promise was before the law, and the covenant of grace antecedent unto the covenant of works. Not to speak of the federal transaction between the Father and the Son which the Scripture frequently mentions as commencing from all everlasting, the promise or revelation of this eternal covenant was exhibited to the church long before the Sinai dispensation.

Again, as Sarah was the mistress and Hagar the maid, so the gospel is the mistress to which the law was subservient. If Hagar had kept her station without departing from that subordination she owed to Sarah, she might then have been of singular use in the patriarch's family instead of raising the broils and animosities which were afterward occasioned by her. For a servant bearing rule is one of Solomon's unseemly things (Prov. 19:10), and among other things which the earth cannot bear, and for which it is disquieted, he mentions an odious woman when she is married and a handmaid that is heir to her mistress (Prov. 30:23). So if the legal covenant be kept in its own room and place, she may greatly serve the covenant of grace; she may be remarkably useful to convince of sin and to endear a Savior. For the law, as the apostle affirms, is good if a man use it lawfully (1 Tim. 1:8). But if this bondmaid (the law) assumes the sole dominion and rivals her mistress, to whom she should humble herself—that is, if she takes upon her to justify and save—she then works wrath and is fatally pernicious. And this the event proved.

The Bondwoman: Law before Promise Brings Bondage

Hagar is taken (unseemly as it was) into the bed of Sarah. This seems to have prefigured that the law should be taken into the room of the gospel: for as Abraham, after he was married to the free woman, turned aside to the bondmaid, so his posterity, after they received the promise, from whence alone they should have looked for justification and everlasting life, turned aside to the law, which was added for other ends, and expected from the law that which the promise can only confer. Whoever they be, whether of the Jewish or Christian denomination, that depend upon their own righteousness, either as the sole or partial cause of their salvation, they are guilty of the same fault in the mystery that Abraham was in the letter when he permitted Hagar to ascend the bed of her mistress.

Though Sarah was long barren, Hagar is not. The birth of Ishmael is not nearly as difficult as the birth of Isaac. It is a far easier matter for the law to engender children into bondage than for the promise to bring forth children unto liberty. Jerusalem above, or the true gospel church, labors indeed to bring forth spiritual children. But, ah! How few are the children of this free woman to the vast shoals of legal professors who desire to be under the law! The most eminent preachers of the gospel have had ground of complaining, "Lord, who hath believed our report?" And that they labored in vain, and spent their strength in vain, and for naught. But as the womb of Sarah was at last opened, after it had been long shut, so of the gospel church, her antitype, the prophet cries, "Sing, O barren, thou that didst not bear; break forth into singing, and cry aloud, thou that didst not travail with child: for more are the children of the desolate than the children of the married wife, saith the LORD" (Isa. 54:1).

The insolent behavior of Ishmael, the son of the bondmaid, when he mocked the child of promise, who was nobler than himself, is an emblem of the persecuting spirit of self-justifiers against the true believers in all ages. For as he who was born after the flesh persecuted him who was born after the Spirit, even so it is now. Witness the enmity of the Jews against the spreading of the gospel. Witness the papists' bloody rage. Witness, ye flames that reduced to ashes the bodies of so many noble martyrs. Yes, and "all that will live godly in Christ Jesus" must be content, in one shape or another, to "suffer persecution" (2 Tim. 3:12).

Lastly, the sentence of exclusion from Abraham's family pronounced by the Scripture against the bondwoman and her son was a sure presage of the irrevocable doom of all the children of the law, though (like the circumcised but mocking Ishmael) they are born in the church and wear the professor's badge. "Abraham" says the Scripture, "rose early in the morning, and took bread, and a bottle of water, and gave it unto Hagar,…and the child, and sent her away: and she departed, and wandered in the wilderness of Beersheba" (Gen. 21:14). Even so, the carnal Jews, though Abraham's natural seed, are now cast out from the church and wander through the world. And all who remain under the law and are not, as Isaac was, the children of the promise shall be in like manner cast out from the presence of God and excluded from the heavenly inheritance.

BOOK 3
Typical Places

1

The Cities of Refuge
Numbers 35:9–34; Joshua 20:1–9

To inspire the minds of the Israelites with the greater horror at the dreadful sin of murder, it pleased God, their Judge and Lawgiver, not only to appoint that the murderer should be put to death but to permit the avenger of blood, or the near kinsman, to kill with impunity from men the unfortunate manslayer, who, without malice or design, was the instrument of taking away the life of his neighbor. But to counterbalance this permission, and to protect an unhappy man from the effects of rash resentment, it pleased the same good God to appoint cities of refuge in his commonwealth to which the manslayer might fly as his sanctuary from the avenger. These cities were six in number: three in the land of Canaan and three on the other side of Jordan. They belonged to the tribe of Levi (Num. 35:13–15). The roads to them were prepared by authority. And that nothing might retard the flight of the hapless manslayer, to whom every moment was precious, they say that the breadth of the road was thirty-two cubits; that where there happened to be water, it was laid over with a bridge; and that, at the cross ways, the inscription of *Refuge, Refuge*, directed where to bend his course.[1] In the city of

---

1. Editor's note: Information about the roads to the cities of refuge is not found in Scripture but in that compendium of rabbinical thought, the Talmud. See the entry "Asylum" in *The Jewish Encyclopedia* (New York: Funk and Wagnalls, 1903), 2:258, which states, "Corresponding to the care for the proper location of these cities were the other ordinances referring to them. The roads leading to them were marked by

refuge he was supplied with all necessary accommodations, and his life once more was protected by the laws of the realm. He was not, however, to venture without the precinct of the hospitable town, for if the avenger of blood should find and kill him, he would not be punished as a murderer for doing it. The death of the high priest was the first thing that released him from his confinement and left him at liberty to go wherever he pleased. Even so, by the death of the Great High Priest the guilty sinner is rescued from bondage and confinement into the glorious liberty of the sons of God.

But what we intend chiefly to notice here is the resemblance between the flight of the manslayer to the cities of refuge and of the sinner to Jesus Christ as the hope set before him. And perhaps it will appear very probable that the method of our salvation was typified by this Mosaic law; at least that here is no contemptible allegory.

The Guilty Sinner and the Inexorable Justice of God

Let the manslayer be an emblem of the guilty sinner who, by violating the precept of the holy law, butchers his own soul, murders his neighbor, and in some manner assassinates God Himself, whose very being is struck at by the commission of every sin.

Let the avenger of blood denote the inexorable justice of an angry God, whose wrath it is alike impossible to shun or to endure; the dreadful curse of the condemning law, whose quiver is filled with the arrows of every divine threatening; the envenomed sting of a resentful conscience, which infixed in the soul can make it a terror to itself, and all around; or death, the grisly king of terrors, the universal destroyer of the nations through fear of whom many are held in bondage all their lifetime. Yea, what creature is not ready, at the slightest intimation of the divine will, to start up an avenger of its Creator's quarrel against the obnoxious criminal?

---

sign-posts at the crossroads, with the inscription 'Miklat' (Refuge); the roads were very broad—32 ells, twice the regulation width—smooth and level, in order that the fugitive might not be hindered in any way (Sifre *l.c.*; Tosef. *l.c.* 5; Mak. 10*b*; B. B. 100*b*)."

Immanuel the Sinner's Refuge

Let the cities of refuge represent the glorious Immanuel and His blessed mediation. These cities pertained to the Promised Land and were to be found nowhere else. So the salvation of Jesus Christ is exhibited in the church: "But upon mount Zion shall be deliverance" (Obad. 1:17), and "God is known in her palaces for a refuge" (Ps. 48:3). They belonged to the priestly tribe. And the priestly office of Christ is that branch of His character which affords the most immediate relief to the sin-burdened soul. They were six in number and scattered through the territories of Israel at convenient distances, that wherever the misfortune should happen, the manslayer might not have far to go to one or other of them. May not this put us in mind that our Redeemer is a "present help in trouble" (Ps. 46:1)? To find Him we need neither climb up into heaven nor dive into the bottom of the sea, for the Word is nigh unto us (Deut. 30:14; Rom. 10:8). And in this Word the great Jehovah brings near His righteousness and His salvation. The patency and plainness of the roads that led to these cities of protection may occasion our reflecting on much the same thing. Guilty, condemned, trembling sinner, see how thy city of refuge expands her gates! How the stumbling blocks are removed! How the way is prepared! How the law is satisfied, justice atoned, and God reconciled! How the wayfaring man, though a fool, needs not err in the way of holiness! Nothing, nothing ought to retard thy present flight unto the hope set before thee or hinder thy present trusting in Christ for everlasting salvation from sin and its dreadful consequences.

Who Flies for Refuge to Jesus Christ?

But who is he that thus flies for refuge to Jesus Christ from the inexorable justice of an angry God and from the dreadful curse of a condemning law?

If the manslayer had not been conscious of the deed, and apprehensive of the kinsman's resentment on that account, he would not have judged it necessary to save himself by flight. And if he could have thought of a better expedient to ensure his safety, he would not have fled to a city where he must long remain a prisoner and in exile. But necessity, hard necessity, drove him to it as his only sanctuary. Even so, the refugee who flies to Jesus Christ from the avenging wrath of God is a person in whose heart is wrought a conviction of his guilt, an apprehension of his danger, and a despair of every refuge.

Formerly he had a very favorable opinion of himself, and his convictions of moral guilt were so general and moderate as to sit easy upon his mind without wounding his rest. He thought it no difficult matter to elude the divine threatenings and imagined himself secure because he was thoughtless of danger. The secrecy of sin, the example of the multitude, the hope of long life, the distance of the day of judgment, the presumption of God's mercy, his privileges and reputation as a member of the church—these, and such like things, he fled unto as a sanctuary from his melancholy thoughts. Or perhaps he stilled the enemy and avenger of an accusing conscience with business, with recreation, and with sensual indulgences.

But now a dreadful sound of vengeance is in his ears. He sees the heinous guilt of his iniquities, hears with Adam the voice of God, knows not where to hide his guilty head, looks on his right hand, and beholds, but there is no shelter. All refuge fails him, and no man cares for his soul. The method of salvation by Christ unfolds unto his view. "This is the way, walk ye in it," says the voice from heaven; and, "Turn to this strong hold, thou prisoner of hope." And as the man who flies for his life from a pursuing enemy will cast away from him anything, however valuable, that would cumber and detain him, so he parts at once both with his sins and with his own righteousnesses, and what things were gain to him, he counts "loss," that he may "win Christ" and "be found in him" (Phil. 3:8–9). He cries unto him and says, "O Lord…Thou art my refuge…. Attend unto my cry; for I am brought very low: deliver me from my persecutors; for they are stronger than I" (Ps. 142:5–6).

An Abiding Refuge in Our Great High Priest

It was not only required of the manslayer that he should fly to the city of refuge for once, but he was to remain there till the death of the high priest. Nor is it sufficient to believe in Christ for once, without abiding in Him as our sure defense. Our High Priest never dies, therefore should we abide in our refuge forever, for "in returning and rest shall ye be saved; in quietness and in confidence shall be your strength" (Isa. 30:15).

The protection afforded to all, both Jews and Gentiles—for there was no difference—who fled to these cities of refuge is no despicable representation of the ability in Jesus Christ "to save them to the uttermost that come unto God by him" (Heb. 7:25). As soon as the wretched manslayer reached the wished town, where he was legally secure of life and where (they say[2]) no weapons were allowed to be made or sold, he could talk with the avenger without turning pale, though before his throbbing heart beat high with the impulse of fear while he thought that every man he met would slay him. Even so the miserable sinner, who has obtained a discovery of his guilt and been harassed perhaps for some considerable time with a fearful looking for of judgment, his soul draws nigh unto the grave and his life to the destroyers: the moment he finds his rest in Christ by believing in Him for life and salvation, he can sit and answer all his accusers and talk with every enemy and avenger. "O thou enemy, destructions are come to a perpetual end" (Ps. 9:6). "Who shall lay any thing to the charge of God's elect? It is God that justifieth.... It is Christ that died" (Rom. 8:33–34). Produce your charge,[3] O law, and "O death, where is thy sting?" (1 Cor. 15:55).

A Superior Refuge to the Cities of Refuge

We shall, lastly, observe the superior excellence of our New Testament refuge to these ancient cities of protection. In all things He

---

2. Editor's note: I.e., the rabbis in the Talmud. See the entry "Asylum" in *The Jewish Encyclopedia* (New York: Funk and Wagnalls, 1903), 2:258, which states, "Dealing in weapons or implements of the chase was forbidden in the cities of refuge. Furthermore they had to be situated in a populous district, so that a violent attack by the avenger of blood might be repelled, if necessary (Sifre, Num. 159; Tosef., Mak. l.c. 8; Mak. 10a)."

3. Editor's note: The author is alluding to the language of Isaiah 41:21: "Produce your cause..."

has the preeminence (Col. 1:18). None was to be finally privileged in these cities but the manslayer, who was not indeed guilty of any crime but rather ill-fated and unhappy. If the willful murderer had fled to any of them, or even to God's altar, he was to be dragged from thence to suffer condign punishment (1 Kings 2:28–34). But none were ever dragged from Jesus Christ, who fled unto Him by faith, to return again into condemnation, however atrocious their crimes, however flagrant their guilt. Here murderers, adulterers, blasphemers, persecutors, and the most execrable miscreants that ever the sun beheld have been forever delivered from their Judge.

These ancient towns defended only the natural life from the avenger's sword, which was to be, however, soon paid as a debt to nature. But if Jesus Christ is our refuge, He will rescue us from everlasting vengeance; He will give unto us eternal life, and we shall never perish.

The refugees in the old cities of refuge were indeed secured in their lives by the laws of the land. But the *promise* of God that cannot lie, and the *oath* of God which cannot be recalled, are "two immutable things" by which their eternal happiness is secured, who have "fled for refuge" to lay hold on the hope set before them (Heb. 6:18). Happy believer, thy consolation is strong indeed: stronger than the afflictions of life, stronger than the fear of death, and stronger than the terror of judgment. Why shouldst thou not dismiss thy fears when thy never-ending safety from the most dreadful dangers is so amply secured that God Himself, for whom it is impossible to lie, would (O blasphemous thought!) be perjured should thou ever come into condemnation? The eternal God is thy "refuge and strength, a very present help in trouble. Therefore we will not fear, though the earth be removed, and though the mountains be carried into the midst of the sea; though the waters thereof roar and be troubled" (Ps. 46:1–3).

2

The Tabernacle in the Wilderness
Exodus 26

The tabernacle which Moses made in the wilderness, by the special appointment of the God of Israel, was the first religious structure in which the eternal Majesty vouchsafed to dwell on the earth. It was a sort of a portable temple and not unfitly esteemed the center of the ceremonial worship. The materials of it were collected by the voluntary contribution of the children of Israel, who, upon this occasion, offered so liberally that Moses found it necessary to stop them by a new proclamation. The pattern of it was minutely described to Moses in the mount by God Himself, who ordered him to be very exact in executing the heavenly plan. Two famous artists, whose names were Bezaleel and Aholiab, were inspired by the Spirit of God with most exquisite and masterly skill to finish the holy fabric and its utensils according to the divine plan (Ex. 31:2, 6). If you are curious to know the construction of this sacred tent, you may take this short description of it.

The Description of the Tabernacle
First of all, there was a spacious *court*, a hundred cubits long and fifty broad. It was hung round with curtains of fine twined linen that were fastened with silver hooks to pillars with sockets of brass filleted with silver.

The *gate* by which you entered to this wide area was a hanging of twenty cubits, of blue, purple, and scarlet, and fine twined linen, wrought with needlework and suspended by four pillars. This outward court the whole nation might enter on their solemn festivals, as it is said, "Enter into his gates with thanksgiving, and into his courts with praise."[1] Here, under the open sky, stood the altar of burnt offering and the brazen laver.

Within the circumference of this wide and open court was the *tabernacle* itself, into which none but the tribe of Levi were allowed to enter to accomplish the service of God. It was a close tent, twenty cubits long, ten cubits broad, and its height equal to its breadth. It was constructed of boards of shittim wood[2] of regular dimensions, running into one another. These boards were supported beneath with sockets of silver, and corroborated behind with bars of the same wood overlaid with gold, and fastened by golden rings through which they passed. Do you ask, What was the roof of this magnificent tent? First, it was covered with ten curtains of equal measure, of fine twined linen, and blue, and purple, and scarlet, embroidered with cherubim, and coupled with loops of blue and taches[3] of gold. Then it was covered with eleven curtains of goats' hair, hung together by taches of brass. Next it was covered with rams' skins dyed red. And above all, there was a covering of badgers' skins to protect the tabernacle and its coverings from the injuries of the weather.

But though these boards and curtains, thus joined together, made but one tabernacle, this one tabernacle was divided into two apartments (Ex. 26:33). The first was called *the Holy Place*, into which you entered through a veil or hanging of blue, purple, and scarlet,

---

1. Editor's note: This is a quotation from the 1650 Scottish Psalter version of Psalm 100, which with Psalm 23 ("The Lord's my Shepherd") still retains an affectionate recognition in Presbyterian worship across the English-speaking world in the twenty-first century.

2. Editor's note: This "shittim wood" is thought to be from the Red Acacia (*Vachellia seyal*), native to North Africa and parts of the Middle East.

3. Editor's note: The "taches" were clasps designed to hold the curtains in place around the tabernacle. The word is used in the KJV (Ex. 26:6, 11, 33, and elsewhere) but is effectively extinct in modern English, except for its appearance in the word *moustache*.

and fine twined linen, curiously embroidered, supported with the pillars of shittim wood, overlaid with gold, and their bases of brass, and fastened with golden hooks. Here stood the golden table, the golden candlestick, and the golden altar. The second was called *the Most Holy Place*, into which the high priest, and none but he, did enter once in the year through a second veil of the same materials with the first, embroidered with cherubim, and fastened by golden taches to four pillars of shittim wood, overlaid with gold, and their bases of silver. In this secret chamber of the deity were deposited the most sacred symbols of the divine presence. Here was the ark of the covenant, covered by the mercy seat, and over it the cherubim of glory, between which Jehovah Himself was said to dwell. Here was the golden pot that had manna and the miraculous rod of Aaron that budded. And here the appearance of the glory of the Lord is supposed to have resided and been seen on special occasions.

Such was the structure of this holy tent, which was built in the taste of heaven, reared up by the inspiration of the Holy Spirit, and consecrated by Moses. And we must not forget this one thing, that it was a movable pavilion and therefore so contrived as to be easily taken down and set up again. While the peculiar people sojourned in the wilderness, the tabernacle shared the same fate, being transported from place to place by the ministry of the Levites. When they possessed the Promised Land, at first it rested in Gilgal, afterward in Shiloh, in the days of Saul it seems to have been in Nob, and when Solomon began to reign over Israel it was pitched at Gibeon. But at the last it was altogether superseded by the magnificent temple built by that glorious monarch, and probably the costly materials of it were lodged among the sacred treasures of the house of the Lord.

What Is the Significance of the Tabernacle?
What shall we then say to these things? Did "the high and lofty One" (Isa. 57:15), "whose dwelling is not with flesh" (Dan. 2:11), who resides not in "temples made with hands" (Acts 7:48; 17:24), did He stand in the least need of this movable habitation? Glorious as it was, can we reasonably think it to have been a suitable apartment for the

deity or at all adequate to the inconceivably glorious, immense, and eternal Spirit? What a contemptible idea of the true God would such a supposition inspire into the mind? Away with such a groveling thought, so unworthy of God and shocking to reason herself!

But if we suppose that these holy places made with hands were figures of heaven, of Christ, and of the church, and exhibited as such to the believing Israelites, then doubtless we will be reconciled to that very particular regard the high God was pleased to show to the worldly sanctuary. Then we shall be able to account for that ardent affection the ancient believers confessed on all occasions to the tabernacles of the Lord of Hosts. Then it will not appear absurd that the same God who spent but six days in creating the universal frame of nature should spend no less than forty in prescribing the little frame of the tabernacle. And that these holy places made with hands were figures of heaven, of Christ, and of the church, we are now to declare.

The Tabernacle as a Figure of Heaven

First, then, the tabernacle of Moses was a figure of heaven itself, that glorious high throne from the beginning. For this interpretation we have the express words of an inspired penman of the New Testament, who speaking of our Great High Priest plainly declares that "Christ is not entered into the holy places made with hands, which are the figures of the true; but into heaven itself, now to appear in the presence of God for us" (Heb. 9:24). Perhaps we should not err though we should think that, as the Jewish high priest went through the outward court and passed through the Holy Place into the holiest of all, so Jesus Christ, when He ascended on high, passed through the first heaven of clouds, and the second heaven of stars, into the third heaven of angels. But though the Most Holy Place was by itself alone, the most eminent figure of the heavenly sanctuary, this hinders not to regard the whole fabric as an emblem of the same blissful mansion.

Was the tabernacle of Moses *divided* into several parts? We know Him that said, "In my Father's house are many mansions" (John 14:2).

Was it a place of great *splendor* and magnificence even to the eye? "Glorious things are spoken of thee, O city of God" (Ps. 87:3).

Was it the dwelling of Jehovah, where the visible tokens of His presence were seen? In the heavenly mansions He unveils the brightness of His glory to all the saints around Him.

Did priests *always* officiate there? The saints in light are both kings and priests unto God.

Were the curtains embroidered with *cherubim*? In the celestial abodes are the innumerable company of angels (Heb. 12:22).

Was it replenished with all necessary *furniture and provision*? In heaven is the true light and the living bread, fullness of joy, and pleasures for evermore.

Did the voice of *praise* continually resound in the earthly tabernacle? The eternal regions are forever filled with loud hosannas.

Was *holiness and legal purity* required in all who trod the venerable courts of God's ancient dwelling place? Nothing that is defiled can enter the heavenly Jerusalem (Rev. 21:27).

And, lastly, as the tabernacle was *sprinkled with blood* by the Jewish high priest when he penetrated its innermost recesses once in the year, with the names of all the tribes engraved on his heart, even so the blood of Jesus Christ has consecrated that high and holy place, that sinners of the human kind might not be forever excluded from dwelling in the beatific presence of Jehovah. When the everlasting gates of heaven were by sin barred forever against us, the blood of Christ was the key that opened them again (Ps. 24:7, 9), and the believers in His atoning blood may enter into heaven itself with greater boldness than the high priest when he went into the holiest of all (Heb. 10:19), than the Levites when they officiated in the Holy Place, or than the people when they approached the outward court.

The Tabernacle as a Picture of Christ

A second thing which the tabernacle of Moses did most undoubtedly represent was the person and future incarnation of the Messiah Himself, who was made flesh in the appointed time and tabernacled among us (Rev. 21:3), and who spoke of His own body when He said to the Jews, "Destroy this temple, and in three days I will raise it up" (John 2:19).

Was the tabernacle a work of *heavenly architecture*? The human nature of our Lord was prepared by His heavenly Father and curiously wrought, by the operation of the Holy Spirit, in the lower parts of the world.

Was it the *habitation of the deity*? In Him dwells "all the fulness of the Godhead bodily" (Col. 2:9).

Was it *anointed* with holy oil? The most holy humanity of our Lord was anointed with the Spirit, which God gave not by measure unto Him.

Was it *embellished* with a variety of ornaments? He was adorned with every divine grace.

Was it taken down by the Levites and removed from place to place, till at last it was conveyed to Jerusalem, where it *remained* in the temple? The human nature of our Lord was dissolved by death, reared up again by His resurrection, and, lastly, translated into the heavenly temple, which must contain Him to the time of the restitution of all things.

Was the tabernacle the place where God *met with Israel*? Here He communed with them; here they presented their gifts, and slew their sacrifices, and even prayed with their faces toward it, though at the remotest distance.

It is easy to see here a lively figure of the one mediator between God and man (1 Tim. 2:5). In Christ alone we have a clear revelation of the divine will, and by Him must we present our spiritual sacrifices and do in His name whatsoever we do, whether in word or deed. We shall only add that, as there were two apartments, the Holy Place, which made, however, but one tabernacle, so in Christ there is a human nature, signified by the Holy Place, and divine nature, represented by the holiest of all; yet these two natures are mysteriously united in one person.

The Tabernacle as a Prefiguring of the Church

The third and last thing prefigured by the tabernacle is the church, that holy society and mystical body of Jesus Christ (Eph. 5:23; Col. 1:18), which, in Scripture style, is the house and temple of the living God, in which He dwells and walks. We shall enumerate some of the most glaring parallels between them. The tabernacle was planned by the wisdom of God Himself, who condescended to adjust the minutest particulars—as the loops, the taches, and the pins—and peremptorily required that all things should be done according to the original pattern. And who knows not that all things in the gospel church are planned by the same unerring wisdom and how much the sovereign Architect has testified His displeasure in every age against the inventions of men in things pertaining to God? "Ye shall not add unto the word which I command you, neither shall ye diminish ought from it, that ye may keep the commandments of the LORD your God which I command you" (Deut. 4:2). This is all the law, this is the prophets, and this is the doctrine of Christ and His apostles.

The tabernacle was executed by the inspiration of *the Holy Spirit*, who rested on Bezaleel and Aholiab, to fit them for this service, without whom they were no more capable of it than other men. It was the same Spirit that descended on the blessed apostles, the wise master builders of the gospel church, without which they could not have been qualified for their honorable work. Yea, it is the Holy Spirit who, by His common gifts, makes ordinary ministers workmen that need not be ashamed.

The tabernacle was composed of very *different materials*, as gold, silver, wood, brass, scarlet, blue and purple cloth, fine linen, rams' skins, badgers' skins, and goats' hair: yet all these different materials, combined by the workman's skill, conduced each in their kind to the beauty and perfection of the structure, and the gold could not say to the brass, nor the scarlet to the goats' hair, "I have no need of you" (1 Cor. 12:21). So in the spiritual house, the materials of which it is composed (that is, the believers in Christ Jesus) are men of diverse nations, different stations in life, unlike natural tempers, unequal gifts and graces, and various ministries; yet being "fitly framed together" by the operation of the Holy Spirit, they grow into "an holy temple in the Lord" (Eph. 2:21). The symmetry of the ancient tabernacle, the nice conjunction of the boards by mortises and bars, and of the curtains by loops and taches, was not so delightful to the eye of the body as it is pleasant to the eye of the mind to see brethren dwelling together in unity (Ps. 133:1), perfectly "joined together in the same mind and in the same judgment" (1 Cor. 1:10), and carefully "endeavouring to keep the unity of the Spirit in the bond of peace" (Eph. 4:3).

The tabernacle was covered with *many coverings*, with fine twined linen; with blue, purple, and scarlet; with rams' skins dyed red; with goats' hair and badgers' skins. By this means it was rendered extremely close and finely protected from the injuries of the weather. May not this recall to our mind the ample protection and security of the gospel church from the heat of God's anger, and from all worldly tribulations, under the rich, the strong, and the broad purple covering of Immanuel's righteousness? For "the LORD is thy keeper: the LORD is thy shade upon thy right hand. The sun shall not smite thee by day, nor the moon by night. The LORD shall preserve thee from all evil: he shall preserve thy soul" (Ps. 121:5–7).

The tabernacle was *ornamented* with gold and silver and curious embroideries, and though without it was not inelegant, it was, however, most magnificent within. Even so, the beauty of the gospel sanctuary does not so much strike the eye of sense that looks at the outward appearance as it is obvious to the spiritual sight that looks at unseen things. Would you discern the true glory of the spouse of Jesus Christ, look not at her face, because the sun hath looked upon her; but "the king's daughter is all glorious within" (Ps. 45:13).

The tabernacle was *anointed with oil* when Moses consecrated it, and the church has "an unction from the Holy One" (1 John 2:20).

The tabernacle was divided into several *partitions*. The outward court might denote the church; the Holy Place is an emblem of the church invisible; and the holiest of all represents the church triumphant in glory, to which none are admitted but the royal priesthood. By baptism we enter into the first, by regeneration into the second, and by death into the third. O death, it is thine to pull aside the veil of mortality that interposes between the Holy and the Most Holy Place. Happy they who enter by faith, and not by a visible profession only, into His sanctuary which He has sanctified forevermore. For as there was no possibility of coming to the holiest of all, but by passing through the Holy Place, even so it is impossible, if we are not now partakers of His holiness, to be hereafter sharers of His glory.

3

The Temple of Solomon
1 Kings 5–6

The second and last material habitation of Jehovah was the temple of Solomon, which that magnificent monarch reared upon the hill of Moriah in Jerusalem, the metropolis of his kingdom, to the honor of the God of Israel (2 Chron. 3:1). The plan of it was dictated by the Spirit unto his father David, who was prohibited from executing it himself because of the bloody wars he had waged in the course of his life (1 Kings 5:3; 2 Chron. 22:7–8). The workmen were partly Israelites and partly Gentiles of Tyre. The materials were the best trees, the most precious metals, and large hewn stones, prepared and fitted for one another before they were laid upon the foundation, that the noise of axes and hammers might not be heard as the building rose (1 Kings 6:7). The structure itself was sixty cubits long, twenty broad, and thirty cubits high and like the tabernacle consisted of two apartments, the "holy" and the "most holy place," or "oracle" (1 Kings 6:16). You entered this temple on the east by a stately porch, which was higher than the edifice itself by ninety cubits and may be considered as the steeple of that sacred palace (2 Chron. 3:4). The length of this porch was equal to the breadth of the principal house, and the breadth was the half of that length. Here stood the two famous brazen pillars, whose names were Jachin and Boaz—that is, *stability* and *strength*, though they were placed there not for the support but for the ornament of the house (1 Kings 7:15–22).

Two open courts surrounded the whole fabric, and side chambers were built around about against the wall; a row of narrow windows that sloped within illuminated the dome. The strength and beauty of God's sanctuary were the main things that distinguished this finished piece of architecture: for the dimensions were far from being wide, but it was supported by a strong foundation of large and costly stones and ornamented within in the most splendid manner, with planks of cedar, plates of gold, glittering diamonds, and figures of palm trees and cherubim.

This was that holy and beautiful house which the Chaldeans were permitted to demolish for the first time, and the Romans for the second time, a thousand years after the first foundation was laid.[1] Seventeen hundred years have now elapsed since the final desolation of this solemn temple, which never more shall rise beneath the builder's hand: for it is the will of God that in every place, and not in Jerusalem alone, He should be worshipped in spirit and in truth (John 4:24).

The Temple as a Figure of Heaven, Christ, and the Church

As the temple of Solomon was built for the same end with the tabernacle of Moses, without all doubt the typical meaning of the one and the other was also the same. Was the tabernacle a figure of heaven, of Christ, and of the church? So also was the temple.

It was a figure of heaven, the glorious habitation of God and angels, where "the righteous…flourish like the palm tree" that were carved on the walls (Ps. 92:12) serve Him continually like the priests that entered into the sanctuary, and go no more out, being established forever like the pillars that graced the porch of that holy place. And as the stones which Solomon used were all hewn and prepared before they were brought there, so all the stones of the celestial house, or the members of the triumphant church, are afore prepared unto glory. Now is the time when their natural roughness and asperity is

---

1. Editor's note: The Jewish temple was destroyed by the Romans in AD 70. Only the "wailing wall" remains.

taken away by the skillful operation of the divine Spirit, and the various afflictions of this life, which exercise them in this vale of tears, that they may rest forever and ever in the calm regions of everlasting peace, where no jarring sound is heard, any more than there was of axes and hammers in the building of the temple. It was also a figure of the humanity of the Messiah, who spoke of the temple of His body when He said, "Destroy this temple, and in three days I will raise it up" (John 2:19). But, without resuming what has already been hinted on this head, let us only further observe that the temple was, equally as the tabernacle, a figure of that holy society the church, which is His body, whether we consider the plan, the materials, the workmen, or the building itself.

The Temple's Plan Designed by God

The plan of the temple was designed by God no less than that of the tabernacle. Nor could any wisdom inferior to divine have adjusted the model of the spiritual house, which the angels themselves admire. The materials were prepared and the stones fitted to one another before they were compacted together, so that noisy tools were wholly unnecessary as the building arose. An expressive emblem this, of that peaceful harmony which ought to reign among the builders of the church as they carry on this holy work, and which would be easily attained if none but polished lively stones, or persons duly qualified, were admitted to become a part of the fabric. The workmen were Gentiles of Tyre as well as Israelites. Was not this a prelude of the future vocation of the Gentiles, that even the sons of the strangers, and those that were afar off, should bear a part in building the walls of the gospel church?

The Temple Building as a Type

Chiefly let us consider the building itself. It was supported by a strong foundation. What should this be in the antitype but Jesus Christ, the foundation which God hath laid in Zion, on which all the apostles and prophets have built themselves and others from the beginning of the world, and to which alone the church is indebted for that unshaken stability which laughs at all opposition?

It was *illuminated with many windows*. For the church is a lightsome house, in which the true light shines. It was surrounded with side chambers, emblems perhaps of the different visible churches which belong to the same universal body.

It was *adorned with gold and cedar*, and its very floor was crusted with the most precious metal. This may remind us of the invisible glory of the church, where the meanest office is honorable and the meanest member excellent.

It was *engraved with cherubim and palm trees*. This may denote the ministry of angels in the church and the eternal verdure of all that are planted in the house of the Lord.

It was *fronted with pillars*. Though ill, alas! did they answer their name. Where was their stability, where was their strength, when the Chaldeans carried them away? But though the pillars of heaven tremble, the pillars of the church shall stand, and thus the gracious promise runs to every the meanest believer: "Him that overcometh will I make a pillar in the temple of my God, and he shall go no more out" (Rev. 3:12).

It was *inhabited by God* and was a "house of prayer for all people" (Isa. 56:7). So in the church are the visible tokens of the divine presence, and holiness becomes it forever. It was replenished with costly furniture. And in Christ Jesus the gospel church really possesses all the holy utensils of the ancient temple. But this must be more largely declared.

3.1

The Ordinance of the Ark and Mercy Seat
Exodus 25:10–22

Where should we begin in enumerating the holy utensils and furniture of the tabernacle and temple but with the sacred chest, commonly called the *ark*, sometimes the ark of His strength, the ark of the covenant, the ark of the testimony, and the ark whose name is called by the name of the God of Israel? Well may we esteem it the heart of the worldly sanctuary. It was the first holy implement the inspired artist Bezaleel formed (Ex. 37:1ff.), and resided in the most venerable apartment of the holy places made with hands. Its dimensions were small but its materials were rich and magnificent. It was made of the best cedar or shittim wood and overlaid with pure gold both within and without. It was edged round with a border or coronet and covered above with a lid of the same precious metal, called the mercy seat. For the convenience of carriage from place to place, in the ambulatory state of their commonwealth, there were fastened to its four corners so many golden rings, into which they put staves of shittim wood, overlaid with gold, that were never taken out but suffered to remain even after the ark rested in the temple and ceased to be a burden on the shoulders of the Levites.

The Contents of the Ark
Within the splendid chest were deposited the two tables of stone that were hewed by Moses, after the first were broken, and inscribed with the finger of God. Before it (as is most probable) were laid up the

miraculous bread that was preserved in the pot and the miraculous rod of Aaron that blossomed and brought forth fruit. The first was a standing memorial of the choice regard of heaven to the whole nation of Israel, and the last was a perpetual sign of His favor to the priestly tribe of Levi and family of Aaron.

The Mercy Seat
Above it two cherubim of beaten gold, arising out of the two ends of the mercy seat and looking toward it and one another, stretched out their wings. Besides these small cherubim there were two others of gigantic stature, which Solomon reared up in the Most Holy Place of the temple. But their precise shape is perhaps impossible for us, at the distance of time, certainly to be defined. This was that venerable utensil which it was death to touch or look into, unless by the persons appointed for that purpose. The sudden fate of Uzziah, and the severe correction of the men of Bethshemesh, are dreadful instances of its vengeance. When Israel marched through the wilderness, the ark is said to have gone before and explored a place of rest for the congregation. The parted wave of Jordan and the falling walls of Jericho confessed its power. Once it was a prisoner in a heathen temple; but, Philistines, short was your victory, small was your cause of triumph. Soon were the proud enemies obliged to refund their spoil, and Dagon could neither defend himself nor his worshipers from perpetual infamy. Once it blessed the house of Obed-edom. But at last, after many removals, the splendid temple of Solomon received it for several ages, whereas is most likely it perished in the common ruin of that holy and beautiful house. But the subject of our present inquiry is the mystic signification of that sacred instrument, for the reception of which both the tabernacle was reared up and the temple built.

A Visible Representation of the Throne of God
And, first, it was a visible representation of the throne of Jehovah, the King of Israel, whose royal palace was the temple. The law in the midst of the ark, on which He sat, signified the equity of His

government, or that justice and judgment are the habitation of His throne. The cherubim at both ends of the mercy seat were doubtless emblematical figures of the blessed elect angels that surround His throne and fly swiftly to execute His high commands. The gold of which they were framed may signify the purity of their essence. The number 2 may perhaps denote the perfect harmony and mutual love of the innumerable company of angels. The position of their faces toward each other may intimate the same thing. The adoring attitude of their bodies may represent the profound veneration they have for their eternal Sovereign. And their flying posture (for their wings were expanded and touched one another) did surely indicate the expeditious alacrity with which they fulfill the heavenly commissions.

A Repository for the Ten Commandments
It was also a repository for the Tables of the Law, which were the instrument of that solemn covenant made between God and that peculiar people (an emblem of the covenant of Adam), and hence it was a perpetual pledge of the divine favor and protection to their nation, if they fulfilled their obligations to the King of heaven, and a witness against them, if they should prove unfaithful. The gold and cedar was a fit emblem of the invaluable worth, the spotless purity, and the perpetual duration of the enclosed law. In imitation of this ordinance of the God of Jacob, the sacred chests of the heathen seem to have been invented to contain the holy books or mysteries of their superstition.

A Figure of Jesus Christ
But especially it may be considered as a figure of Jesus Christ, the promised Messiah, whom all the holy things seem to have pointed out with one consent. There will appear to be no contemptible likeness between Him and this most holy vessel if we attend unto the following things: the materials of which it was framed, the *depositum* which it contained, its ornaments, its uses, its virtues, and, lastly, its removals from one place to another till it rested in the temple.

The *materials* of the ark were cedar and gold. What hinders us from this to think upon the constitution of His wonderful person, whose humanity is like the cedar, the fruit of the earth, but not subject to corruption, and His divinity, like the gold in the ark, embosoms His human nature, ennobles, but is not blended with it?

The *depositum* it contained were the second Tables of the Law, for the first tables were broken before. In Jesus Christ we may see that Law which Moses had broken (Ex. 32:19) preserved inviolate and perfectly fulfilled in the immaculate obedience of His holy life, who says of Himself, "I delight to do thy will, O my God: yea, thy law is within my heart" (Ps. 40:8).

Its *ornaments* were the border of gold resembling a crown, which reminds us of the Messiah's regal dignity, and the cherubim of glory, which signified, say some, the two natures of that glorious person who was signified by the whole workmanship, say others, the twofold church of the Jews and Gentiles. But rather they were emblems of the angels—these bright and glorious creatures who are supported in their happy state by Jesus Christ as the cherubim were by the ark—who desire to look into the mystery of man's redemption and pry into it with the most unwearied attention, the most sublime satisfaction, the highest wonder, and the profoundest adoration (1 Peter 1:12), and who are all ministering spirits (Heb. 1:14), ascending and descending upon the Son of Man (John 1:51).

The *uses* of the ark were various and important. Here God was enthroned. So God is in Christ reconciling the world unto Himself. Here the Law was covered from all eyes. So Jesus Christ, our true propitiatory, interposes Himself between us and that condemning law, which never fails to curse and kill all who presume to meddle with it but as fulfilled in Him; for when the commandment comes without Him who fulfilled it, sin will revive, and, like the men of Bethshemesh, we will die (Rom. 7:9). Here oracles were given, and here, said God to Moses, "I will meet with thee, and I will commune with thee from above the mercy seat, from between the two cherubims which are upon the ark of the testimony, of all things which I will give thee in commandment unto the children of Israel" (Ex.

25:22). So Christ is the meeting place of God with man, in whom He deigns to reveal His gracious will and pleasure to the fallen creature: hence is He called "The Word of God" (Rev. 19:13; cf. John 1:1–5) and is said to declare God the Father, who never was, and never can be, seen by any man. Jesus says to Philip, "Have I been so long time with you, and yet hast thou not known me, Philip? he that hath seen me hath seen the Father; and how sayest thou then, Shew us the Father?" (John 14:9).

And, lastly, here *prayers were presented* and *offerings were accepted*: for the most holy Israelite durst not approach the presence of Jehovah but as he sat upon the mercy seat sprinkled with blood. Nor could the holiest Christian presume to hope for the acceptance of his best duties were it not for the mercy of God through Christ Jesus.

The Virtues of the Ark

The virtues of the ark are such as these: It searched out a resting place for Israel in the wilderness. So Christ is to His people the breaker of their way, who goes before them, gives them rest, and prepares for them a place. It opened a passage for the ransomed tribes through the river Jordan. O Jesus, by Thee we safely pass through the river Jordan of death, and have abundant entrance ministered into the heavenly kingdom, because these waters shall not overflow them who have His presence with them, according to His promise. It overturned the walls of Jericho when carried round them seven days. So shall the walls of Babylon fall and every high thing that exalts itself against God be cast down by the preaching of His gospel, who is the power of God and wisdom of God. It overthrew Dagon of the Philistines in his own temple, maimed his brute image, and utterly abolished that monstrous idol. So shall he that sits in the temple of God, and shows himself that he is God, be destroyed by the spirit of His mouth and brightness of His coming. It sanctified the places to which it came, in the opinion of Solomon himself, and blessed the house of Obededom, where it transiently resided. It is the presence of Christ that makes us holy and happy, and in Him we are blessed with every spiritual blessing (Eph. 1:3). The removals of the ark from place to place in the wilderness and in Canaan, till it rested in the temple, shall we say bear some faint resemblance to the humbled Redeemer, going about doing good while He was upon the earth until the everlasting doors of heaven were opened to receive Him? Or was the bearing of the ark about upon the shoulders of the Levites a figure of the ministers of Christ bearing His name among the Gentiles, in all the corners of the world? The staves remained always in the ark, perhaps to intimate that no place or nation is absolutely secure against His departure from them who have no suitable esteem for His gracious presence with them in the dispensation of the eternal world.

It is long since the Babylonians destroyed this glory of Israel, but we have an ark whereunto they have no right to approach who serve the tabernacle. John saw it in the heavenly temple. The Old Testament ark, like the covenant it confirmed, is vanished away. But the New Testament ark, in whom the new covenant stands fast, shall abide forever in the presence of Jehovah. Nor is it death for any to look into this ark, for the Word of Life was looked upon with the eyes and handled with the hands of men. Let it be our one and chief desire that all the days of our life we may abide in His house, behold His beauty, and inquire in His temple.

3.2

The Ordinance of the Golden Table
Exodus 25:23–30

The table of the showbread was a principal part of the apparatus of the middle court or sanctuary, and a piece of very nice and costly workmanship. Like the ark, it was made of gold and cedar, ornamented with a golden order and crown, furnished with golden rings for carriage and with golden dishes and other necessary utensils. On this pure table were laid twelve loaves, according to the number of the tribes. They were made of fine flour and piled up in two rows, crowned with frankincense. Thus they stood continually before the Lord but were renewed every Sabbath morning, and the stale bread was to be eaten by none but the priests in the Holy Place. As to the meaning of this service, perhaps it was a continual thank offering, whereby the Israelites testified their gratitude for the fine wheat of Canaan. But it seems likewise no contemptible figure of Christ Jesus, both personal and mystical, which is to be now declared.

And, first, it seems to represent Christ Jesus Himself. It was a golden table to denote His most invaluable worth, who is precious to them that believe. It was a crowned table to signify His royal dignity and the "royal dainties" wherewith He feeds His people, who eat the bread of the mighty (Gen. 49:20).

It was a *movable* table, for the dispensation of His gospel is not confined to any particular spot of earth but has been frequently removed from one place to another. It was a furnished table, furnished both with provisions and vessels. In Christ we have "all things that pertain unto life and godliness" (2 Peter 1:3); "For it pleased the Father that in him should all fulness dwell" (Col. 1:19).

An Emblem of Christ

Let us consider the provision wherewith this table was loaded, and we shall see how fitly it quadrates to Jesus Christ. It was covered with loaves of bread. What bread is to the body, Christ is to the soul—that is, the staff of life. Like bread, He is of the most universal use, of the most absolute necessity, and prepared for our spiritual food by various sufferings, as bread-corn is bruised.

The loaves were *fine* flour. Jesus Christ is the finest of the wheat, in whom there was found no bran of sinful corruption, being holy, harmless, undefiled, and separated from sinners.

They were *twelve* in number, for every tribe a loaf. There is enough in Christ to supply the wants of His people, who may say, "Of his fulness have all we received" (John 1:16).

They were continually present before the Lord. Jesus Christ is the "angel of his presence," who appears before the Lord continually as the representative of Israel (Isa. 63:9).[1]

They were *crowned with frankincense*. This is an emblem of the acceptableness of His sacrifice and intercession, or of their sweet-smelling savor unto God.

They were *renewed every Sabbath* morning by the priests. For the doctrine of Jesus Christ, or the spiritual provision exhibited on the table of the gospel, in order that it may prove always palatable to the hearers, the ministers of the Word ought, as the legal priests, to renew it every Sabbath, not indeed by preaching novel doctrines but by clothing old truths in a new dress; or, to use the expression of our Lord, they are to "[bring] forth out of [their] treasure things new and

---

1. Editor's note: Matthew Henry comments on Isaiah 63:9, "But this is rather to be understood of Jesus Christ, the eternal Word, that angel of whom God spoke to Moses (Ex. 23:20, 21), whose *voice Israel was to obey*. He is called *Jehovah*, Ex. 13:21; 14:21, 24. He is the angel of the covenant, God's messenger to the world, Mal. 3:1. He is the *angel of God's face*, for he is the *express image of his person;* and the glory of God shines in the face of Christ."

old" (Matt. 13:52). By this means the attention will be fed, weariness relieved, and appetite increased.

They were *eaten by the priests* in the Holy Place after they were removed from the presence table. So Christ the bread of God must be eaten (that is, believed in), that we may receive from Him both life and strength. The ministers of the gospel must feed on that same Christ whom they exhibit unto others; and all the saints are that royal priesthood, whose privilege it is to eat this bread of God. And if others are admitted to the most holy ordinances, the table of the Lord is contemptible indeed. I shall only add that unless this heavenly bread had been first presented unto the Lord, He would not have been presented to men as food to the hungry soul.

An Emblem of the Church

Let us now consider the showbread as an emblem of "the church, which is his body" (Eph. 1:22–23), of which it is also said, "we being many are one bread" (1 Cor. 10:17). Indeed, the number of the loaves, corresponding to the number of the tribes, did certainly intimate that they represented "the Israel of God" (Gal. 6:16). Christ is that corn of wheat which fell into the ground and died, that He might not abide alone (John 12:23–24), and from Him believers grow as their parent root. Christ is that golden table that continually supports and presents them before the Lord.

They were *crowned with frankincense*: for their prayers are directed to God as incense, and the intercession of Jesus Christ perfumes at once their persons and works, as with all the powders of the merchant.

They were disposed in *two regular rows*, which may denote the comely order of the churches.

They were *renewed every week*. So one generation of Christians succeeds another. Or perhaps we may take occasion to think how distasteful unto God are stale and moldy professors,[2] who have "left

---

2. Editor's note: Not professors in the sense of academics and teachers, but mere "professors" of faith, who, says the Lord, "draw near me with their mouth, and with their lips do honour me, but have removed their heart far from me" (Isa. 29:13).

[their] first love" (Rev. 2:4) and are, like "Ephraim," as cakes "not turned" (Hos. 7:8).

They were, lastly, to be *eaten by the priests*. May we be allowed thus to allegorize this last particular? When the faithful have served their generation and are removed from further usefulness in this world, they are not rejected as useless altogether, but they become the inheritance of Jesus Christ, the true priest, as the old bread was not cast away, but fed upon by the typical priesthood in the Holy Place.

3.3

The Ordinance of the Golden Candlestick
Exodus 25:31–40

Over against the table there was a golden candlestick set on the north side, that the sanctuary might never be dark. It consisted of a large stalk with six branches, and every branch was in three different places adorned with a bowl, like an almond, a knob, and a flower. The tongs and snuff-dishes were pure gold, as the candlestick itself. At the extremities of the stalk and branches were seven lamps, which were fed with pure olive oil and lighted every evening by the priests, who burned incense at the same time.

An Emblem of the True Light
Was not this an emblem of "the true Light, which lighteth every man that cometh into the world" (John 1:9)? Not only is Jesus Christ, in many texts of Scripture, resembled unto the light of the sun, but it is said in one place, "Thou art my lamp, O LORD: and the LORD will lighten my darkness" (2 Sam. 22:29).

The *pure beaten gold* of this candlestick may denote the spotless holiness and the invaluable worth of Jesus, who was beaten, if we may so speak, with the hammer of adversity and made perfect through suffering (Heb. 5:8–9).

The *oil* that nourished the lamps is an emblem of the Holy Spirit that anointed Christ to preach glad tidings to the meek (Isa. 61:1; Luke 4:18–21).

The *number* of the lamps, which was seven, imports the perfection of His light. The sanctuary where they shone is the church, and the priests that trimmed them are the ministers of the gospel, whose office it is to elucidate "the mystery of Christ" (Col. 4:3).

The *light* which was shed all around from this candlestick may represent the light of the knowledge of the glory of God in the face of Jesus, which shines into the hearts of all the royal priesthood (2 Cor. 4:6; 1 Peter 2:9), or the light of the Scriptures, which are the rays of Jesus Christ, and to which we do well to "take heed, as unto a light that shineth in a dark place" (2 Peter 1:19).

An Emblem of the Church
That the golden candlestick was also a figure of the church will appear very probable when we consider that Zechariah, an Old Testament prophet, saw in the visions of God, as her emblem, a golden candlestick, supplied with golden oil from two olive trees (Zech. 4:1ff.); and John, a New Testament apostle, when he was in the Spirit, beheld our Great High Priest in sacerdotal robes, walking in the midst of the seven golden candlesticks, which were the seven Asian churches (Rev. 1:10-13). But let us, for further proof, observe the likeness of this sacred utensil to the whole and every particular church.

We shall, first, consider the candlestick itself. Its use was to receive the materials of the light and then to spread it abroad. Even so, the church receives the truth in the first place and then holds it forth by purity of doctrine and sanctity of life.

Its *matter* was pure and beaten gold. The church may be a lamp despised in the thoughts of worldly men and esteemed as an earthen pitcher, yet in the eyes of the Lord she is comparable to fine gold. O how the gold becomes dim in the presence of faith and holiness! She is pure gold, being purged from the dross of reigning corruption by the blood, by the Spirit, and by the word of Christ. She is beaten gold, being partaker of the afflictions of the gospel. By these means she is a vessel made meet for the Master's use.

For *shape*, it was divided into six branches, united by one common stalk. This signifies the coalition of all true churches and sound believers into one great society, which is founded upon their common relation to Jesus Christ, the center of the union.

The *ornaments* of almonds, knobs, and flowers, which decorated all the branches, may denote the various gifts and graces with which every church should be adorned, that she may with greater dignity hold forth the word of life.

The *tongs and snuff dishes* were not more necessary appendages to the golden candlestick than church censures and brotherly admonitions are to every society of Christians. By means of these instruments the lamps burned clear, and the floor of the Holy Place was not sullied. So the discipline of the church is an excellent means of preserving the lamp of gospel light from defilement by the "superfluity of naughtiness" (James 1:21).[1]

The *oil* burning in the seven lamps of the candlestick is an emblem of the Holy Spirit in His various gifts who resides in the church, is compared to oil and fire, and of whom the apostle John speaks in this enigmatical manner when he saw the visions of the Almighty: "And there were seven lamps of fire burning before the throne, which are the seven Spirits of God" (Rev. 4:5). So much for the candlestick itself.

An Emblem of the Gospel Ministry

Let us now glance at the ministry of the priests about this holy vessel. They were to supply it with oil, to trim the lamps, and light them every evening and to burn incense at the same time. Might not this signify the watchful care of Jesus Christ, the minister of the sanctuary and true tabernacle (Heb. 8:1–2), who walks in the midst of the seven golden candlesticks, imparts unto them all necessary supplies of the heavenly unction, quenches not the smoking flax, but strengthens the things that remain and are ready to die, while at the

---

1. Editor's note: Four centuries on, the AV/KJV "superfluity of naughtiness" sounds more like a silly euphemism than a solemn indictment of bad behavior. The Greek περισσείαν κακίας literally means an "overflow" of "wickedness" and is better rendered "rampant wickedness" (ESV) or "overflow of wickedness" (NKJV).

same time He offers unto God the grateful incense of His prevalent intercession in their behalf (Heb. 7:25)?

And may it not further adumbrate the duty and office of all the ministers of the gospel, who in the evening of the world are to light the lamp ordained for God's Anointed? "They shall teach Jacob thy judgments, and Israel thy law: they shall put incense before thee, and whole burnt sacrifice upon thine altar" (Deut. 33:10). It is their province, while they direct unto God the incense of fervent prayer, to make their lamps burn clear by supplying them with the oil of pure doctrine and trimming them with the tongs of wholesome discipline and salutary admonition. "For Zion's sake will I not hold my peace, and for Jerusalem's sake I will not rest, until the righteousness thereof go forth as brightness, and the salvation thereof as a lamp that burneth" (Isa. 62:1).

3.4

The Ordinance of the Golden Altar
Exodus 30:1–10; 34–38

In the inner part of the sanctuary there stood a foursquare altar of shittim wood, overlaid with gold. It was encompassed with a golden crown; furnished with golden rings for carriage, like the ark and table of showbread; and graced with four golden horns at its four corners. To this secret altar none but the priests were to approach—not to offer propitiatory sacrifices, as upon the altar of burnt offering, but to burn incense of sweet spices morning and evening before the Lord. The confection of this sacred perfume is minutely prescribed, with a strict prohibition of imitating it for any other use. It was a figure of the intercession of the Great High Priest before the throne, or the altar of burnt offering was a figure of His satisfactory oblation upon the earth. Let us first attend unto the altar and next unto the incense.

The Altar Is an Emblem of Christ's Heavenly Intercession
The altar itself was, first, a golden-crowned altar, which signifies the glorious dignity of the royal intercessor, who is a priest upon His throne and is set down on the right hand of the heavenly Majesty.

It was a *square* altar, equally respecting the four corners of the world, to denote how accessible He is to all the ends of the earth.

It was a *movable* altar, capable of being transported wherever the church of Israel went: an emblem of His perpetual presence in all places where His name is recorded or where His people are afflicted. A jail, an isle of Patmos, a lion's den, a fish's belly, a fiery furnace are all alike to Him who never leaves, never forsakes His chosen and His called.

It was a *hidden* altar, to which none approached except the sons of Levi. To know Christ as their interceding priest is the distinguished privilege of all the royal priesthood. These only see Him by faith, whom the world seeth no more (John 14:19). But as the way to the golden altar of incense was to pass by the brazen altar of burnt offering, so none can come to Jesus, as ever living to make intercession for them, who come not to Him as dying once to atone for their guilt and put away their sin by the sacrifice of Himself.

It was a *horned* altar. And what should these four horns at its four corners portend but the strength and prevalence of His intercession whom the Father heareth always, and "who is able to save unto the uttermost all who come unto God by him" from the four winds of heaven?

It was an altar *stained with blood*, for though no sacrifices for expiation were offered upon it, yet Aaron was commanded to tip its horns every year with the blood of atonements. The blood of Jesus Christ the righteous is the strength of His advocacy. This blood presented forever before the throne of God enforces all his suits with louder cries than ever the blood of Abel sent from the ground, imploring vengeance on the first murderer.

The Incense Is an Emblem of the Merits of Jesus Christ

From the altar let us come to the incense burned upon it (Ex. 30:34–38). It represents both the merits of Jesus Christ and the prayers of all saints. The merits of Jesus Christ is that incense in which the prayers and tears and works of all the saints are clad and wherein they ascend, like Manoah's angel, before the presence of Jehovah (Judg. 13:20–21).

That incense was composed of sweet spices that *shed a rich perfume* (Ex. 30:34–35), but not so grateful to men as the sweet-smelling sacrifices of Christ was savory unto God (Eph. 5:2).

That incense was *burned in the sanctuary* while the people were praying without. The appearing of our High Priest in the heavenly sanctuary with the sweet odor of His merits by no means supersedes the prayers of saints on earth. For these things will God be not only solicited by the intercession of His Son but "enquired of by the house of Israel, to do it for them" (Ezek. 36:37).

That incense was *continually burned* before the Lord and was a perpetual incense throughout their generations. The intercession of Jesus Christ is everlasting because He "ever liveth" (Heb. 7:25). Never, never shall it be discontinued till all its ends are fully reached and the elect vessel be prayed home to glory.

That incense was *not to be counterfeited* or imitated for any other purpose: "And as for the perfume which thou shalt make, ye shall not make to yourselves according to the composition thereof: it shall be unto thee holy for the LORD. Whosoever shall make like unto that, to smell thereto, shall even be cut off from his people" (Ex. 30:37–38). Therefore, detest the impiety of the harlot church which confides in the merits of any saint, living or dead, on whatsoever pretense, thereby ascribing the Mediator's glory to another. But the time approaches when this counterfeit incense, the commodity of Babylon, shall no more be bought from the merchants of the earth, for the fall of "Babylon the great" will cause "the merchants of the earth" to "weep and mourn over her; for no man buyeth their merchandise any more" (Rev. 18:2–3, 10–11).

The Incense Is an Emblem of the Prayers of Saints
"The prayers of saints" are also said to be directed as incense before the Lord and are likened by a New Testament writer to "odours" preserved in "golden vials" (Rev. 5:8). Prayer is that incense which, according to Malachi's prediction, shall be offered to the name of the Lord in every place.

Was the holy incense compounded of various *sweet spices* (Ex. 30:34–35)? The graces of the Holy Spirit are the precious ingredients in the effectual prayer of the righteous. Some of them were beaten very fine (Ex. 30:36; Lev. 16:12), perhaps to intimate that brokenness of heart and contrition of spirit which "the high and lofty One… whose name is Holy" requires in the worshipers at His footstool (Isa. 57:15).

The *fire* that burned the incense may denote the fervency of spirit required in acceptable worship. But take heed of the sparks of your own kindling and lift up holy hands without wrath (1 Tim. 2:8), for incense must not be kindled with fire from the kitchen, but the altar (Rev. 8:3–5).

Was the incense burned morning and evening *continually*? And can we reasonably think the incense of prayer and praise should be less frequently addressed to the God that dwells in the heavens? Jesus Christ is the altar; Jesus Christ is the priest who stands with His golden censer; by Him your incense of prayer, and your incense of praise, shall go up for a memorial before God and meet with gracious acceptance! Without Him, even "incense is an abomination" unto God (Isa. 1:13), and the most solemn duties are a smoke in His nostrils (Ps. 18:7–8) and "a fire that burneth all the day" (Isa. 65:5).

3.5

The Ordinance of the Brazen Altar
Exodus 27:1–8

Let us next consider the altar of burnt offering, which was a chief part of the holy furniture both of the tabernacle and temple. Its materials were brass and cedar wood; its shape was foursquare; its station was in the outward court. It protected criminals that fled unto it, sanctified gifts, and provided meat for the priests. It was ornamented with four horns of brass flourishing from its corners, and upon it the sacred fire was kept perpetually alive. The ceremonies of its consecration lasted for seven days, and it is called by God "an altar most holy" that should impart a legal holiness to everything that touched it (Ex. 29:37; 40:10). In ordinary cases it was not lawful to offer sacrifices upon any other altar but this alone.

This Altar Is Emblematic of Jesus Christ
That Jesus Christ is the antitype of this altar, the apostle to the Hebrews permits us not to doubt; for, speaking of Him, he says, "We have an altar, whereof they have no right to eat which serve the tabernacle" (Heb. 13:10). He says not *altars*, as if they were many, but an altar speaking of one, and this altar is Christ. As the intercession of Jesus Christ was typified by the golden altar of incense, so the altar of burnt offerings represented both His satisfaction in general and His godhead in particular. Let us begin with the first.

It Is a Figure of Christ's Satisfaction for Sin
It represented the person of our Redeemer as the propitiation for our sins. It was a brazen altar. Was it not the same glorious person whom Ezekiel saw, like a man "of brass, with a line of flax in his hand" to measure the temple (Ezek. 40:3) and whose feet are described in the visions of John "like unto fine brass, as if they burned in a furnace" (Rev. 1:15; 2:18)? Brass is a cheap and common metal. When by Himself He purged our sins, He shone not with golden luster, for His "visage was so marred more than any man, and his form more than the sons of men" (Isa. 52:14). Brass is a strong metal and fit to endure the fire. Our strength was not the strength of stones, our flesh was not of brass, to "dwell with the devouring fire" and abide "with everlasting burnings" (Isa. 33:14): but Christ was the mighty One, who felt the power of God's anger and was not devoured by the fiery indignation.

It was a *horned* altar. This signifies the strength of His atonement both to satisfy the justice of God and pacify the conscience of men.

It was a *foursquare* altar, an emblem of His perpetual stability, who is "the same yesterday, and to day, and for ever" (Heb. 13:8).

It was a *public* altar, for the death of Christ was to be a transaction of the most public kind (see John 3:14).

It was a *burning* altar on which the fire never went out. The Holy Spirit is that eternal Spirit of judgment and of burning through whom He offered up Himself unto God and who dwells forever in the Son. With this holy fire the Great High Priest inflamed His legal sacrifice of atonement, and with this holy fire the royal priesthood ought to kindle their moral "sacrifice of praise," which they offer "by him...continually, that is, the fruit of our lips giving thanks to his name" (Heb. 13:15).

It was an *only* altar and, by the law of Moses, admitted not any rival. So Jesus Christ is the one mediator between God and man. To multiply mediators is no less condemned by the New Testament than to multiply altars by the Old.

It was an altar *most holy* that sanctified all gifts. Whether we present unto God the meat offering of alms, the drink offering of tears, the peace offering of thanksgiving, the heave offering of prayer, or the whole burnt offering of body and soul, by Him alone they are sanctified and accepted, as the altar sanctified the gift. It was an altar that protected criminals who fled unto it, though for some crimes they were to be dragged from it to suffer condign punishment. In Jesus Christ the guilty sinner finds a refuge from legal condemnation, nor can they fail of making peace with Him who by faith take hold of His strength, be their crimes ever so atrocious.

It was an altar that *nourished* the Levitical priesthood who served at it and were partakers with it. Even so, the happy persons who are made priests unto God, and partakers of Christ, receive from Him not a natural but a spiritual and eternal life, for as Christ Himself declares, "As the living Father hath sent me, and I live by the Father: so he that eateth me, even he shall live by me" (John 6:57).

It Is a Figure of Christ's Godhead

But in a particular manner His deity seems fit to be called *the altar* on which He offered His humanity: for He was His own altar no less than ours. It was not the wooden cross on which He died that served Him for an altar. Far less can the material table on which the holy memorials are exhibited in the sacrament of the Lord's Supper deserve any such glorious epithet. Hear what He Himself says about the altar and the gift: "Ye fools and blind: for whether is greater, the gift, or the altar that sanctifieth the gift?" (Matt. 23:19). Will any dare to say that the wooden cross was greater than the soul and body of the Redeemer who expired on it? Or that the table of the Supper is greater than the consecrated symbols of His body and blood? If it be impossible to find anything greater than the humanity of the Lord and Savior except His own divinity, His own divinity and nothing else must be the altar.

Did the altar support the gift or victim while it was burning upon it? It was the godhead of Christ that supported the manhood from sinking under these direful sufferings He patiently endured.

Did the altar sanctify the gifts that touched it? It was the deity of Christ that sanctified the gift of His humanity and imparted a dignity and value to the sacrifice of His body and soul. The sins of many are fully expiated by the sufferings of one, because He is God, and there is none else; besides Him there is no Savior. Therefore, says He, "Look unto me, and be ye saved, all the ends of the earth: for I am God, and there is none else" (Isa. 45:22).

Christ Must Be Your Altar
Blessed be God for such a High Priest, such a temple, such a sacrifice, such an altar of burnt offering and incense. We have an altar not only in the midst of the land of Canaan but in the midst of the land of Egypt, to which sons of the strangers may bring their sacrifices. We have an altar which God will never cast off, a sanctuary which He will never abhor. The great atoning sacrifice is already offered up; what remains for us but to render unto a gracious God the calves not of the stall but of the lips and "the sacrifice of praise…continually" (Heb. 13:15)?

3.6

The Ordinance of the Brazen Laver
Exodus 30:17–21

The divers washings enjoined in the law of Moses were no doubt a very significant branch of that ritual economy: for not only did the heathen nations adopt this custom in their false worship of imaginary gods, but a shadow of it is still retained in the Christian baptism, the initiating ordinance of the church. The daily illustration of the Levitical priesthood we shall presently glance at.

At the entrance of the tabernacle of the congregation, before you came to the brazen altar, was set, by the appointment of the Lord, a pure vessel or laver of polished brass. The materials of it were furnished by some religious women who complimented their "lookingglasses" for this purpose, consecrating these instruments, perhaps of vanity, to the sacred use of adorning the worship of the true God (Ex. 38:8).[1] Though the shape of this vessel is not minutely described by Moses, it was certainly so contrived as the water it contained might be emptied by vents or pipes: for the priests were ordered, on pain of death, to wash their hands and feet at this laver when they went into the tabernacle or approached unto the altar. At first this washing pot was probably of small size, but when Solomon built his magnificent temple, he made also a laver of large

---

1. Editor's note: The ESV helpfully clarifies this incident: "He made the basin of bronze and its stand of bronze, from the mirrors of the ministering women who ministered in the entrance of the tent of meeting."

dimensions, which, on account of the huge quantity of water it was capable to hold, was called a "molten sea" and set it on a base of "twelve oxen" of brass, not without the direction of heaven, as we may well presume (1 Kings 7:23–26).

The Laver Speaks of Spiritual Purification

Did the pure and holy God intend by this law only to require from His worshipers the putting away the filth of the flesh, which might be done with material water, and by such as had neither their hearts clean nor their hands pure? Is washing the body with the purest water an adequate preparation for coming into the presence of that God in whose sight the heavens are not clean? Far be it from us to harbor so foolish a thought. The purification of the soul from spiritual pollution was the thing intended by this carnal ordinance. The laver is Jesus Christ Himself, who cleanses all the royal priesthood from the foul contagion of sin by the word which He speaks unto them, by the Spirit which He sheds upon them, and by the blood He poured out for them.

Was the laver a *pure and cleanly vessel*? This may denote the innocence and spotless purity of the glorious Immanuel, together with His fitness to preserve all that are in Him holy and unblamable.

Was it a *large and capacious vessel* and therefore styled a "sea"? This may remind us of that vast and inexhaustible fullness which ever dwells in the New Testament laver, by which He is able to "sprinkle many nations" (Isa. 52:15) and wash away the crimes of all who "come unto God by him" (Heb. 7:25).

Was it an *open vessel* that stood in the most public situation? A prophet styles the blessed Redeemer "a fountain opened to the house of David and to the inhabitants of Jerusalem for sin and for uncleanness" (Zech. 13:1).

Was it a *consecrated* vessel? For Moses anointed the laver and his foot with the holy anointing oil. Christ Jesus was consecrated forevermore to His saving office and anointed with the Holy Spirit in the most ample measure.

Was it *supported by twelve oxen* in the temple of Solomon? These brazen figures that looked to all the winds of heaven may not absurdly be viewed as emblems of the twelve apostles, who bore Christ's name to the Gentiles, who poured the doctrine of salvation in all the quarters of the world. For not only does the number of the oxen correspond to the number of the apostles of the Lamb, but the servants of Christ are in other passages held forth under the emblem of these robust, laborious, and useful animals.

The Laver Speaks of Life and Death

But the use which the priests under the law were commanded to make of this vessel on all occasions, under the severest penalty, is the most remarkable circumstance we are to attend unto. They were to wash their hands and feet with the water of this vessel when they entered the tabernacle, *on pain of death* (Ex. 30:21). These priests are figures not only of all office-bearers in the church, who ought to be pure and holy, but of all the holy nation of Christians, who having a Great High Priest over the house of God ought to draw near with true hearts and in the full assurance of faith, having their "hearts sprinkled from an evil conscience" and their "bodies washed with pure water" (Heb. 10:22).

It is true, they are washed and justified already in the name of the Lord Jesus and by the Spirit of our God; yet still they need to wash their hands and feet. The sins of daily walk demand fresh application to the laver of His atoning blood, even from the honest saints on earth. Faith is the hand by which this purifying water is applied to the conscience. Would we approach to God in holy duties? Would we ascend the hill of the Lord and stand in His holy place? Then in a special manner must we lay aside "all filthiness and superfluity of naughtiness" (James 1:21),[2] resolving with the sweet singer of Israel,

---

2. Editor's note: The author loves James 1:21 and has quoted it a number of times in these studies. But it is well for us to remember that the seventeenth-century English words "superfluity of naughtiness" today seem merely quaint and no longer carries the weight of the Greek, which means "overflow of wickedness" in modern English.

"I will wash mine hands in innocency: so will I compass thine altar, O Lord" (Ps. 26:6). But whoever they be that prefer the mire of their sin to the laver of His blood and think to wash away their stains with the nitre and soap of their own righteousness (Jer. 2:22), they shall die before the Lord, be excluded from His beatific presence, and forevermore "shall be an abhorring unto all flesh" (Isa. 66:24).

3.7

The Ordinance of the Anointing Oil
Exodus 30:22–33

In Jesus Christ we have also the antitype of the legal anointings, no less than of the divers washings and sacrifices, which is to be declared. The Jewish lawgiver is commanded, in a very particular manner, to take unto him of the "principal spices, of pure myrrh five hundred shekels, and of sweet cinnamon half so much, even two hundred and fifty shekels, and of sweet calamus two hundred and fifty shekels, And of cassia five hundred shekels, after the shekel of the sanctuary." These precious ingredients were to be compounded by the apothecary's art in a hin of olive oil (Ex. 30:23–24). The use of this holy oil was to anoint the tabernacle, and its furniture, and Aaron with his sons (Ex. 30:26–30). But it was strictly forbidden to apply it to any other use, to put it upon any stranger, or to make anything like it, after the composition of it. "This," said God to the Israelites, "shall be an holy anointing oil unto me throughout your generations" (Ex. 30:31–33). Let us come to the concealed mystery of this ordinance.

The Oil Is an Emblem of the Lord's Anointed
Then was this type fulfilled when the Lord's Anointed was endued with the gifts and graces of the Holy Spirit, which God gave without measure unto Him (John 3:34). Hear what He Himself declares by the mouth of the prophet Isaiah: "The Spirit of the Lord is upon me, because he hath anointed me" (Luke 4:18, quoting Isa. 61:1). And therefore the disciples of Christ are styled *Christians* because

it is supposed they have also "an unction from the Holy One" (1 John 2:20).[1]

Surely it is not without sufficient reasons that anointing with oil and receiving the gift of the Holy Spirit are phrases of the same import in the language of inspiration.

If oil is of a *healing nature* and fit to appease the anguish of rankled wounds, the Spirit of God is that mollifying ointment by which the "wounds, and bruises, and putrifying sores" occasioned by the fall (Isa. 1:6) are gradually healed until at last the cure is so completely wrought that not a scar remains.

If oil is of a *beautifying quality* and makes the human face to shine, by the benign agency of the sanctifying Spirit our souls are made as the wings of a dove covered with silver and are presented at last in presence of His glory, without spot or wrinkle or any such thing.

If oil is *savory to the taste*, imparting to her esculents[2] an agreeable flavor, without the Spirit, what is the Word itself but a dry morsel? But when He sheds His kindly influences, then do we find God's "words" and "eat them," and His Word is to us "the joy and rejoicing of [our] heart" (Jer. 15:16).

If oil is of an *exhilarating virtue*, greatly refreshing the animal spirits of them who are anointed, this puts us in mind of the reviving operations of the "Comforter" who is the Holy Spirit of truth (John 14:16, 26; 15:26; 16:13), the true "oil of gladness" (Ps. 45:7; Heb. 1:9) whose fruit is "joy and peace" (Rom. 15:13). In the same manner we might apply the strengthening, softening, preserving, insinuating properties of this staple commodity of Canaan to the like operations of the divine Spirit.

---

1. Editor's note: The word *Christ* is a title—not a surname—and means literally "Anointed." The author here makes the connection between Jesus's disciples, first called "Christians" in Antioch (Acts 11:26), and their Lord and Savior, Jesus Christ, as involving their anointing of God by His Holy Spirit.

2. Editor's note: Esculents are things fit to be eaten, from the Latin *esculentus*, "edible."

The Special Qualities of the Anointing Oil

But let us rather reflect upon the special qualities of the holy anointing oil, which Moses made according to divine dispensation.

It was compounded of various *costly ingredients* to represent, perhaps, the great variety of heavenly gifts and graces which are conferred by the Spirit of the Lord and the diversities of His operations.

It shed a most *delightful perfume*, even to a proverb, when poured on the head of Aaron (Ps. 133:2). Of a greater than he it is said, "All thy garments smell of myrrh, and aloes, and cassia" (Ps. 45:8), and again, "Because of the savour of thy good ointments…therefore do the virgins love thee" (Song 1:3).

The *quantity* which Moses made was considerably large and sufficient to anoint both the priests, the tabernacle, and all its sacred vessels. May not this faintly adumbrate the fullness of the Spirit, by which He is able not only to anoint our Great High Priest but likewise all the sanctified vessels that are made meet for the Master's use?

It was *unlawful* to make anything like it; and the Jews affirm, with great probability, that it was never but once prepared, though they fabulously add that it wasted not by use for many generations.[3] This may denote how displeasing it is to God to counterfeit His Holy Spirit; and as we are to try the spirits, whether they be of God, so in all generations there is but "one Spirit," as there is "one body" mystical and "one hope of [our] calling" (Eph. 4:4). The prohibition of putting any of it on a stranger may signify that the spiritual unction is the peculiar privilege of saints, which, to use the expression of our Lord, "the world cannot receive" (John 14:17).

And lastly, as this anointing oil did *sanctify* the persons and things to which it was applied, consecrated them forever to the service of

---

3. Editor's note: *The Jewish Encyclopedia* (New York: Funk and Wagnalls, 1903), 1:612, cites some of this teaching in its entry "Anointing": "The oil of holy ointment prepared by Moses in the wilderness (Ex. xxx. 23 *et seq.*) had many miraculous qualities: it was never absorbed by the many spices mixed therewith; its twelve logs (1.68 gallons) were sufficient for the anointment of all the kings and high priests of Israelitish history, and will be in use in the Messianic time to come. During the reign of Josiah this oil was hidden away simultaneously with the holy ark, to reappear in the Messianic time (Hor. 11*b et seq.*; Sifra, Milluim, 1)."

God, and entitled them to His protection, so the happy souls who have "received, not the spirit of the world, but the spirit which is of God" (1 Cor. 2:12) are "sanctified…in the name of the Lord Jesus, and by the Spirit of our God" (1 Cor. 6:11), are "sealed unto the day of redemption" (Eph. 4:30), and the "anointing which [they] have received of him abideth in [them]" (1 John 2:27). Because of this anointing, their yokes shall be destroyed. "Touch not mine anointed, ye enemies of their salvation," will the Lord say, "and do no harm to my peculiar people" (see Ps. 105:15). Let others "drink wine in bowls, and anoint themselves with the chief ointments" (Amos 6:6), but give us, O Lord, this holy oil forevermore, "even life for evermore" (Ps. 133:3).

4

The Land of Canaan
Genesis 17:8

The land that flowed with milk and honey deserves a particular consideration among the other shadows of good things to come (Heb. 10:1). God promised to the fathers of the holy nation, "Unto thee will I give the land of Canaan, the lot of your inheritance; when ye were but few, even a few, and strangers in it" (1 Chron. 16:18–19). This promise He performed to their posterity at the appointed time, when, under the conduct of Joshua, He drove out the heathen and planted them. But was this all which God provided for His people?

Are Earthly Inheritances Enough?

Was the promise of an earthly inheritance the blissful hope that supported the believing patriarchs in the few and evil days of their pilgrimage? Was there no other rest remaining for the people of God but that which Joshua gave them? Then indeed they would have been, upon the whole, considerable losers by their religion, and God would have been "ashamed to be called their God" (cf. Heb. 11:16). It is true the earthly Canaan was a delicious country—a land of brooks of water, of fountains and deeps that sprang out of the valleys and hills; a land where they did eat "butter of kine, and milk of sheep, with fat of lambs, and rams of the breed of Bashan, and goats, with the fat of kidneys of wheat," and they did "drink the pure blood of the grape" (Deut. 32:14–15); a land whose rich soil produced whatever could fill the cup of joy or load the board of plenty. But alas! what cruel mockery had it been to propose no more sublime enjoyments than these to the lovers of His blessed name? Are such things an adequate portion to the immortal spirit in man? Besides, the patriarchs themselves "sojourned in the land of promise, as in a strange country" (Heb. 11:9) and had not so much as a grave to call their own, till bought with money. And their posterity, the people of His holiness, possessed it but a little time. What was the language of all this? Did it not proclaim, in loudest accents both to the patriarchs and their seed, "Arise ye, and depart; for this is not your rest" (Mic. 2:10)? "I have provided for you, O My people, a better heavenly country, of which this pleasant land is but the pledge and shadow." Beyond all doubt the godly patriarchs regarded the Promised Land in this amiable light; and it is hard to imagine how Moses, that wise and great lawgiver, could have been so passionately desirous to see, before he died, that good land beyond Jordan if he had not considered it as a pledge of God's eternal rest. Let us add to all this the sublime encomiums that are everywhere bestowed upon Canaan in Moses and the prophets. Surely there was nothing about that little spot of earth to entitle it to such high eulogiums as "the glory of all lands" (Ezek. 20:6), "the pleasant land" (Ps. 106:24), and "thy land, O Immanuel" (Isa. 8:8). But when we view it as a type of the heavenly inheritance, the propriety of these grand epithets immediately discovers itself. Let us see where the resemblance lies.

Canaan Is an Emblem of the Heavenly Inheritance
Canaan was a land *originally possessed by other nations*, whom the Lord drove out for their wickedness. It is revealed in the Scriptures that the celestial mansions were first inhabited by these once pure but now apostate spirits, who, for rebellion against their eternal Sovereign, were driven out from God and bliss, and their places in heaven shall know them again no more.

It was a land of amazing *fertility*. And such is the tender condescension of the heavenly Father as to describe, by earthly similitudes, that fullness of joy in His beatific presence and all the rich variety of spiritual and eternal blessings. The plenty of Canaan, where they did "eat bread without scarceness" (Deut. 8:9), was an emblem of the fatness of God's house (Ps. 36:8). In heaven they shall not want any good thing that can be perfective of their natures or conducive to their true felicity. There, to use the prophetic style, "the mountains shall drop down new wine, and the hills shall flow with milk" (Joel 3:18; Amos 9:13). They shall not hunger nor thirst, for the tree of life forever hangs out his golden fruit, and the water of life forever rolls its silver stream.

It was a *promised* land, and promised long before the possession was actually taken, to the father of their nation, four hundred and thirty years before the Law of Moses (Gal. 3:17). Even so, eternal life was promised to Christ, "The everlasting Father" (Isa. 9:6), not only antecedent to the good works of His seed but before the world (John 17:5, 24; Eph. 1:4; 2 Tim. 1:9; Titus 1:2), and though the Lord is not slack concerning His promise (2 Peter 3:9), yet we have need of "faith and patience," even though we have done the will of God, that we may "inherit the promises" (Heb. 6:12).

It was a land which *their own righteousness could not merit* and which their own sword could not procure. Their induction into it is ascribed in the strongest terms to the sovereign grace and "outstretched arm" of God (Deut. 26:8–9), who has "shewed his people the power of his works, that he may give them the heritage of the heathen" (Ps. 111:6). Should we vainly arrogate unto ourselves the honor of deserving, by our best works, our access to the heavenly inheritance, there is one that condemns us, even Moses in whom we trust: "Speak not thou in heart," says that great lawgiver to his people, "for my righteousness the LORD hath brought me in to possess this land.... Not for thy righteousness, or for the uprightness of thine heart, dost thou go to possess their land.... Understand therefore, that the LORD thy God giveth thee not this good land to possess it for thy righteousness; for thou art a stiffnecked people" (Deut. 9:4–6). Can any be so absurd as to affirm that though the earthly inheritance could not, yet the heavenly inheritance may be merited by works of righteousness that we have done?

It was a land to which they went through many *hardships* and difficulties, through floods, and wildernesses, and legions of opposing foes. They had both real and imaginary discouragements to grapple with. Even so, "the kingdom of heaven suffereth violence" (Matt. 11:12), and "we must through much tribulation enter into [it]" (Acts 14:22), though it be a "purchased possession" and a promised inheritance (Eph. 1:14; Acts 7:5). But as neither Sihon, king of the Amorites, nor Og, king of Bashan (Ps. 135:11–12), nor the formidable giants the sons of Anak (Judg. 1:20) could hinder the Israelites from their promised rest (1 Kings 8:56), so neither shall the power of the enemy, however great and dreadful, be able to retard the lowliest saint who takes unto him the whole armor of God and with determined ardor fights the good fight of faith and lays hold on eternal life (1 Tim. 6:12).

It was a land which many *despised*, and through unbelief they came short of the promise and their carcasses fell in the wilderness. And many—alas!—prefer the present pleasures of sin to all the ravishing prospects of eternity. Instead of seeking this better country all the days of their life, it is the land which they abhor.

Lastly, it was a land which the Israelites obtained not till Moses was dead. None are brought to heaven till they be "dead to the law by the body of Christ" (Rom. 7:4). He is the true Joshua, or "the captain of…salvation," who brings "many sons unto glory" (Heb. 2:10) and conducts them through the Jordan of death, into the "inheritance incorruptible, and undefiled, and that fadeth not away, reserved in heaven" (1 Peter 1:4).

5

The Holy City of Jerusalem and the Holy Hill of Zion
Psalm 2:6

We must not "forget thee, O Jerusalem," thou famed metropolis of Judea, nor that adjacent hill of Zion, the royal residence of David, where the temple also stood. Such glorious things have been spoken of this city and mountain as can by no means agree to them when viewed only in the letter. It is long, very long, since Zion was ploughed as a field, since the palaces of Jerusalem have been leveled with the ground: "Go ye up upon her walls," said God to the victorious Roman army, and "take away her battlements; for they are not the LORD's" (Jer. 5:10). But still there is a spiritual Zion, on which the Lamb stands with His redeemed tribes; still there is a heavenly Jerusalem, to which the general assembly and church of the firstborn are said to come. What should this spiritual Zion and heavenly Jerusalem be but the militant and triumphant church of Christ, of which the earthly Zion and the worldly Jerusalem were the shadow and type? The old Mount Zion was equally with Mount Sinai a mount that might be touched, being a corporeal substance, and the old Jerusalem was a city that might be razed to its foundations; but the true Zion is a spiritual thing which cannot be touched, and the new Jerusalem is a city that hath foundations and never can be moved.

Places Where God Chose to Dwell
There were hills more eminent than Zion and towns more potent than Jerusalem, yet no mountain or city makes so distinguished

a figure in the Scriptures. It was not the natural elegance of Zion and Jerusalem, nor the fortified situation of these places, that could entitle them to such high eulogiums as are everywhere bestowed upon them by the inspired writers. It is true indeed, the beautiful situation of Mount Zion and the compact form of Jerusalem, which was comely to a proverb, deserved their due praises (Ps. 48:2), and their strength both of nature and art was far from being despicable. It may be also affirmed that the Holy Spirit intended a faint representation of the invincible strength and spiritual beauty of the church in the strength and beauty of these holy places. But the extraordinary regard which the great Jehovah was pleased to testify toward His holy hill of Zion and His beloved city of Jerusalem is the chief thing which exalted that little hill above the great mountains of the world and ennobled that metropolis above all other cities, however populous or magnificent.

"Why leap ye, ye high hills?" Why do ye exult against the little hill of Zion, as if you were superior to it? This is the hill which God desires to dwell in: "The LORD will dwell in it for ever" (Ps. 68:16). This makes it a high hill, a high hill as the hill of Bashan; this renders it the perfection of beauty and the joy of the whole earth. Exactly so, it is the distinguishing favor and sovereign love of God bestowed upon His church that ennobles it beyond all other societies, however inferior to them in the beauty of earthly splendor and worldly dominion. Let us see, then, what are the marks of the divine regard to these sacred places which rendered them fit emblems of the real church in all ages.

Places Where God Set His King
Jerusalem and Zion were places where God set His king and the thrones of the house of David. That illustrious monarch who founded the long line of the Jewish kings, having rescued Jerusalem and Zion from the Jebusites by force of arms, he fortified them and made them the places of his royal residence (2 Sam. 5:6–10). The spiritual Zion is "the city of the great King" (Ps. 48:2; Matt. 5:35)—that is, of Jesus Christ, who won it out of the hands of idolatrous

Gentiles, who boasted of their idols, though lame and blind. Christ is the true David, who indeed was signified by all the kings of Israel, His lineal successors, who hath gained this notable victory over the Gentile world and in those very places where superstition reigned has built His church, fixed His throne, and issued forth His righteous laws. If it was a distinguishing privilege of the ancient Zion and Jerusalem to be the seat of a king of heaven's election, how greatly superior is the New Jerusalem and gospel Zion in being the seat of the King of Kings, who sits upon the throne, shall never perish, and has the key of David (Isa. 22:22; Rev. 3:7)? "Cry out and shout, thou inhabitant of Zion: for great is the Holy One of Israel in the midst of thee" (Isa. 12:6).

Places Where God Established His Worship
Jerusalem and Zion were places where God established His worship and to which the tribes of the Lord resorted because of His house at Jerusalem (Ps. 122:4). Here the voice of His praise was heard, and sacrifices came with acceptance upon His altar. Jerusalem was the city of Jewish solemnities, and it is foretold by the prophets that the once hostile nations round about them should pay them annual visits and join in their holy festivals (Zech. 14:16). Yea, says the prophet Isaiah, "From one new moon to another, and from one sabbath to another, shall all flesh come to worship before me, saith the LORD" (Isa. 66:23). Now, it is evident, these high predictions were never accomplished in the earthly Zion and Jerusalem: yea, it is impossible they can be accomplished in their literal sense; the nature of things forbids it. But to the spiritual Zion and heavenly Jerusalem, they have been fulfilled and shall be more and more accomplished: for this holy hill may be found in all places of the world, and we may come to the city of the living God without a pilgrimage.

Places Protected by Divine Providence
They were places for whose protection the divine providence has oftentimes awoke in a very extraordinary manner. Assembled kings have come with hostile design against these highly favored places;

but instead of executing their cruel purpose, the joyful Israelites, after their departure, upon the most narrow inspection of their towers, palaces, and bulwarks, could not observe that any of them was battered down or even defaced (Ps. 48:12–14). This was not owing to their own strength, but to the presence of their God: "God is in the midst of her; she shall not be moved: God shall help her, and that right early" (Ps. 46:5; Zeph. 3:17). But this glorious prerogative—of being in the peculiar care of heaven—is now transferred to the gospel church and all her true members: "They that trust in the LORD shall be as mount Zion, which cannot be removed, but abideth for ever" (Ps. 125:1).

5.1

The Feast of Tabernacles
Leviticus 23:33–44

The Feast of Tabernacles[1] was one of the three grand festivals in which all the males of Israel appeared before God in Jerusalem.[2] It began on the fifteenth day of the seventh month, which was four days after their mournful fast on the Day of Atonement,[3] and was celebrated with all possible demonstrations of joy and natural gladness. It lasted eight days and was the longest of all their solemnities, and the last day is called in the New Testament "that great day of the feast." Upon this day, we are informed, "Jesus stood and cried, saying, If any man thirst, let him come unto me, and drink" (John 7:37), alluding, as is commonly thought, to a ceremony they usually performed on that occasion with great pomp, though it be not commanded in the

---

1. The acceptable celebration of the following articles being fixed, by divine appointment, to Jerusalem, they are introduced here to explain and illustrate the great importance of that city as a typical place, though, in another view, they might rather appear to belong to the head of typical things.

2. Editor's note: These were the feasts of Tabernacles/Booths (seventh month: Tishri/September–October), Weeks/Pentecost (third month: Sivan/May–June), and Unleavened Bread (first month: Abib/March–April). The other feasts—Passover, Firstfruits, Trumpets and the Day of Atonement (Yom Kippur)—were not less significant for not requiring all males to attend.

3. Editor's note: The author calls it "the day of expiation," no doubt in order to highlight the sufferings of Christ as the atonement that expiates/cancels the penalty of sin for all who would believe on Him.

law.[4] On all the eight days they were to offer the sacrifices, which are minutely condescended upon by Moses: on the first day thirteen young bullocks, two rams, and fourteen lambs of the first year, and one kid of the goats for a sin offering, beside the continual burnt offering. But it is worthy of our notice that the bullocks diminished by one every subsequent day, till on the seventh day but seven were to be offered; and upon the eighth and last, though the great day of the feast, they offered but one bullock. Did not God intend, by this gradual abatement as the solemnity advanced, to exhibit unto His people a representation of the decaying nature of that dispensation they were under, that a time should come when these sacrifices should vanish away altogether and give place to more spiritual oblations, which should please the Lord better than any bullock that hath both horns and hoofs?

But the ceremony that gave the name to this joyful feast was their *dwelling in booths* the first seven days. These booths were made of olive branches, pine branches, myrtle branches, palm branches, willows of the brook, and branches of other goodly trees they cut down and carried about in their hands. And that none might be at a

---

4. Tremellius, on John 7:37, observes from the Talmud that on the eighth day of this feast the Jews used to march round the altar seven times, singing Hosanna with palm branches in their hands in memory of the Israelites marching round Jericho seven times on the day of its fall, in the time of Joshua. He also informs us from the same authority that on this day they drew water with great joy from the brook Siloam, at the foot of Mount Zion, and carried it to the priests of the temple, where they made a libation of it, mingled with wine, upon the altar. In the time of drawing the water, they sang that cheerful ditty of the prophet Isaiah, "With joy shall ye draw water out of the wells of salvation." They pretended that the prophets Haggai and Zechariah were the institutors of these rites, and they imagined that the Holy Spirit was so delighted with their carnal mirth and vociferation as to impart to them on this occasion a prophetical afflatus, which happened, they say, to the prophet Jonah. The same writer observes that as the Jews had miserably perverted this ordinance by the additions of their own magical ceremonies, so Christ intended to reprove and silence their mad vociferations when He cried with a loud voice, and to lead them away from the terrestrial water to the water of life, and to Himself the only scope of this feast, and of all the other ceremonies. [Editor's note: Immanuel Tremellius (1510–1580) was an Italian Jewish convert to Christianity. At first a Catholic, within a year he became a Protestant and later was imprisoned for some time as a Calvinist.]

loss to know the meaning of this ordinance, it is expressly declared by God Himself: "That your generations may know that I made the children of Israel to dwell in booths, when I brought them out of the land of Egypt" (Lev. 23:43). So prone are human minds to bury in oblivion those mercies that are past, that such rememorative institutions have been always held necessary and expedient. And surely the divine power and goodness displayed to the forefathers of the Jews, in miraculously providing all necessary accommodations for them in a desolate wilderness, deserved anniversary celebration no less than their exodus, or departure from Egypt.

Praising God for His Goodness
By this glad feast, they *praised God* for that good land into which He had brought them, as if they had said, "Our ancestors once wandered in the wilderness, in a solitary way. They found no city to dwell in, but 'Oh that men would praise the LORD for his goodness!' (Ps. 107:8). 'He led them forth by the right way, that they might go to a city of habitation' (Ps. 107:7). Instead of those dreary prospects our fathers had in the wilderness forty years, we their posterity are introduced to this delicious country, where we sow fields and plant vineyards that yield us fruits of increase, whose rich and generous soil supplies us with these 'goodly trees' (Lev. 23:40) from whence we pluck these verdant branches."

Recognizing We Are but Pilgrims Here
And we may add, with great probability, that their dwelling in booths so many days every year was a solemn recognition that they were *still in a wandering state*, though settled in Canaan (Lev. 25:23); that they looked on themselves as "strangers…on the earth" (1 Chron. 29:15), even in the land of promise, as the patriarchs, from whom they sprung, confessed by dwelling in tents and tabernacles in this same land; that they were but pilgrims here and expected a better heavenly inheritance (Heb. 11:13, 16; 13:14).

Truly this has been the universal acknowledgment of good men in every age, who have esteemed their felicity to arise not so much from their present enjoyments as their future prospects. They have not only counted themselves pilgrims and sojourners when struggling with adversity and wandering from one country to another, without a fixed abode, but when elevated to the very summit of fortune and enjoying the most profound repose which this terrestrial state affords.

Our Bodies Are Earthly Tabernacles
A *tabernacle* is the common appellation of a dwelling place in the Old Testament. In the New Testament the body in which the soul is lodged is styled by the great apostle the "earthly house of this tabernacle," which is "dissolved" by death and resigns to a more permanent house: "a building of God, an house not made with hands, eternal in the heavens" (2 Cor. 5:1). David, a glorious king, called his palace "the tabernacle of my house" (Ps. 132:3); and Jesus Christ, when He lived on the earth, at least after He began to act in His public character, had no proper home but chose to be the guest, sometimes to one and sometimes to another, of His followers. Whatever other reasons might be assigned for this conduct of our Lord, it seems as if He had designed to exhibit to all His genuine disciples an illustrious example of superior indifference to all sublunary things and to inculcate, in the strongest manner, upon their minds, "Arise ye, and depart; for this is not your rest" (Mic. 2:10).

Set not your affections, O my people, on this transitory scene of things; remember the glorious hopes you entertain of admission into the celestial mansions, and learn of me not to regard this world as your home. Then do we keep the Feast of Tabernacles in a special manner when we raise our ardent hopes to those glad regions where God our Father, where Christ our elder brother, and all the holy saints and blessed angels inhabit forevermore—when we view these earthly mansions, and even the grave itself, as but our short home and places of transient residence in comparison of eternal habitations.

The Feast Is a Figure of Joy in the Lord
But the Feast of Tabernacles seems chiefly to be a figure of that holy joy and spiritual gladness which is both the duty and privilege of the

true "circumcision" (Rom. 2:28–29), who "worship God in the spirit" (Phil. 3:3; John 4:24). It is long since this solemnity was discontinued, for God has made all their feast days to cease, and there is no warrant in the Scriptures for us under the Christian economy to revive this ceremonial ordinance. But still we have the substance of this shadow and ought to keep this feast, though not in a carnal manner (1 Cor. 5:8): for a prophet of the Jews foretells the conversion of the Gentiles in phrases which evidently import that these joyful rites are figures of gospel worship.[5] The Christian joy, both in the present and future life, seem to have been prefigured by this Jewish festivity.

Christian Joy Flows from the Great Atonement
It began soon after the sorrowful day of expiation, in which they afflicted their souls and had a lively representation of the great atonement. Exactly so, the Christian joy treads upon the heel of godly sorrow, and it is the prerogative of "the high and lofty One… to revive the spirit of the humble, and…the heart of the contrite ones" (Isa. 57:15). The bloody death and meritorious sufferings of the great sacrifice of the Christ is the source from whence it springs. It is strange, but certain, the sinner's unspeakable joy arises from the Savior's unutterable woe. Well may they keep a Feast of Tabernacles who have received the atonement by Jesus Christ; well may they shout for joy whose "iniquity is pardoned" (Isa. 40:2), whose "transgression is forgiven, whose sin is covered" (Ps. 32:1), and "to whom the Lord will not impute sin" (Rom. 4:8); for though He was angry with them, His anger is turned away and He comforts us (Isa. 12:1).

Christian Joy Is for the Whole Course of Life
As this solemn feast lasted eight days, the Christian's joy is not like "the joy of the hypocrite but for a moment" (Job 20:5), for it should be perpetuated through the whole course of his life. "Rejoice evermore"

---

5. Zechariah 14:16, "And it shall come to pass, that every one that is left of all the nations which came against Jerusalem, shall even go up from year to year, to worship the King, the Lord of hosts, and to keep the feast of tabernacles, &c."

is a New Testament precept perpetually obliging (1 Thess. 5:16). There are times when carnal mirth may be very unseasonable and highly improper, but what should forbid that joy in the Holy Spirit, which is "the gladness of [God's] nation" to be indulged at all times (Ps. 106:5)? It is a joy that may exist in the same soul together with the most unfeigned sorrow (John 16:20–22) and most lively contrition (Ps. 34:18). It may even comport with the most afflicted state in this world and abound in the greatest tribulations (Ps. 30:5). It is a continual feast, which the unparalleled afflictions of Paul were not capable of interrupting: "I am," he says, "exceeding joyful in all our tribulation" (2 Cor. 7:4). Job could say, "Blessed be the name of the LORD," in the most complicated distress (Job 1:21). And "although the fig tree shall not blossom, neither shall fruit be in the vines; the labour of the olive shall fail, and the fields shall yield no meat; the flock shall be cut off from the fold, and there shall be no herd in the stalls," it was the firm resolution of Habakkuk, "Yet I will rejoice in the LORD, I will joy in the God of my salvation" (Hab. 3:17–18).

However, it must be owned, the feast is kept here but imperfectly. We are "in heaviness through manifold temptations" (1 Peter 1:6) and must not expect to have all tears wiped away in a place of sin and sorrow. The principal celebration of this festival is in heaven, where alone there is fullness of pure, unmixed joy. In comparison of this blessed state, how imperfect is the present! It may be resembled to the sorrowful day of expiation that preceded this joyful feast. But as the Jews of old for one day of sorrow had eight days of gladness, so momentary affliction shall there give place to everlasting joy (2 Cor. 4:17). The beloved apostle describes the heavenly state in allusion to the ceremonies of this feast: "After this I beheld, and lo, a great multitude, which no man could number, of all nations, and kindreds, and people, and tongues, stood before the throne, and before the Lamb, clothed with white robes," and, as the Jews were wont at the Feast of Tabernacles, they had "palms in their hands" and sang "with a loud voice" the great Hosanna: "Salvation to our God which sitteth upon the throne, and unto the Lamb" (Rev. 7:9–10).

5.2

The Fast of Anniversary Atonement
Leviticus 16; 23:26–32; Numbers 29:7–11

Upon the tenth day of the seventh month (a month distinguished in the Jewish rubric for the great number of festivals observed in it), the whole body of the people in Israel were required to keep a solemn fast to afflict their souls for sin and to abstain from all manner of servile work (Lev. 16:29). But the chief solemnities of the day consisted in those rites by which the high priest was to make atonement for the sins of his nation, which rites were never practiced but upon this occasion (Lev. 16:34). Whatever our Great High Priest has done for the salvation of His people in earth beneath or in heaven above was prefigured in these venerable solemnities. This the inspired writer to the Hebrews having at great length illustrated to our hand, it will not be necessary to enlarge upon it. Let it suffice briefly to enumerate the sacerdotal actions reserved for this memorable day and then to hint at their typical sense.

The Actions of the High Priest
How, then, was the Jewish high priest to equip himself for the service of the day? He was to put on his holy linen garments after washing himself. He was to furnish himself with a bullock for a sin offering and a ram for a burnt offering to be offered for his own sins and the sins of his family. He was also to take of the congregation two kids of the goats for a sin offering and a ram for a burnt offering. The two goats, making but one offering together, were not to be used in the

same manner. One of them was to be offered unto the Lord after the manner of a sin offering, the other presented alive before the Lord and then dismissed a scapegoat into the wilderness. The sacrifices being prepared, he proceeded in the following manner.

First, he killed the bullock to atone for himself and his family; and taking in his hand a censer full of burning coals from off the altar and a quantity of sweet incense sufficient to raise a cloud that should cover the mercy seat, taking also the blood of his bullock in a vessel, he went also into the sanctuary, set the incense on fire, and sprinkled the blood upon and before the mercy seat (Lev. 16:11–14).

The sacrifice for himself being thus performed, he returns out of the sanctuary and kills the goat of the sin offering for the people; and bringing his blood again within the veil, he sprinkles it, as he had done with the blood of the bullock, upon the mercy seat, and likewise upon the golden altar. "And," said the lawgiver of the Jews, "there shall be no man in the tabernacle…when he goeth in to make an atonement in the holy place, until he come out" (Lev. 16:15–19).

The next ceremony is this: he brings the live goat and, laying his hands upon the head of the creature, confesses over him all the iniquities of the children of Israel, putting them upon the head of the goat, and sends him by some fit man into the wilderness. "And the goat," said the Lord, "shall bear upon him all their iniquities unto a land not inhabited" (Lev. 16:20–22).

This done, he goes into the tabernacle of the congregation, and stripping himself of his linen garments, he deposits them in the Holy Place, washes himself, puts on his golden garments for glory and beauty, comes forth to the people, and offers the two rams for a burnt offering: the one for himself and the other for the people (Lev. 16:23–24).

Lastly, the fat of the sin offering is burnt upon the altar, and the bodies of the bullock and goat, whose blood had been carried into the Holy Place, were burned without the camp (Lev. 16:25).

The Imperfections of the Annual Atonement Sacrifices

Such is the order of the holy rites to be practiced on this great anniversary, and the happy effects of it are said to be a cleansing from all their sins. Now, it is evident these carnal ordinances have many marks of weakness and imperfection If we speak of *real* atonement, it was utterly impossible that the blood of these bullocks and goats could take sin away as pertaining to the conscience.

They were but *brute creatures*, of inferior nature to the priest that offered them and to the people for whom they were offered.

They were offered by *a sinful man*, who needed atonement for himself.

They were offered *year by year* continually, and in them a remembrance was again made of sin every year. Now, if they could have made the comers to them perfect, would they not have ceased to be offered? Most certainly they would, because the worshipers once purged should have had no more conscience of sin.

The High Priest of Our Profession

In all these things the "High Priest of our profession" has the preeminence (Heb. 3:1; Col. 1:18). He, being harmless and undefiled, needed not to offer for Himself, like Aaron and his successors. He needed not to shed the blood of others, for He was able to offer up Himself. He needed not repeat His sacrifice oftener than once, or suffer often from the foundation of the world, for by one offering He had forever perfected all them that are sanctified. These necessary allowances being made of the vast disparity between the type and Jesus Christ, we shall proceed to enumerate some of these grand evangelical mysteries that were enigmatically preached unto the Jews in the transactions of this day.

That *in future time* a true and proper atonement should be made for the sins of Israel, or, to use the style of the prophet Zechariah, that God would "remove the iniquity of [His] land in one day" (Zech. 3:9), this seems to have been the leading doctrine held forth in all the sacrifices, but especially in those that were offered on this occasion. Yet a little while, and God will exhibit a propitiation in the promised

Messiah, who shall "finish...transgression" and "make an end of sins" (Dan. 9:24) and perfectly do that will of God, which cannot be done by sacrifice for sin and burnt offerings. And how shall this great event be brought to pass? How shall the Messiah "redeem Israel from all his iniquities" (Ps. 130:8)? What shall He do? What shall be done unto Him? How shall He begin, and in what manner shall He finish the arduous work? These questions may all be answered by these anniversary rites.

It was signified that the great Maker of atonement should *assume the nature* of those for whom it should be made, for their high priest was one of their brethren, and taken from among men (Heb. 5:1, 5),

- That when Christ should come into the world to do the will of God, He should not make a splendid figure nor array Himself with all that glory of which He is truly possessed. Thus, the high priest of the Jews, upon the Day of Atonement, put not on at the first his best suit of apparel but was content with the holy linen garments he wore in common with other priests (Lev. 16:4).

- That He should be constituted a *public person* and *represent* a great number of individuals, in whatever should be done by Him. For the high priest did not officiate in the garments which he commonly wore but in these public robes that were the badges of his public character as the representative of the people.

- That the *sins of all the redeemed should be transferred upon Him* and become His own by legal imputation. For all the iniquities of the children of Israel were solemnly confessed over the head of the scapegoat before he was dismissed into the wilderness (Lev. 16:21).

- That when thus charged with guilt, He should *suffer the punishment of death* and His life be violently taken away. For the other goat, the bullock, and the two rams were killed for sin offerings and burnt offerings, and "without shedding of blood is no remission" (Heb. 9:22).

- That the blood of Jesus should be shed in a public manner "without the gate" (Heb. 13:12) is indicated by the bodies of these beasts being burned outside the camp (Lev. 16:27).

- That He should, however, live even when dead, as to His divine nature, and be a glorious conqueror of the grave by *His resurrection* is also signified, for the scapegoat, which was the half of the sin offering for the people, was not to be killed, as the other goat.

- That He should, when the work of purging our sins was finished, disappear on earth and *enter "within the veil"* of these aspectable[1] heavens, into that happy place where God resides among the blessed angels (Heb. 6:19). For when the high priest had shed the blood of the bullock and the goat, he went out of the sight of the Israelites, entering within the veil into that venerable apartment, where were the symbols of the divine presence and where Jehovah sat enthroned between the cherubim.

- That this most precious blood should be *the key to open the everlasting gates*, or should procure His welcome reception into the presence of God. For unless the high priest had offered up the appointed victims, he durst not have presumed to see the face of God in the Most Holy Place.

- That though the heavens should contain Him and the world see Him no more, He should still be *carrying on His priestly work in the presence of Jehovah*. For when the Jewish priest entered within the veil, he perfumed the mercy seat with incense and sprinkled it with blood. Truly, unless the high priest had gone into the holiest of all with his blood and incense, he had not discharged the most glorious part of his work. If he had only offered the victims and gone no further than the middle court, the inferior priests had been upon a level with him, for these things they did as well as he. So if Jesus Christ were still on earth, where He offered up Himself; if He had not gone to the Father and retired from the view

---

1. Editor's note: I.e., visible, capable of being seen.

of men, He could not be a priest in the most eminent sense of the word, the most glorious part of His function were still to be discharged, and the resemblance between Him and the Jewish high priest would be very lame and imperfect.

But rejoice, O ye that believe in His name and ye who make His atonement the principal basis of your comfort: for "we have a great high priest" that was once on earth but is now "passed into the heavens, Jesus the Son of God" (Heb. 4:14). There He appears as "a Lamb as it had been slain" (Rev. 5:6) and stands with His golden censer, to offer up the incense of His intercession with the prayers of all saints (Rev. 8:3).[2] A time will come when the interposing veil shall be drawn aside and the Great High Priest return with sound of trumpet to bless His expecting people and absolve them from all their iniquities before an assembled world: for "unto them that look for him shall he appear the second time without sin unto salvation" (Heb. 9:28).

---

2. Editor's note: Matthew Henry comments on Revelation 8:3, "It is very probable that this other angel is the Lord Jesus, the high priest of the church, who is here described in his sacerdotal office, having a golden censer and much incense, a fulness of merit in his own glorious person, and this incense he was to offer up, *with the prayers of all the saints, upon the golden altar* of his divine nature."

5.3

The Feast of Firstfruits and of Pentecost
Leviticus 23:9–21

As it was the will of God that His people should dwell alone and be divided from all nations of the world by a wall of partition till the Messiah should come to pull it down (Eph. 2:14), so, besides a great number of other peculiarities, they must not plough nor sow nor reap in the same manner as other people. The rites with which they began and finished their harvest are not unworthy of a particular notice. Besides the charitable regulation they observed in not making a clean riddance of the corners of their field, nor gathering any gleanings, nor returning to fetch a forgotten sheaf (for these were the perquisites of the poor stranger, the fatherless, and the widow [Lev. 23:22]), they were commanded to begin their harvest with offering to the Lord a sheaf of the firstfruits and to end it in a holy convocation and an offering of two loaves, with other solemnities.

The Firstfruits of the Land

The beginning of harvest in the Holy Land was on the morrow after the feast of the Passover (Lev. 23:4–8), when they presented their firstfruits unto the Lord, not only for the whole congregation but, it would seem, for every particular family (Lev. 23:9–10). The form of words to be pronounced on this occasion by him that offered the firstfruits is expressly recorded in the Jewish law,[1] and the wise

---

1. Deut. 26:3, "I profess this day, that I am come unto the country which the

king of Israel enforces the obedience of this religious precept with the assurance of the heavenly benediction: "Honour the LORD with thy substance, and with the firstfruits of thine increase: so shall thy barns be filled with plenty, and thy presses shall burst out with new wine" (Prov. 3:9–10). They were themselves forbidden to taste the produce of the year, whether "bread, parched corn, or green ears," till they had brought the appointed offering to their God, as an acknowledgment of His dominion and expression of their gratitude (Lev. 23:14). It seems to have been a significant ceremony intended to revive that law of nature that the all-bounteous Giver should be honored with our first and best. And truly, the observance of this rule is not only enjoined everywhere in the Mosaic ritual but may be traced as high as the offering of the first martyr, Abel, who brought unto the Lord of "the firstlings of his flock," whereas no such thing is observed of the first murderer, Cain, to whose offering the Lord had no respect (Gen. 4:4–5).

Besides, when He who crowned the year with His goodness (Ps. 65:11) required a sheaf to be given Him, it might impress upon their minds such momentous truths as these: that we can give nothing to God but what we first receive from God, that what we present unto God cannot be profitable unto Him, and that what He requires is nothing to what He bestows. What is a single sheaf to all the treasures of the harvest? Would he not be a foolish Israelite who should have regarded his puny sheaf as an equivalent or price that deserved at God's hand the rich productions of the year? Nor is it less absurd for any to imagine that their most useful actions can deserve the gift of eternal life (Rom. 6:23), that joyful harvest of "light [that] is

---

LORD sware unto our fathers for to give us. A Syrian ready to perish *was* my father, &c." [Editor's note: The full passage is Deuteronomy 26:3–10, which describes the dialogue between the worshiper and the priest: "And thou shalt go unto the priest that shall be in those days, and say unto him, I profess this day unto the LORD thy God, that I am come unto the country which the LORD sware unto our fathers for to give us. And the priest shall take the basket out of thine hand, and set it down before the altar of the LORD thy God. And thou shalt speak and say before the LORD thy God, A Syrian ready to perish was my father, and he went down into Egypt."]

sown for the righteous" and "gladness" that is sown for "the upright in heart" (Ps. 97:11).

The end of harvest was upon the fiftieth day after it begun.[2] This day was solemnized with a religious assembling and with abstaining from servile work (Lev. 23:21). The husbandman had seen the fruits of his ground brought to maturity and testified his gratitude by the sheaf which he offered, with holy rites upon the first day; and now he offers upon the fiftieth day two large loaves of fine flour baked with leaven, which are also called "the firstfruits unto the LORD" (Lev. 23:17) and were a thank offering, as well as the sheaf, to that good God who had reserved for them the appointed weeks of the harvest. On the beginning of Pentecost they offered with the sheaf a lamb without blemish for a burnt offering; but now their gratitude must rise in proportion to the favors they receive, and not one lamb but seven lambs, one young bullock, and two rams must smoke upon God's altar (Lev. 23:18).

Two Pentecosts

We are informed by the historian[3] of the New Testament that this fiftieth day coincided with the most remarkable event of the descent of the Holy Spirit upon the first founders of Christianity. "And when the day of Pentecost was fully come, they were all with one accord in one place. And suddenly there came a sound from heaven as of a rushing mighty wind, and…there appeared unto them cloven tongues like as of fire, and it sat upon each of them. And they were all filled with the Holy Ghost, and began to speak with other tongues, as the Spirit gave them utterance" (Acts 2:1–4). By inspecting the history of the Israelites' march from Egypt, it will also be found that upon this very day the Law was given at Mount Sinai (Ex. 34:28–29). The conjunction of these two grand events on the last day of Pentecost seems not without some special intention in the Holy Spirit. Fifty days after the

---

2. Editor's note: *Pentecost* is Greek meaning "the fiftieth."
3. Editor's note: Luke, "the beloved physician" and writer of the third Gospel and the Acts of the Apostles.

deliverance from Egypt was the killing letter, or the fiery law, given; and fifty days after the resurrection of Christ, our better deliverance, was the quickening Spirit dispensed, to write the law not on hard tables of stone but on the fleshly tables of the heart and to qualify the apostles to begin a new harvest far more important than what was now happily finished—a harvest not of corn but of men, to be reaped by putting the sickle of the Word of God into the field of the world.

The Firstfruits of the Spirit

Such were the sacred rites with which the Jews began and finished their harvest; and, in the language of the New Testament, whatever thing is the beginning, pledge, and earnest of more of the same kind is styled *firstfruits*. So the "firstfruits of Achaia" denotes the most early converts to the Christian faith in that part of the world (1 Cor. 16:15), and those begun graces and consolations of the Holy Spirit that are the earnest of the eternal inheritance are denominated the "firstfruits of the Spirit" (Rom. 8:23). But we shall chiefly observe the application of this epithet to Christ and to believers.

The Risen Christ as Firstfruits

"Christ," says the inspired apostle, is "risen from the dead, and become the firstfruits of them that slept" (1 Cor. 15:20). May we not hence affirm that as the harvest is a natural emblem of the end of the world and general resurrection, so the Jewish firstfruits did represent the resurrection of the Son of God? The bodies of the saints, when deposited in the grave, may be compared to that seed which the husbandman commits to the furrows of the field. One would imagine that the grain once buried under the clod would never more emerge from under it. But constant experience assures us that by the combined influence of vernal showers and suns it will burst the confinement of the furrow and reward the laborer's toil with copious fruit. So, at the destined hour, the sleeping dust of saints "shall revive as the corn" (Hos. 14:7), the earth shall cast forth her dead and shall no more cover her slain (Isa. 26:21), and what was "sown in dishonour" shall be "raised in glory" (1 Cor. 15:43). The "resurrection" of the corn is an event in the world of nature that illustrates something of God's raising the dead.

- The resurrection of Jesus Christ—a true resurrection after a true bodily death—advances further still and evidently proves the certainty of our bodies arising from the dust. This joyful event not only proclaims in loudest accents that the dry bones can live if it is the pleasure of God to send forth His quickening Spirit (Ezek. 37:3) but asserts, in the strongest manner, that "he will revive us…he will raise us up, and we shall live in his sight" (Hos. 6:2).

- Were the firstfruits reaped before the rest of the harvest? So "Christ the firstfruits" was raised from the grave, and "afterward they that are Christ's at his coming" shall be raised to life (1 Cor. 15:23).

- Were the firstfruits a pledge and earnest to the Israelites, that the whole harvest should be reaped in due time? The resurrection of Jesus Christ ensures the resurrection of all His people at the appointed season. So runs the joyful declaration in the prophet. "Thy dead men shall live, together with my dead body shall they arise. Awake and sing, ye that dwell in the dust: for thy dew *is as* the dew of herbs, and the earth shall cast out the dead" (Isa. 26:19).

The Redeemed of the Lord as Firstfruits

But as the firstfruits are an emblem of Jesus Christ, they no less represent the faithful and the redeemed from among men. "Israel," says a prophet, "was holiness unto the LORD, and the firstfruits of his increase" (Jer. 2:3). And the Lord's brother affirms that "of his own will begat he us with the word of truth, that we should be a kind of firstfruits of his creatures" (James 1:18). Let us see the resemblance.

The firstfruits were the *unalienable property* of the God of Israel, with which it had been sacrilege to intermeddle. Even so, the redeemed are the portion of the Lord; they are not their own, and all who devour them shall offend.

The firstfruits were *given by God* to the priests as a part of their maintenance. This puts us in mind of that saying of our High Priest, "Thine they were, and thou gavest them me" (John 17:6).

The firstfruits were but a *small part* of the harvest. This may denote the paucity of saints, who, in comparison of the multitude, are like "an handful of corn in the earth" (Ps. 72:16).

But, lastly, as the firstfruits did *sanctify and bless the whole crop*, and in their use were better than the rest, even so, the people of God, though few and small, are a blessing in the midst of the land, however much they may be undervalued by worldly men, and are "the excellent" of the earth, "whom," says the Lord, "is all my delight" (Ps. 16:3).

5.4

The Feast of the New Moon
Numbers 28:11–15

As the feast of the new moon is placed among the "shadow of things to come" (Col. 2:16–17) by the apostle of the Gentiles, we must not altogether pass over it. Though the beginning of the seventh month was peculiarly sacred, the beginnings of all the other months were also dedicated unto God and solemnized with holy rites and exercises of devotion. On their new moons they refrained from servile work, offered extraordinary sacrifices,[1] resorted to the prophets, feasted together, and blew the silver trumpets. Let us try if we can assign the probable reasons of this service or the moral instructions that may be learned from this "statute for Israel, and a law of the God of Jacob" (Ps. 81:4).

Praise to the Creator of All Things
And, first, might it not be designed as an ascription of praise and thanksgiving to that glorious Being who suspended that silver lamp in the blue vault of heaven, that it might smooth the shades of night

---

1. The sacrifices for the new moon appointed in the Mosaic law are two young bullocks, one ram, seven lambs, &c. (Num. 28:11). Ezekiel mentions but one young bullock, six lambs, and a ram (46:6), though the church-state which he describes is supposed to be more glorious than the former one. We see from this the ceremonial law was not designed to be unalterable, for not only the priesthood being changed (which the apostle observes [Heb. 7:12]) but the sacrifice also being changed (according to Ezekiel), there is made of necessity a change also of the law.

with its cheerful borrowed rays, turn the ocean in its bed, divide our time, and serve the purposes of vegetation as well as the golden ruler of the day? They acknowledged by this festival that God who is above was the prime mover of this and other heavenly luminaries, that to Him they were indebted for all the beneficial effects of these excellent creatures. Had they intended to address their homage to the host of heaven themselves and not Him who formed them by the breath of His mouth, they would no doubt have rather blown their trumpets to the rising sun or to the moon at her full, when she walks in brightness. But God, who is jealous of His glory, required that He should be praised for this good creature, not when she appears to her greatest advantage but when she is altogether invisible, or dimly seen, like that inconsiderable streak of light which the *new* moon is. By this precaution none can suspect but the sacred rites were in honor of Him who made "the sun to rule by day" and "the moon and stars to rule by night: for his mercy endureth for ever" (Ps. 136:8–9).

Praise to the Lord of All Our Times
Might it not also be intended as a solemn recognition that God was the sole proprietor of their "times," which are wholly in His "hand" and ought to be dedicated unto His service (Ps. 31:15)? The first days of their month might be offered to God for the same reasons as the firstfruits of their ground. Hereby they disclaimed the superstition of the heathen, who were dismayed at the signs of heaven and esteemed some parcels of their time ill-fated or unlucky. As every creation of God is good, so no time is evil, being sanctified by the same word of God and prayer. If the firstfruits be holy, so is the lump; and if the first day of every month be holy, the subsequent days are consecrated by it.

Praise to the Lord for His Messiah
But chiefly, as one is apt to look for some notices of the Messiah in all the legal ordinances, might not this monthly festival, and especially the feast of trumpets in the seventh month of their civil but first of their sacred year, be viewed by them as a faint shadow of the future renovation of all things by Jesus Christ? Though we must not

be bold in fixing our own conjectures upon the Holy Spirit, as His undoubted meaning there seems, however, to be a considerable likeness between the blowing of the trumpet at the new moon and the voice both of the gospel and the archangel.

First, it might perhaps be a figure of the *new face the church should wear in the age of the Messiah*. In other places, the universal church is compared to the moon (Rev. 12:1),[2] and the preaching of the gospel is resembled to the blowing of "a great sound of a trumpet" (Matt. 24:31). What though we should consider the old moon as an emblem of the Jewish economy, which, like that waning orb, decayed, waxed old, and vanished away. But the Christian dispensation may be compared to the new moon, which, though small at first, did gradually increase, while the sound of the gospel trumpet, the voice of our Great High Priest, did go into all the earth and His words unto the end of the world. Who knows but the believing Jews might, by this feast, express their faith and joy in that happy revolution, which the apostle calls the abolishing "in his flesh the enmity, even the law of commandments contained in ordinances; for to make in himself of twain one new man, so making peace" (Eph. 2:15).

Or, lastly, may we not discern in this monthly festival a shadow of the awful transactions in *the great and terrible day of the Lord*, which shall, however, be a joyful period to all true Israelites and the time of the restitution of all things? This visible world itself may be resembled to a waning moon, as the fashion of it passes away. But as the new moon succeeded the old while the priests did blow with their trumpets, so when the "last trump" shall sound, "the dead shall be raised incorruptible, and we shall be changed": "So when this corruptible shall have put on incorruption, and this mortal shall have put on immortality, then shall be brought to pass the saying that is

---

2. Editor's note: Revelation 12:1–2: "And there appeared a great wonder in heaven; a woman clothed with the sun, and the moon under her feet, and upon her head a crown of twelve stars: and she being with child cried, travailing in birth, and pained to be delivered." This is a picture of the church as Christ's light-bearer in the world, bringing forth a godly progeny but facing imminent persecution from the enemies of the Lord.

written, Death is swallowed up in victory" (1 Cor. 15:52, 54). Then shall that blessed state commence when, according to the sublime prophet, thy sun, O Zion, "shall be no more thy light by day; neither for brightness shall the moon give light unto thee: but the LORD shall be unto thee an everlasting light, and thy God thy glory. Thy sun shall no more go down; neither shall thy moon withdraw itself: for the LORD shall be thine everlasting light, and the days of thy mourning shall be ended" (Isa. 60:19–20).

5.5

The Metaphorical Priesthood of All Christians
Leviticus 8–10

Although the Levitical priests were chiefly designed to prefigure the Great High Priest, as has been said, this hinders not to view them also as emblems of all the saints, who in every age are caused to approach unto God, that they may dwell in the house of the Lord forever. It is true indeed, the great propitiatory sacrifice is already offered, never to be repeated again; and we cannot sufficiently detest that sacrilegious usurpation of the Redeemer's glory by the pretended priests in the Roman Church, who, without the slightest warrant from the Scriptures, give out to their deluded votaries, that they offer in the Mass I know not what unbloody sacrifice for the sins of the living and the dead. O impiety! O absurdity! for can anything be more wicked and foolish than to imagine that Jesus Christ has not by His "one offering…perfected for ever them that are sanctified" (Heb. 10:14) but left His work to be completed by a wretched, mumbling, mortal priest? We Christians must acknowledge that all priesthood, in the strict literal sense, is now ceased in "Christ…the end of the law" (Rom. 10:4).[1] But still there is a metaphorical priesthood, which the New Testament ascribes not to the office-bearers in the Christian church but to all Christians without exception. It was the promise of God to His ancient people that they should be unto

---

1. Editor's note: Christ is the "end" of the law in the sense of accomplishing its positive "goal" (the Greek τέλος).

Him "a kingdom of priests" (Ex. 19:6), and the phrase is adopted by a New Testament apostle, who says to the whole body of the believers to whom he wrote, "Ye are...a royal priesthood" (1 Peter 2:9). It was foretold by the holy prophets that men should call the professors of the true religion "the Priests of the LORD" and "the Ministers of our God" (Isa. 61:6), that the Gentiles should be taken "for priests and for Levites" (Isa. 66:19–21), that the priestly tribe should have an offspring numerous as the host of heaven and the sand of the sea (Jer. 33:22), that in every place which "the rising of the sun" and "the going down of the same" surveys, "incense...and a pure offering" should be offered to the true God (Mal. 1:11). These great and precious promises have already been, and still more shall be, fulfilled. The company of the redeemed were seen by John in vision "arrayed in white robes" (Rev. 7:13), the badge of their priestly character (Lev. 16:4), and he heard their heavenly song of praise to that loving Savior that washed them from their sins "in his own blood" and "hath made us kings and priests unto God" (Rev. 1:5–6; 5:9). Though the analogy of the legal and metaphorical priesthood may not perhaps be so striking as between Aaron and Christ Jesus, there is not wanting a considerable resemblance.

- Were the Levitical priests chosen by God and separated to His peculiar service? God hath chosen the faithful from the rest of mankind and "set apart him that is godly for himself" (Ps. 4:3).

- Were the Levites taken by the Lord "instead of all the firstborn among the children of Israel," to whom the right of priesthood seems to have originally belonged (Num. 3:41)? The people of Christ are "the general assembly and church of the firstborn," as all God's children are (Heb. 12:23).

- Were they all descended from Aaron and Levi (for unless they could prove their genealogy, they were put from the priesthood as polluted)? So all the saints are descendants from Jesus Christ, their everlasting Father, and ought to ascertain their heavenly extraction by the documents of a holy conversation.

- They were washed with water at their consecration and were always to use the great laver that stood in the entry of the tabernacle when they ministered in the sanctuary. This puts us in mind of the washing of regeneration that all Christians partake at first and of the frequent recourse to the fountain of Christ's blood in their holy services.
- The oil that anointed them signified the unction of the Spirit, which the faithful receive from the Holy One.
- The white raiments of fine linen is an emblem of the righteousness of the saints.

They were not allowed a share of the earthly Canaan, as the other tribes, for the Lord spoke unto Aaron, "Thou shalt have no inheritance in their land, neither shalt thou have any part among them: I am thy part and thine inheritance" (Num. 18:20). Was not this a lively type of the superior privilege of His beloved, who are delivered from the men of the world who have their wretched portion in this transitory life (Ps. 17:14)? But the Lord is their portion, and therefore in Him they may hope, be their outward state ever so indigent (Ps. 16:5). The ceremonial purity required of them that bore the vessels of the Lord denotes that holiness becomes the house of the Lord forever (Ps. 93:5) and all who worship in His temple (Ps. 96:9).

But what are their sacrifices? Let an apostle speak this; they are "spiritual sacrifices, acceptable to God by Jesus Christ" (1 Peter 2:5). Perhaps we might say, to use the legal style, there is the meat offering of charitable distributions; the drink offering of penitent tears, issuing from a broken, contrite heart; the heave offering of prayer and elevated desires; the peace offering of praise and thanksgiving; and the whole burnt offering of the whole man, when the body is presented unto God a living sacrifice, when every lust is mortified and the very life surrendered for the honor of God in martyrdom, which sometimes is a reasonable service. These are the sacrifices which all the saints should offer, not to an unatoned but to an atoned God.

They themselves are their temples; and, besides, they have access by faith into heaven, the holiest of all. Christ is their altar that sanctifies all their gifts. His Spirit is the fire that inflames, and His merit is the salt that powders all their sacrifices when they come with acceptance before the presence of Jehovah.

An Evangelical History

of

the Birth, Life, Death, Resurrection, and Ascension of Jesus Christ, the True Messiah, in Whom All the Types of the Old Testament Are Fulfilled

An Evangelical History

The seventy weeks of Daniel were now elapsed, and they who looked for salvation in Israel were wrapped in silent expectation of the Messiah coming in the name of the Lord to save them (Dan. 9:24–25). Long had the Gentile nations walked in their own ways and the Jews practiced the ceremonies of Moses. But neither could the precepts of the philosopher retrieve the ruins of our fall, nor could the carnal ordinances of the law make them perfect who had recourse unto them, as touching the conscience. For as yet the daily oblation had not ceased, nor the temple smoked in ruin, into which the messenger of the covenant, according to an ancient prediction, was suddenly to come (Mal. 3:1). The scepter of David was now sunk into the hatchet of a carpenter, and his "tabernacle" was "fallen down" (Acts 15:16). Tiberius swayed the scepter of Rome (Luke 3:1); Herod was king in Judea (Matt. 2:1); John the Baptist had lain six months in the womb, who was to be the harbinger of His coming (Luke 1:36; Mal. 3:1; Mark 1:2–3); and a profound peace reigned over the world, as a presage of His birth, whose name is called the "Prince of Peace" (Isa. 9:6). When the almighty King, who is "ever…mindful of his covenant" (Ps. 111:5), dispatches from the blessed abodes the angel Gabriel (none of the least of the heavenly throng, and not now first employed in embassies of love to man) to salute the blessed virgin, the mother of our Lord (Luke 1:26ff.), the obedient angel flies and punctually discharges his commission.

The Virgin Birth of the Incarnate God
But, O ye papists, though he honors her as a saint, he worships her not as a goddess. A new thing indeed it was in the earth, that "a virgin [should] conceive" (Isa. 7:14), but by no means impossible unto the Holy Spirit to bring about by His overshadowing power. If once a woman was formed out of the substance of a man, why should not

that same divine power be fully able to produce a man out of the substance of a woman? May we not humbly judge that it came from Him who is "wonderful in counsel, and excellent in working" (Isa. 28:29), that for the general honor of our nature the Savior did spring from that feeble sex which was first in the transgression (Gen. 3:6)? For "as the woman is of the man, even so is the man also by the woman; but all things of God" (1 Cor. 11:12). O condescending Savior, blessed, beyond all peradventure, was "the womb that bare thee, and the paps which thou hast sucked" (Luke 11:27): nor is it easy to conceive how a sinful woman could be more highly honored than to carry Thee in her womb (Luke 1:28, 42) unless by having Thee formed in her heart.

Here let us forgo all idle speculations about what other methods were possible to God by which to send forth His Son into our lower world, and let us rather be willing to discern the character of wisdom that is evidently stamped upon this dispensation, such as it is. For had a body been prepared Him of nothing, of the dust of the ground, or of some heavenly materials, He would not be of the same flesh and blood with those He intended to redeem. Or had it been produced in the ordinary method of human generation, He would have been involved in the same guilt of Adam's originating sin with the rest of mankind, whom He represented in the first broken covenant. As in the former case His relation to us would (for what appears) be too remote, so in the latter He would (in all appearance) be too like us, not only in the qualities of our natures but in the guilt of our persons. But he is "made of a woman" (Gal. 4:4) and therefore of our bone and our flesh. And because His mother is a virgin, we easily understand how He is holy, undefiled, and separated from sinners. But here a difficulty arises to our thoughts: for if she is a virgin that shall be "with child by the Holy Ghost" (Matt. 1:18), who shall preserve her character from the unjust aspersions of the world? It is far more fitting that her "holy child Jesus" shall confirm the truth of His divine extraction (Acts 4:30) by the tenor of His deportment, when adult, than that she should be the asserter of it. Therefore she is betrothed unto a husband, who is at once the witness and the guardian of her virginity (Matt. 1:18).

The Advent of Jesus Christ

But leaving the sacred embryo to be "curiously wrought in the lowest parts of the earth" by the fingers of the Almighty (Ps. 139:15), let us next see in what manner the heavenly infant was ushered into the light. "But thou, Beth-lehem Ephratah, though thou be little among the thousands of Judah," says the prophet, "yet out of thee shall come forth unto me that is to be ruler in Israel" (Mic. 5:2). But though the blessed virgin can trace her genealogy from David, and from Abraham, she is a resident of Nazareth, from whence no prophet was expected to arise. How, then, shall the prediction be accomplished? The emperor of Rome issues a royal edict, that all his large dominion shall be taxed. He meant to fill his coffers with money, but a greater Sovereign than he intended the fulfilling of His promise.

While every man repairs to his city to be taxed in obedience to the imperial mandate, Joseph, His father, as was supposed, repairs among the rest to Bethlehem, the city of his family, being of "the house and lineage of David" (Luke 2:1–4). And now he is arrived with Mary, his espoused wife, who being near the time of her delivery had been directed by providence, or special instinct, to accompany her husband on this occasion. No costly palace receives our wearied travelers. A common inn is the place of His nativity, perhaps a silent intimation that He Himself should be a common Savior? Nor even in the inn could a commodious apartment be spared to the Lord of heaven and earth. Ye men of Bethlehem, what a guest did you exclude! The coarse accommodation of the manger was all His mother could obtain for her tender infant. Lo! there He lies wrapped in swaddling clothes (Luke 2:7) whom the "heaven of heavens cannot contain" (1 Kings 8:27)!

Immanuel, God with Us

He is associated with the herds in the stall, whom all the angels adore! For this is He—believe it, ye children of men!—whose name is "Emmanuel, which being interpreted is, God with us" (Matt. 1:23). This is He who from all everlasting was "the brightness of his [Father's] glory, and the express image of his person" (Heb. 1:3), who was "daily his delight, rejoicing always before him" (Prov. 8:30). This is He who was "in the form of God, [and] thought it not robbery to be equal with God" (Phil. 2:6); but for our salvation He is clothed in flesh and blood, and now become a helpless, feeble infant! O ye beautiful scenes of the creation, thou glorious sun, thou silver moon, and all ye glittering stars, in you the invisible things of God are clearly seen; but now you are eclipsed by the more excellent glory, "God... manifest in the flesh" (1 Tim. 3:16).

Come hither, ye that thirst for curious knowledge, and lose yourselves in thankful admiration. For the person of the eternal Word (John 1:1), by whom all things were made (1 Cor. 8:6), is found in the likeness of man (Rom. 8:3), is become as our brother, that sucked the breasts of our mother (Matt. 12:50). Not that He stripped Himself of any divine perfection or ceased to be what He was, but by a most ineffable act of condescension and power, He has veiled the glory of His divinity and become what He was not, by assuming a portion of our humanity to subsist in His own personality (Phil. 2:7). O mysterious infant, the glory of our race, who "is not ashamed to call [us] brethren" (Heb. 2:11). Now Thou art fully able to give our ransom unto God, and the redemption of our souls, though precious, shall not cease forever.

From Bethlehem to Egypt

What charming melody is that breaking the silence of the night and tasting strong of heaven? It is "a multitude of the heavenly host" praising God in strains of highest rapture (Luke 2:13). O shepherds, blessed were your ears to hear such early tidings of a Savior born in the city of David (Luke 2:11). Though your heads were wet with dew and your locks with the drops of the night, yet none of the princes of this world could boast of such an honor. But lo! three eastern sages, conducted by a wondrous star, or glittering meteor, come from a far country to seek and worship the princely babe of Bethlehem (Matt. 2:1–2). They are not scandalized at the inglorious figure the infant king did cast; but perceiving the rays of deity, even through the veil of flesh—such is the power of faith—they not only offer unto Him costly presents but address Him with divine honors (Matt. 2:11). A sad presage, ye children of the kingdom, that "many shall come from the east and west, and shall sit down with Abraham, and Isaac, and Jacob, in the kingdom of heaven. But the children of the kingdom shall be cast out into outer darkness" (Matt. 8:11–12). In vain does the besotted tyrant of Judea think to reverse the high decrees of heaven by issuing out a bloody mandate to murder the tender innocents (Matt. 2:16). While their infant blood defiles the streets of Bethlehem, Egypt herself shall be a sanctuary to the young Prince of Peace (Matt. 2:13–15, quoting Hos. 11:1). Be comforted, ye mothers, whose lovely babes have perished in so good a cause and received such an early crown. In a little time the cruel murderer shall feel the weight of so many just curses upon his guilty head, and the Messiah shall reign in spite of his infuriate and feeble rage.

About His Father's Business

We cannot reasonably doubt but the young Redeemer gave early proofs of His divine original. It was no doubt a very pleasing employment to the highly favored parents to rear up this tender plant by a thousand endearing offices, to mark the first buddings of His genius more than mortal, and to observe the blossoms of every heavenly grace that adorned His holy soul. But as it hath seemed good to the wisdom of the Holy Spirit to be very sparing in the history of His private life, after He called His Son out of Egypt, we must be content to remain in ignorance of what is not revealed (Matt. 2:19–23).

Yet as a specimen of the rest, one remarkable occurrence is transmitted down to our knowledge concerning the holy child Jesus. He had numbered but twelve revolving years when accompanying His religious parents to the solemn festival of the Passover; young as He was, He could maintain a dispute even with the doctors in the temple. His parents, not suspecting where He was, seek Him with sorrowful hearts, and the third day restores Him to their longing eyes (Luke 2:41–46): "And he said unto them, How is it that ye sought me?" (Luke 2:49). They did not realize that He had the business of His heavenly Father to look after and that He needed not their paternal care. For though His parents should both forsake Him, the Lord will take Him up (Ps. 27:10). Ye learned doctors, little thought you that the amazing child who talked with you, to the great admiration of every beholder, was He of whom the prophet says, "Unto us a child is born, unto us a son is given:...and his name shall be called Wonderful, Counsellor," and "The mighty God" (Isa. 9:6).

Announced as God's "Beloved Son"
For the space of thirty years He lurked in obscurity in the contemptible village of Nazareth. Who would have suspected that the Son of the carpenter was Himself the "everlasting Father" and "the Creator of the ends of the earth" (Isa. 9:6; 40:28)? But now the time is come when He shows Himself unto Israel.

What venerable person is this who, like the ancient Esau, wears a hairy garment and in the villages of the wilderness preaches the doctrine of repentance, talks of the kingdom of heaven being at hand, of the axe to the root, the fan to the wheat, and the chaff to the fire (Matt. 3:10–12)? It is the forerunner of Christ: "the voice of one crying in the wilderness, Prepare ye the way of the Lord" (Luke 3:4). See how the multitudes flock after him, to his baptism; even Christ Himself condescends to be baptized of him. The hoary baptist wonders that the Master should come to the servant, who was not worthy to perform the meanest office to such an exalted dignitary. But thus it became Him to fulfill all righteousness (Matt. 3:15). Once He was circumcised to sanctify the church that then was, to honor the divine ordinances, and to testify that He was a debtor to do the whole law. And now He is baptized to sanctify the church that is to be and to confirm His faith by this expressive sign in the promise of His everlasting Father. For though He needed not "the washing of regeneration" (Titus 3:5), as we do, when he descended into the baptismal water, it signified the large effusion of the Spirit upon His sacred humanity, to qualify Him fully for His high and saving work. And may we not also think that when He ascended from the consecrated stream, into which He went down with willing steps, He was then assured that in like manner He should lift up His head above the waters of adversity and emerge victorious from under the billows of His Father's wrath? O Jordan, it was a strange thing that befell thee when thy waters drove back their course at the presence of God (Josh. 3:14–17; Ps. 114:3) and when Elijah smote them with his mantle (2 Kings 2:8). But much more strange is this, that He who poured them into thy bed and made "heaven, and earth, and the sea, and the fountains of waters" (Rev. 14:7) is now washed in thy hallowed wave, while from on high the heavens are opened, a voice is heard "from the excellent glory" (2 Peter 1:17), and the Holy Spirit, in the likeness of a dove, descends upon Him (Matt. 3:16–17).

Tempted in the Wilderness by the Devil

Now let us follow the illustrious Redeemer from the banks of Jordan unto the solitary wilderness, where Moses the giver, and Elijah the restorer of the law, fasted forty days and where the ancient Israelites provoked Him forty years. There, too, during the space of forty days, the great Fulfiller of the law abstains from food, being supported by a divine power and fed with holy contemplation (Matt. 4:1–11). But afterward He feels the gnawing power of hunger, to expiate the luxury of Adam in the garden of paradise and to demonstrate the truth of His humanity (Luke 4:2). When lo! The subtle enemy is permitted to assault His virtue by sundry ensnaring artifices. But all his efforts are baffled by this "captain of [our] salvation" (Heb. 2:10). Think it not strange, O humble soul, if this malicious spirit shall tempt with restless importunity even the most atrocious crimes and shall abuse even the sacred oracles to this vile purpose. He came unto the glorious Head "in all points tempted like as we are" (Heb. 4:15). But being resisted by "the sword of the Spirit, which is the word of God" (Eph. 6:17), Satan betakes himself to shameful flight (Luke 4:13; cf. James 4:7).

He Dwelt among Us

Let us now proceed to trace the most interesting steps of our Redeemer's life, when He "dwelt among us" in our flesh (John 1:14). And shall we first listen unto Him as "a teacher come from God" (John 3:2)?

With what inimitable authority (Matt. 7:29)! And with what irresistible wisdom, impartial freedom, undaunted boldness, unwearied diligence, burning zeal—with what homely plainness, condescending humility, tender compassion, amiable meekness, long-suffering patience, divine delight—did He "[preach] righteousness in the great congregation" (Ps. 40:9–10)! How eloquent! How full of pathos! How mighty in the Scriptures! But who can enumerate all the wonderful works which by His own power, and for the manifestation of His own glory, He effected (Ps. 40:5)? The raging element of water He stills with a powerful word and walks upon its rolling surges (Matt. 14:26). Trees withered at His rebuke (Matt. 21:19); fishes have paid His tribute (Matt. 17:27). How often did He give sight to the blind, hearing to the deaf, speech to the dumb, strength to the weak, health to the diseased, and purity to the defiled (Luke 7:22, etc.)? Even strong death could not retain his prisoners when He gave the high command (John 11:43). Never were words as gracious as those He spoke. Never were works as glorious as those He did.

Perhaps it might be inquired in what palace He dwelt, what riches He possessed, what princes was He acquainted with? But though He calls the silver and the gold His own, if He pays tribute, a fish supplies Him with money (Matt. 17:27); if He rides, He must borrow an ass (Matt. 21:2–5). He built the sky and had nowhere "to lay his head" (Matt. 8:20). He prepares the corn and was fed at the table of others (Luke 7:36). O poverty! How dost thou expose to contempt even the greatest wisdom, and most solid virtue, in this degenerate world! But "though he was rich, yet for [our] sakes he became poor, that [we] through his poverty might be rich" (2 Cor. 8:9).

A Man of Sorrows Acquainted with Grief

The faithless and perverse generation among whom He conversed—not content with rejecting His heavenly doctrines, blaspheming His miracles, and staining His moral character with the most odious imputations—arrived at that enormous pitch of wickedness as on many occasions to thirst for His blood. Sometimes they take up stones to cast at Him as an abominable wretch, unworthy to breathe

the vital air (John 8:59); and sometimes they lead Him to the brow of a hill (Luke 4:29), with an impious intention to cast Him down, though in the village where He was born and though a while before they wondered at the gracious words that proceeded out of His mouth (Luke 4:22).

Nor was the conclusion of the scene unlike its beginning. Even to the last we find Him "a man of sorrows" (Isa. 53:3). "Is it nothing to you," O ye children of men (Lam. 1:12)? Much every way. For by His bloody sweat you are purged, by His condemnation you are absolved, by His bonds you are loosed, by His death you are quickened, and "with his stripes [you] are healed" (Isa. 53:5; 1 Peter 2:24). Nor must we regard the last dismal sufferings of the Redeemer in the light of an affecting tragedy, but of an evangelical history.

Obedient unto the Death of the Cross

Already He had made His triumphant, though lowly, entrance into Jerusalem, riding upon an ass, amid the acclamations of the populace, in accomplishment of an ancient prediction (Matt. 21:4–5). His eye had melted with tender compassion over the bloody city (Matt. 23:37–39). He had eaten the last Passover (Matt. 26:17–25) and instituted the new solemnity of the Supper (Matt. 26:26–29). Many excellent discourses He had made to His sorrowful disciples, and by the significant ceremony of washing their feet (John 13:5ff.), He strongly inculcated how by love we should serve one another in all humility (John 13:14).

Gethsemane: Betrayal and Arrest

But as once we saw Him in the wilderness, let us now attend Him into that garden of Gethsemane, the scene of His dreadful agony, where He trod the winepress alone (or rather was trodden in the winepress of His Father's wrath), where He was in all the mysteries of woe, where He beheld the angry face of God (cf. Rev. 14:20) and felt the sting of death, long sharpened (if we may use the expression) upon the stony tables of the law, infixed into His very soul (Matt. 26:36–46). See how He lies all prostrate on the ground and pressed out of measure with an invisible load, till large red drops of blood issue from every opened pore (Luke 22:44)! What words are these, O Savior, that dropped from Thy lips in this sore and bloody conflict, when in the most fervent manner Thou didst deprecate the bitter cup (Matt. 26:39)? Was it the prospect of Thy cruel death? Was it the terror of Thy crucifixion that made Thee to stand aghast and to shrink back with shuddering horror? O no—Thy martyrs have rejoiced even in the sternest tribulations, have bid defiance to all the variety of torture, and resolutely met "the king of terrors"[1] in his most formidable armor. For they beheld the face of God clad with sweet smiles, while their afflictions did abound. But Thine it was to know the power of God's anger: "Who knoweth the power of thine anger? even according to thy fear, so is thy wrath" (Ps. 90:11). O Lord Jesus, it was the burden of our guilt, and it was the lively sense of the Almighty's indignation, that filled Thee with such amazing anguish and extorted from Thy human nature confession of distress, in tears and groans, and prayers unto "him that was able to save [thee] from death" (Heb. 5:7).

But He survives the bloody sweat, being strengthened by an angel and supported by His own divinity, when, lo, the perfidious traitor comes and dares approach with a treacherous kiss to salute those lips that knew no guile.[2] For the wretched gain of thirty pieces of silver—the price of a slave when pushed by an ox that he died, and a goodly price that he was prized at by them (Ex. 21:32)—did this miserable sinner betray his Lord and Master (Luke 22:48). O cursed lust of gold! To what enormous crimes canst thou urge on the human mind! But who are these he brings along with him? Romans

---

1. Editor's note: As Bildad the Shuhite describes the death as the punishment for "him that knoweth not God" (Job 18:21).

2. Editor's note: This is an allusion to Proverbs 24:26, which the AV/KJV translates, "Every man shall kiss his lips that giveth a right answer." The ESV gives the sense more clearly: "Whoever gives an honest answer kisses the lips." The NIV may be best of all, "An honest answer is like a kiss on the lips." The point is that Judas is not honest; he has lying lips, and so the kiss of betrayal—ever since appropriately called a "Judas kiss"—is the antithesis of commitment and affection. The "treacherous kiss" is, in the British vernacular, "a punch on the kisser"!

and Jews sent from the high priests. "Why do the heathen rage, and the people imagine a vain thing," to plot "against the Lord, and against his anointed?" (Ps. 2:1–2). Against whom do they come thus equipped "with swords and staves" (Luke 22:52)? But what is this? They "went backward, and fell to the ground" (John 18:6). Understand, ye wicked, that He is able to slay you with "the breath of his lips" (Isa. 11:4) and cast you down beyond the possibility of rising (Amos 8:14). But His hour is now come—take Him and lead Him away. Let the disciples retire at the permission of their Lord. And thou, "Peter, Put up thy sword" (John 18:11)—leave vengeance unto God (Isa. 63:4; Rom. 12:19).

Trial and Condemnation
"The breath of our nostrils, the anointed of the Lord, was taken in their pits" (Lam. 4:20). He is bound like a malefactor, who proclaims "liberty to the captives" (Isa. 61:1). Easily could He act the Samson upon this occasion. But the justice of His Father forbids it, and the cords of His own love, stronger than all fetters, hold Him fast. Where do they lead Him but to the high priest, as a lamb to the slaughter (Isa. 53:7; Acts 8:32)? In vain does the conscience of Pilate remonstrate the innocence of the accused (Luke 23:4–5, 20–25). In vain does the wife of Pilate dissuade from sanguinary methods and tell about her ominous dream the preceding night (Matt. 27:19). The silly judge, intimidated by the threats and dunned by the incessant clamor of the mob, delivers Jesus unto their will and releases unto them the murderer whom they preferred. What barbarous indignities were done unto Him, both before and after He received His sentence, may justly raise our wonder while they excite our detestation. Lo, He is exceedingly filled with contempt, being forced to wear the ludicrous ensigns of majesty (Matt. 27:28). His crown is a wreath of thorns (Matt. 27:29), His scepter a reed. The Judge of Israel is smitten with a rod reproachfully. He hides not His face from shame and spitting (Matt. 27:30). They rest not here, for His back is prepared for the tearing scourge. In these circumstances of disgrace, He is denied by His only apostle who had the courage to follow Him (Mark 14:67–72). O

Peter, hear you not the witnesses accusing Him falsely? Is this your kindness to your friend? Where is your confident boasting now? But so it was foretold by Christ, and for this let us "pass the time of [our] sojourning here in fear" (1 Peter 1:17).

The Death of the Cross

Ah, how have we made Him to serve with our iniquities! For panting and spent with toil, and covered with blood and sweat, He bears His cross. "His visage was so marred more than any man, and his form more than the sons of men" (Isa. 52:14). And now He is arrived at the appointed place for consummating this melancholy scene. His garments are parted (Matt. 27:35). The assembly of the wicked encompasses Him around. They pierce His hands and feet (Ps. 22:16). See how He hangs suspended on the racking cross, between the heavens and the earth! No fountain relieves His parching thirst! No angel strengthens Him from heaven! No Peter draws a sword in His quarrel! His inexpressible torments are not able to command one tear from the unpitying spectators, who shake their head at Him in cruel scorn, wrest His words, and mock His prayers! Even the sun withdraws his light! O golden ruler of the day, didst thou fly the pain of thy Maker? Or was it incensed justice that arrested thy beams from giving light unto the suffering Surety? But more horrid was the darkness of His soul, when Thou, O heavenly Father, withheld the pleasing beams of Thy countenance (Matt. 27:46). "Persecuted, but not forsaken" (2 Cor. 4:9) may be the motto of the suffering saint but not of the suffering Savior. But even in this "hour, and the power of darkness" (Luke 22:53), He casts not His confidence away (Heb. 10:35), but having commended His mother to a beloved apostle (John 19:26–27), and His spirit unto His beloved Father, He bows the head and renders up the Spirit (Luke 23:46). The earth quakes. The dead arise. The temple rends her veil (Matt. 27:51). Then were ye spoiled, O principalities and powers! Then justice was satisfied, the law was magnified. The mighty work which had employed the thoughts of God from all everlasting, and which shall be the subject of the most delightful contemplation to all the redeemed company, world without end, did then receive its consummation.

O that this dying love[3] of God might dwell forever in our thoughts, constrain us to every duty, and deter us from every sin! Must the Son of God expiate with such direful sufferings sin not His own (2 Cor. 5:21)? What, then, must they endure for their own sins, who refuse to learn from their amazing example, the infinite evil of that abominable thing?

Resurrection and Victory over Sin and the Grave

Great was thy victory, O death, when even the Son of God slept in the chamber of the tomb, a prisoner of darkness, a pale and ghastly corpse. But woe unto us if the gospel history had left Him in the silent grave. Then had the expectation of the poor perished; then had His promise failed forever; then had we been still in our sins, unpurged, unpardoned (1 Cor. 15:17). But the third day beheld Him emerging from the darksome grave. In vain they set a watch and seal the stone. It is not possible He can be held. The wounds of His body are miraculously healed; the separated spirit is reunited by a divine power, before He saw corruption (Ps. 16:10); and He arises as a man refreshed with sleep springs from his bed, when the morning shines with a purple radiance. No more shall infirmity clog Thy flesh, or sorrow cloud Thy brow, O risen Savior. No more shall death reduce Thee under his gloomy power. Thy "warfare is accomplished," and Thou hast "received of the LORD's hand double for all [our] sins" (Isa. 40:2).

O earth, why didst thou quake? And what disturbed your repose, ye sleeping bones? It was at the presence of the God of Jacob, who lately was crucified in weakness but now He is raised in power (2 Cor. 13:4). The earth cast forth her dead. Sleep on, ye remaining prisoners of the dust; a time, a time will come, when ye too shall wake and sing and ascend to meet Him in the air (1 Thess.

---

3. Editor's note: I.e., the love of God in giving His Son to die in the place of sinners so as to become the Savior of all who believe. The "love of God" is not "dying," but God's (unchanging) love is *in* the dying of Jesus, in which Jesus suffers under God's just wrath as the substitutionary atonement for the sin of sinners.

4:17). Ye living saints, rejoice that "death is swallowed up in victory" (1 Cor. 15:54). The grave, that hungry monster, catching the bait of His humanity, was not aware of the hook of His divinity and swallowed its own destruction. Now may we rest in full assurance that all our debt is paid, when by the order of the creditor, the Surety is taken from prison and from judgment. For lo, a shining minister, whose countenance is as lightning and his raiment white as snow, descends to roll away the stone from the holy sepulcher! For fear of him the keepers did shake and became as dead men. No doubt He was fully able to have removed the stone who had power to lay down His life and had power to take it up again. For even the pillars of heaven tremble and are astonished at His reproof. But it was the will of the eternal Father that these excellent and glorious creatures round His throne should put this token of respect upon their Lord and ours, even in His lowest humiliation. Hail, happy day, on which a more glorious work was finished than when He planned the heavens and laid the foundations of the earth! May that sweet day of sacred rest be the joy of our souls! Then may we often join with God and angels in remembering this most illustrious work, a finished redemption.

Ascension and Entrance within the Veil

The victory is complete; what remains but that the Victor shall triumph? The atoning sacrifice is offered; what remains but that the High Priest shall enter within the veil? Forty days He converses with His disciples, instructing them in the nature of His kingdom by His heavenly discourses and confirming them in the certainty of His resurrection by His frequent appearances (Acts 1:3). Then does "he led them out as far as Bethany" and the Mount of Olives (Luke 24:50).[4] By that way He once came to His ignominious cross, and by that way He returns to His glorious crown. And how did He employ the last parting moments but in blessing His beloved apostles and assuring them of His being ever present with them in the discharge of their office, even when they should see Him again no more.

---

4. Editor's note: Bethany is a village on the Mount of Olives.

Could we have stood among that favored few who witnessed this glorious transaction, then would we have seen Him slowly ascending from the earth, not snatched as Elijah in a whirlwind, till an obedient cloud receives Him from the sight of the astonished gazers, who had already seen enough to satisfy their faith: "Lift up your heads… ye everlasting doors," the doors of paradise, "and the King of glory shall come in" (Ps. 24:9). Listen to the triumphant shout wherewith the blessed assembly hailed His arrival. Observe the trophies of His victory, the blunted sting of death, and the keys of hell and the grave. Great was the pomp, thou Sinai didst behold, when the Holy One descended on thy top and out of His right hand went a fiery law; but greater doubtless was the pomp when He "ascended on high" and "led captivity captive" (Ps. 68:18; cf. Eph. 4:8), after He had magnified the law and made it honorable.

The Heavenly Rule of the Mediatorial King
Now reign forever, blessed Lord Jesus, upon Thy heavenly throne. Forever shall a crown of glory encircle Thy radiant head. No more shalt Thou complain of a sorrowful soul or a forsaking God. With what infinite satisfaction shalt Thou forever revolve Thy past agonies and see the travail of Thy soul (Isa. 53:11)! Obedient angels cast their crowns before Thee (Rev. 4:10). With Thee shall the church militant swell their song even in this vale of tears.[5] And unto Thee shall the triumphant church ascribe eternal praise, saying with a loud voice, "Worthy is the Lamb that was slain to receive power, and riches, and wisdom, and strength, and honour, and glory, and blessing" (Rev. 5:12). To join the songs on high, may we also in Thy due time be brought!

Amen.

---

5. Editor's note: The expression "vale of tears" is from the Latin *valle lacrimarum*, origin unknown. This appears in the fourth-century Latin Bible (the Vulgate) in Psalm 84:6 to translate "Valley of Baca" (בְּעֵמֶק הַבָּכָא), *Baca* means "weeping."

The Great Matter and End of Gospel Preaching
A SERMON

This sermon was preached by Rev. William McEwen at the ordination of the Rev. Alexander Dick to be Minister of the Associate congregation of Aberdeen on Thursday, December 7, 1758.

The Great Matter and End of Gospel Preaching

For we preach not ourselves, but Christ Jesus the Lord.
—2 Corinthians 4:5

When you consider the occasion of your present meeting, it will not, I presume, be necessary to make any apology for making choice of this text as the ground of discourse.[1] For it is a theme the consideration of which may not only be very suitable to my brethren in the ministry but very profitable to every gospel hearer. I am sure that it is incumbent upon everyone that is vested with the sacred character of a minister of Jesus Christ to join with the apostle of the Gentiles in this solemn and serious declaration: "We preach not ourselves, but Christ Jesus the Lord." O that every minister could say it with the same sincerity and truth!

In these words you have the duty and character of a preacher of the everlasting gospel exhibited to you, both in negative and positive terms. What ought he not to preach? Himself. What ought he then to preach? Christ Jesus the Lord. Do you not observe that all of the three names of our gracious Redeemer are mentioned here? The frequent repetition of the lovely titles of this wonderful person in the writings of this apostle—which, as some observe, is as good as five hundred times—renders them all like boxes of precious ointment, inexpressibly refreshing to every Christian soul.

- He is called *Christ* to signify His unction to the mediatorial offices. For He was anointed a priest to procure, a prophet to reveal, and a king to apply the blessings of redemption.

---

1. This sermon was preached at the ordination of the Rev. Alexander Dick to be Minister of the Associate congregation of Aberdeen, upon Thursday, December 7, 1758. [Editor's note: You will notice that, in the time-honored practice of Presbyterian churches, this includes a charge to the minister and a charge to the congregation.]

- He is called *Jesus* because, in the execution of these offices to which He was appointed, He "shall save his people from their sins" (Matt. 1:21). This name is pregnant with salvation and "highly exalted…above every name" (Phil. 2:9).

- He is called *the Lord* to denote His true and proper deity and His sovereign dominion. A very extraordinary Lord indeed is Jesus Christ. He was the Lord of His forefathers—for David "calleth him Lord" (Luke 20:44)—and He is the "Lord both of the dead and living" (Rom. 14:9).

But to proceed directly to the subject in view: you easily see that the doctrinal truth we are to declare from these words must be the following:

DOCTRINE: "That it is the character of every faithful minister, and should be the study of every gospel preacher, to preach not himself but Christ Jesus the Lord."

In illustrating this proposition, I shall essay:

I. To inquire into the *import* of this declaration of the apostle, we preach not ourselves, but Christ Jesus the Lord;

II. To point forth some of the *reasons* why it ought to be the character and study of every gospel minister not to preach himself but Christ Jesus the Lord; and

III. Then we shall see what *improvement* should be made of the doctrine by making a few obvious reflections from what may be said.

And these things we will do, if God permit. Let us begin with the first.

I. THE IMPORT

What is imported in the declaration here made by the apostle concerning not only himself but all faithful ministers of the gospel: "we preach not ourselves, but Christ Jesus the Lord."

I shall here content myself with observing only two things:

1. It evidently imports that we are not to make the inventions of our own brain, but the doctrine of Christ, the great matter of our preaching.
2. That we are not to make the advancement of our own worldly interest and reputation, but the glory and honor of Christ, the great end of our ministrations. Favor me with your attention while we endeavor to explain at somewhat further length both these particulars. And,

---

FIRST,

it is as if the apostle had said, "we make Christ Jesus the Lord the great matter and theme of all our sermons."

The minister of Jesus Christ must not content himself even with declaring such things as have a general truth in them. Things that are said may be truth and yet not *the truth*, or "the word of the truth of the gospel" (Col. 1:5). But though we should be far from despising the excellent sentiments of moralists, or our own neglecting to preach the duties of the law and inculcate the necessity of personal righteousness, still Christ should be the main argument of every sermon. As in a regular building, the most remote parts of it are supported by the foundation, without which it were nothing but "a bowing wall...and tottering fence" (Ps. 62:3); so whatever the minister of Jesus Christ shall think fit to insist upon, Christ is his everlasting foundation that imparts to every doctrine solidity and consistency.

The Philosophical Haranguer

He is not like your *philosophical haranguer*, whose sermons are generally nothing but stiff and unaffecting declamations on some moral subjects, who waives the peculiar doctrines of Christianity as dry and speculative points and chooses commonly for his theme those topics that are common for all religions. You may hear a course of sermons from a person of this stamp without ever learning what is the great end of divine revelation or how a fallen creature may emerge from the ruins of his apostasy. He talks much about the beauty of virtue and how conducive is morality to the happiness of mankind in social and private life. It is true, he cannot, for shame's cause, altogether omit mentioning the name of Christ. But it is as seldom as possibly he can; and lest it should be shocking to the polite part of his audience, he commonly veils it under some paraphrase, calling him the sacred author of our religion, that finished pattern of obedience, or the like. I have read in a famous author "that some have avoided pronouncing the name of Christ in their discourses, because it is a harsh monosyllable, and likewise clogged with too many consonants."[2]

The Legal Declaimer

Nor is the gospel minister like your *legal declaimer*, whose character it is to be always inculcating the duties but seldom the privileges of Christianity. Instead of making privilege the foundation of duty, he makes duty the foundation of privilege. It is true, he may seem to entertain an abhorrence of the before-mentioned *philosophical haranguer*, and to talk in a more baptized and Christian style, and pay a greater compliment to Christ Jesus the Lord in the strain of his discourse; yea, he will even not scruple to tell his hearers at

---

2. Editor's note: Something similar is said by Isaac Watts in his discourse "The Improvement of the Mind" in *The Works of the Rev. Isaac Watts D.D.* (London: Longman et al., 1813), 8:209, where he says, "I have heard it hinted, that the name of Christ has been banished out of polite sermons, because it is a monosyllable of so many consonants, and so harsh a sound." Watts apparently "heard" this said ("hinted"), and cites no written source, so it seems altogether likely that McEwen picked it up from his reading in Watts.

some times that they cannot merit anything at God's hand, and that they can do nothing in their own strength, and therefore we need to seek the aid of divine grace for the performance of this or the other duty. But alas! These necessary points are so faintly handled and so superficially insisted on as to leave but very faint impressions on the mind. Indeed, though he does not openly go over to the camp of the Roman doctors by crying up the merit of good works and crying down imputed righteousness altogether, he is afraid to insist upon the opposite Protestant doctrines, except upon some rare occasion, as suppose a person in the agonies of death or under the horrors of conscience. He is always exhorting his hearers to perform duties but seldom to believe. He hampers the general gospel call with absolute conditions and impossible qualifications, and turning the gospel into a new law that prescribes easier terms of life than the first covenant allowed of (as sincerity, or repentance), he makes the gospel of Christ of none effect. For if we should speak accurately, the terms of life that are prescribed in the second covenant are so far from being easier than those prescribed in the first that, on the contrary, they are infinitely more difficult than ever: for the redemption of the soul is precious and would have ceased forever without the shedding of blood by a person of infinite dignity.

The Evangelical Preacher of Christ
But the evangelical preacher of Jesus Christ, though he should have ever so deep acquaintance with the scene of philosophy, forgets it when he ascends the pulpit to show unto his hearers the way of salvation; and as Aaron's serpent swallowed up the other serpents (Ex. 7:12), so does the wisdom of the cross all other wisdom (1 Cor. 1:17).

1. Christ as mediator. The glorious person, the mysterious incarnation, the amazing satisfaction of Christ Jesus the Lord, the glories of His exalted state, His mediatorial characters, offices, and relations—these are his darling themes on which he expatiates with a peculiar delight. And whether these topics that have not the most immediate relation to Christ are the subjects of his discourse, yet still it may be

said of all his sermons what the apostle says of Christians: "of him are ye in Christ Jesus" (1 Cor. 1:30). They have no being but in Him; in Him they live and move. Whatever mystery, whatever privilege, whatever duty he chooses to explain, still Christ is "all, and in all" (Col. 3:11).

- If he insists on a divine attribute, he declares how it shines forth in Christ with the brightest evidence (2 Cor. 4:6; Col. 2:9).
- If on a promise, he explains how in Christ it is "yea, and… Amen" (2 Cor. 1:20).
- If on a command, he inculcates the necessity of obedience by motives drawn from Jesus Christ and how impossible it is for us to obey without first being united to Him as the head of the vital influences.

2. Christ as all and in all (Col. 3:11). Christ is the beginning; Christ is the end; Christ is the middle; Christ is the all of every sermon. With Him, he comforts the drooping heart; with Him, he corrects the wandering transgressor. To Him he can apply these emphatic words of Jeremiah:

> Thou art my battle axe and weapons of war:
> for with thee will I break in pieces the nations,
> and with thee will I destroy kingdoms;
> and with thee will I break in pieces the horse and his rider;
> and with thee will I break in pieces the chariot and his rider;
> with thee also will I break in pieces man and woman;
> and with thee will I break in pieces old and young;
> and with thee will I break in pieces the young man and the maid;
> I will also break in pieces with thee the shepherd and his flock;
> and with thee will I break in pieces the husbandman and his yoke of oxen;
> and with thee will I break in pieces captains and rulers.
> (Jer. 51:20–23)

3. Christ as the crucified Savior. Lest any should think that this character of making Christ Jesus the sole matter of our sermons is but chimerical, I shall produce the particular example of this same apostle Paul, in his first epistle to the Corinthians, chapter 2:2: "I determined not to know any thing among you, save Jesus Christ, and him crucified." What, I beseech you, is the language of this? Is it not a lively confirmation of the present truth? Here is a man of genius, who was educated at the famous school of Gamaliel and who was well acquainted with the most eloquent compositions of ancient poets, orators, and philosophers. It was in his power to have entertained these Corinthians with fine poetical and philosophical discourses and have made them admire his wisdom and erudition. "But, O ye Corinthians, it is not (as if he had said) your applause I seek after, but your salvation. Therefore, Christ Jesus is my theme: Christ Jesus in His inglorious cross."

Some, indeed, might have been apt to reply, "Truly, Paul, this subject of a crucified Christ may do indifferently well to preach about in some obscure country village where the people are not great judges of refined sentiment; but when you come to a polite city, like Corinth, what harm would there be, though you should waive your favorite topics of the cross and give the polite citizens some display of your fine taste and universal learning? For we assure you such a doctrine as that will never take in a place like this. So, take it to second thoughts and deliberate upon it, whether this would not be the most prudent method." "Nay," says the apostle of the Gentiles, "I will deliberate no more on such a subject; I am quite at a point about it. It is not rudeness;[3] I could do otherwise. It is not rashness; I have deliberately and peremptorily resolved, and my resolutions never shall be shaken that I dwell on no other subject, even in your fine city of Corinth, but Jesus Christ and Him crucified."

---

3. Editor's note: *Rudeness* is used here in its now archaic usage of being "uncultured" or "simple." Nowadays it means being "discourteous" or "giving offense."

So much for the first thing imported in preaching, "not ourselves, but Christ Jesus the Lord"—namely, that we are to make the doctrine of Christ the great matter of our preaching.

SECOND,

it is as if the apostle had said, "we make not the advancing of our worldly interest and reputation but the honor and glory of Christ the great end of our ministry."

For it is a very melancholy truth that there are persons who may have the glorious Redeemer for the matter of their sermons even when they are not in the least swayed by regard to His glory and honor but are solely animated by sordid interest and groveling pride. A person of this character preaches himself even when he preaches Christ. Though he seems to make as if he wanted his hearers should be in love with his Lord and Master, yet he chiefly intends they should admire himself. When he composes his sermons, he is more solicitous how he shall touch the passions, please the fancy, and tickle the ears of his hearers than how to instruct, than how to persuade, than how to break the heart and espouse the sinner to Christ. That he may be esteemed a man of learning, it is ordinary for him to cloud his meaning with strange words with which the ears of the common people are not accustomed; and how very often we mistake that which is wonderfully dark for wonderfully deep. And that he may be reputed a man of piety, he finds himself under a necessity of counterfeiting those devout affections to which he is an entire stranger. Pride chooses his subjects, invents his ornaments, and animates his delivery. What he is chiefly desirous to know, when the sermon is over, is not what benefit his hearers have reaped but what are their sentiments about himself. If he gain the applause and is extolled to the skies as no ordinary man, his end is reached and he blesses himself in his fancied superiority unto others. But if he shall understand that they consider him as but an indifferent, ordinary preacher, he is extremely mortified, being disappointed in his principal aim.

Christ Must Increase, the Faithful Servant Decrease

How unlike to this is the character of the servant of Jesus Christ, who is constrained by His love and is willing that He should increase and himself should decrease (John 3:30)? He chooses for the ground of his sermons those subjects which will give him the best opportunity for recommending Christ Jesus the Lord rather than of ingratiating himself with the world or displaying his own abilities. He does not clothe his ideas in strange words and unusual language, that he may be admired by the ignorant, but he chooses such expressions as are common and intelligible to everyone rather than high-flown expressions that are not generally understood. For as Augustine says, "An iron key that can open a treasury, is preferable to a golden one not fitted for the purpose."[4]

He does not affect new and unheard-of ways of speaking to illustrate the commonly received doctrines of the blessed gospel, but he will even abstain from those phrases that are capable of a dexterous[5] interpretation if they are offensive to weak Christians. He is ever seeking to adapt himself to persons of common rank and capacity—"not many wise men...not many mighty, not many noble, are called" (1 Cor. 1:26)—and he never discovers in his air, his looks and gestures, contempt and high disdain of those whom he pretends to instruct. If he should happen to win the applause of the common people, he rejoices not greatly in it; and if he miss of their applause, it

---

4. Editor's note: This quotation attributed to Augustine has defied all my efforts to ascertain any source in Augustine's own writings. It seems to be a paraphrase of the words of the English Puritan John Collinges, who says in the preface to his 1683 work *The Intercourses of Divine Love betwixt Christ and His Church* that while he was "yet a very young man," he learned from Augustine ("he saith") that "an iron key is better than one made of gold if it will better open the door, for that is all the use of a key." Many since have assumed Collinges was quoting Augustine (e.g., James Comper Gray and Rev. George M. Adams, *The Biblical Encyclopedia: The Old Testament* (Cleveland, Ohio: F. M. Barton, 1903), 3:452 (note on Jer. 25:1, 11), but no one, Collinges included, cites the source in Augustine's writings.

5. Editor's note: *Dexterous* is used here in an older sense to mean "clever"—in a showy way, unbecoming of plain-speaking gospel preaching. Today, dexterous just means neat and capable; it literally means "right-handed."

is "a small thing" to him to be judged of man's judgment, for "he that judgeth [him] is the Lord" (1 Cor. 4:3–4).

Though the faithful minister of Jesus Christ will not affect a slovenly way of preaching and descend to low familiarities of addiction, taking his images and metaphors from the law and sordid occurrences of life, at the same time he does not hunt after a pompous and gaudy diction, or what is styled by this apostle the "enticing words of man's wisdom" (1 Cor. 2:4). I would not be sought from this observation to cry down all study in a minister to find out acceptable words; indeed, to preach the Lord Jesus Christ with true eloquence is not inconsistent with the greatest humility.

The Eloquence of Scripture
We cannot sufficiently admire the eloquence of the Scripture. There is nothing in Homer himself that can rival the sublimity of the song of Moses, the majesty of Isaiah, the tenderness of Jeremiah, or the loftiness of David. And then the herdsman Amos is justly considered by Augustine, in his book *On Christian Doctrine*, as a great pattern of lofty expression. Nor is this peculiar to the writings of the Old Testament; the most simple writers of the New Testament want not very fine strokes of eloquence. So much did the apostle Paul excel in this that he was actually taken for Mercurius, the god of eloquence, when he was in the town of Lystra (Acts 14:12).

Cautions about Human Eloquence
But permit me here to lay down two necessary cautions to all the admirers of human eloquence in evangelical discourses.

1. That the efficacy of the doctrine must never be ascribed to it. There are too many who allow of no other energy in the word but the moving of the affections by an inspiring orator, while the invisible and irresistible operation of the divine Spirit is altogether forgotten and despised. But though Paul should plant, and Apollos should water, it is God alone that gives the increase (1 Cor. 3:7). Thus, though soldiers should burnish their armor, yet in the day of battle they will not

wound their enemies because they glitter upon the day but because they are of strong and solid temper.

2. That there is a false rhetoric that men are very apt to mistake for the true. For it is not every person that can fill a discourse with crowded similes, forced conceits, bombastic phrases, jingling quibbles, swelling sentences, who may immediately lay claim to the character of "Apollos,…an eloquent man, and mighty in the scriptures" (Acts 18:24). The windows that are most daubed with paint give not the greatest light, and the trees that are most covered with leaves bear not always the greatest quantity of fruit: in like manner, these discourses that are adorned with the greatest profusion of ornaments are not always the most informing or fruitful.

To conclude this observation, sermons that are composed and delivered in this false taste may be known by one of these two marks: either they are heard with contempt and disdain or they serve only to fill the hearers' minds with admiration of the speaker but not at all to inspire with the sentiments he would inculcate. Furthermore, the minister of Jesus Christ, who preaches not himself, considers eloquence and the gospel as the gift and the altar. It was not the gift that sanctified the altar but the altar that sanctified the gift (Matt. 23:18–19): so it is not eloquence that sanctifies the gospel but the gospel that sanctifies eloquence. Having finished what I intended on the first head of this discourse, which was to inquire into the import of Paul's declaration here, "we preach not ourselves, but Christ Jesus the Lord," I will now proceed to inquire,

---

II. THE REASONS

The reasons why every minister of Jesus Christ should make Him the great matter and end of all his sermons. And,

---

FIRST,

as to the reasons why Christ should be the great matter of our sermons.

As I said before, we are very far from despising rational and moral truths, which are excellent in their own nature and which it may be very profitable for a gospel minister to be acquainted with. The duties of the law are also to be preached, as we said before. But let philosophy, let morality beware how they use that room which belongs not unto them. Let them shine in their own firmament, but let them not presume to aspire to a higher dignity than they are originally destined unto. Let not this Reuben seek to ascend his father's bed, lest he lose his excellency (Gen. 49:3–4). Let not this Hagar presume to lord it over her mistress, lest she be cast out (Gen. 21:10). Let not this woman (philosophy), though extremely talkative, speak in church (1 Cor. 14:34). For if we make philosophical disquisitions the subject of our sermons, instead of Christ, then,

A High Indignity to Christ

This is a high indignity to Him who is the foundation of all our hopes and our gracious deliverer from misery and sin. O how dishonorable to Christ to esteem any truth more as it comes from Cicero, Epictetus, or Marcus Antonius[6] than as it comes from the great prophet of the world! It is a notable effect of the atheistic pride of men, who pretend to inculcate obedience unto God, to betake themselves to other rules and directions as more plain, more full, more efficacious than those of the gospel, which are the teachings of Christ Himself, "teaching for doctrines the commandments of men" (Matt. 15:9). How reproachful is it to Christianity for a pretended preacher of it to prefer those topics that are common to it with all other religions, to

---

6. Editor's note: These are all famous Roman orators. Marcus Antonius (d. 87 BC) was the grandfather of the triumvir Mark Anthony (83–30 BC), whose memory is kept alive today by Shakespeare's play *Julius Caesar* and the Hollywood movie *Cleopatra*.

those by which it is peculiarly distinguished from them! "Do ye thus requite the LORD, O foolish people and unwise?" (Deut. 32:6).

Unprofitable to the Hearers
As it is the height of shameful ingratitude, so it is utterly unprofitable to the hearers; for the great end of preaching never can be reached by such discourses. The philosophical haranguer can neither inform the judgment nor affect the heart.

1. He cannot inform the judgment. Even the truths he teaches are not satisfactory to the mind, when separated from Christ, who is "the true Light, which lighteth every man that cometh into the world" (John 1:9). In Christ alone all the lines of truth do center. In Him only they have a firm consistency. If truth is not learned as it is in Jesus, the mind remains in midnight darkness (Eph. 4:1); and, after a long course of attendance on such instructions, one may be as ignorant as a heathen in the knowledge of salvation. Who knows not how the great masters of philosophy have lost themselves in endless disputes about the nature of morality and moral obligation? And what is the reason they scorn the aid of revelation, which would furnish them an easy solution to many perplexing questions? "Professing themselves to be wise, they became fools" (Rom. 1:22). Truly, if you take Christ out of the Bible, the Bible itself will be but an inconsistent composition, and we could no more expect to derive from it the satisfactory knowledge of any divine truth whatsoever. The blindness of the modern Jews bears witness to this, who, though they have the Scriptures of the Old Testament among their hands yet, not finding Christ in them, they are almost as absurd in their doctrinal system as the very heathens themselves.

2. He cannot affect the heart; for, as professors of religion that have no union with Christ are but withered branches, so truths, even of religion, when separated from Him are but dry and sapless speculations. Christ is the fountain of truth (Zech. 13:1), and when water is separated from the fountain, it will soon gather putrefaction and

turn into a puddle. If any should be of the mind that to reform the world, the best way would be preach the moral truths and leave out the peculiar doctrines of Christianity from our sermons, I beseech them seriously to consider the following queries.

- If such discourses are the most effectual means of reforming the world, why did not the great moralists of the Gentiles reform the world? Yea, why did they not reform themselves from the gross irregularities of their own lives by reducing their own refined theories into practice?

- Why did the apostles make a crucified Christ the theme of their sermons? Why did they not rather preach the great beauty of virtue, the great dignity of human nature? Then the offense of the cross would have ceased; then they would not have suffered persecution.

- Was it by preaching of moral truths that the apostles captivated the world to the obedience of faith and triumphed over their inveterate prejudices, their deep-rooted lusts and vicious propensities? Was it thus they laid the "axe...unto the root of the trees" (Matt. 3:10), that "wickedness" might "be broken as a tree" (Job 24:20)? Was it thus they prevailed against the emperor's sword and the wit of the philosopher? No, surely. The world was not reformed by moral haranguers in the days of the apostles, and have we any reason to conclude that such discourses will be more successful in our days? On the contrary, is there not abundant reason to think that God, who is jealous of His Mediator's glory, will not bless such sermons with success?

The Pitiful Reward of Christless Sermons

Let me hear and address every such preacher, in the words of a modern author: "Had you all the refined science of Plato and Socrates, and all the skill of morals attained unto by Zeno, Seneca, or Epictetus: were you furnished with all the flowing oratory of Cicero and the thunder of Demosthenes: were all these talents united in one man and you are the person so richly endowed; and could you employ them in every sermon you preach, you could have no reason to hope that you could convert or save one soul, while you leave the gospel entirely out of your discourses."[7] Such creatures can neither save themselves nor them that hear them. And as they "walk in the light of [their own] fire, and in the sparks that [they] have kindled," is there not ground to fear that "this shall [they] have of [God's] hand," and so "shall lie down in sorrow" (Isa. 50:11)? "O my soul, come not thou into their secret; unto their assembly, mine honour, be not thou united" (Gen. 49:6).

Poor will be the compensation, and pitiful the reward, of those preachers who leave out Christ in their sermons, to be complimented by unbelievers as men of distinguished parts and superior abilities; for though they gain the applause of infidels, "what is the hope of the hypocrite, though he hath gained, when God taketh away his soul?" (Job 27:8).

And what we have said of the philosophical haranguer, we may also affirm of the legal declaimer, who inculcates the precepts of the law without pointing forth Jesus Christ as "the end of the law for righteousness" (Rom. 10:4).[8] Though indeed, in the law righteousness is revealed (Rom. 1:17), yet the gospel is the only ministration of it. The law may demand righteousness, but the gospel confers it. When the law comes, the soul may indeed die, but sin revives (Rom. 7:9); but when the gospel comes, the soul revives and sin dies. It was not without a mystery that Moses could not lead the chosen seed into the Promised Land; for though the natural force of the law is not abated (as it is said of Moses), it is become "weak through the flesh" to give life (Rom. 8:3), and it is the province of Jesus Christ alone—the true Joshua—to give us rest (Matt. 11:28).

---

7. Editor's note: This quotation is from "An Humble Attempt toward the Revival of Practical Religion among Christians" and can be found in *The Works of the Rev. Isaac Watts D.D.* (London: Longman et al., 1813), 4:600.

8. Editor's note: The "end" of the law is not its annihilation or total termination but rather its *telos* or goal. Christ is its "end" in that He is the only perfect lawkeeper and its accomplished purpose.

To conclude then, this is the sum of what I have said: Suppose a minister should come forth, armed with all the literature of the schools and all the thunders of Sinai, he will be but like David in Saul's armor, unable to do any execution; neither will he work any salvation in the earth (compare Ps. 74:12). But Christ Jesus and the Lord, like the small stone taken "out of the brook" of the Scriptures, lights with a vengeance into the forehead of a very high thing that would "defy the armies of the living God" (1 Sam. 17:26, 40, 49).

SECOND,

I will now say a few things about making Christ Jesus the Lord the great end of our ministry.

And I cannot sufficiently express the great iniquity and solidity and danger of having no other end in our preaching but to advance our own interest or gain the applause of men. Consider,

How Great a Sin It Is

Is it thus we resemble the "meek and lowly" Jesus (Matt. 11:29), who sought not "his own glory: but...his...that sent him" (John 7:18; 8:50; 9:4)? Is it thus we requite the condescending Savior, who "made himself of no reputation," by snatching at the honors belonging to Him alone (Phil. 2:7)? Indeed, where pride and self are wholly predominant, it argues a little groveling soul, destitute of the grace of God. Neither is it in the power of any person, who is wholly influenced by them, to do so much as one hour's faithful service unto God.

The Folly Is Equal to the Sin

For pride and self are vices which very commonly have the peculiar happiness of disappointing their own schemes. Alas! If pride is our sovereign principle, if applause is our ultimate end, how miserably will we be disappointed? Fame is a shadow; if you pursue it, it will fly. Fame is a bubble; if you grasp it, it will break. Full often the ambitious preacher stands confessed to the discerning Christian, and instead of the vainglory he is so passionately fond of, he meets with that contempt which he so richly deserves. For this love of fame, or desire of vainglory, like "the ointment of his right hand…bewrayeth itself" (Prov. 27:16). For there is something of that genuine simplicity in the voice, air, and gesture of him who is animated by the love of Christ, which the false pretender cannot imitate by his utmost art. Hence it is very ordinary for such a preacher to seem to be all in raptures when his audience is not in the least affected. For he throws out his vehemence at very improper places, and without discretion, which renders him extremely contemptible.

Dangerous Consequences
Consider, lastly, the dangerous consequences, both to minister and people, that may attend upon such a method of preaching as this. It is not at all to be supposed that a minister of this ambitious turn of mind will be countenanced by God in the discharge of his ministerial function, seeing God resisteth the proud (James 4:6). And though he should be so far assisted by the common influences of the Spirit as to acquit himself in the external duties of his office to the approbation of men—yea, though his labors should be crowned with success in converting and edifying the hearers—yet sure I am it is not at all so probable that this will be the case, as if he were of the contrary temper, for He "giveth grace unto the humble" (James 4:6).

But let us further suppose that he should be universally esteemed among men and his labors crowned with more than ordinary success; yet still he cannot be approved of God nor be entitled unto that glorious reward provided for His faithful servants, who serve Him with their spirits in the gospel of His Son (Rom. 1:9). How shall proud ministers enter these blessed abodes, where proud angels could not stay (see Isa. 14:12–15; Matt. 25:41; 2 Peter 2:4; Jude 6; Rev. 12:9)?

But, on the other hand, when a minister of the gospel has it for his undivided aim to advance the honor of his glorious Lord and Master, such is the goodness of God that he will not ordinarily suffer his reputation to sink even among men; for this is his determined method of procedure in the general course of providence, that "he that humbleth himself shall be exalted" (Luke 14:11). And though his labors should not prove so successful as could be wished, or "though Israel be not gathered, yet shall [he] be glorious in the eyes of the LORD" (Isa. 49:5).

III. THE IMPROVEMENTS

A few obvious reflections, or inferences, from what has been said, shall shut up this discourse.

FIRST,

we may be informed whence it comes about that the public state of religion among us is at such a low pass in the day and time wherein our lot is cast.

"Lord," said the devout sister of Mary, "if thou hadst been here, my brother had not died" (John 11:21). So may I say, "Hadst Thou, O Lord, been in the sermons of our modern preachers, there would not have been so many dead souls in our congregations and so many on the very brink of giving up the ghost." It is reported there are seen in the mines a kind of spirits or fairies who imitate real workmen and seem to be very busy in every part of their work, but after all, there is nothing done. These beings, whether real or imaginary, are but too just emblems of all preachers who leave Christ Jesus the Lord out of their elaborate compositions. Let them be ever so busy, they are busy about nothing.

I have no intention to insult any person whatsoever nor to depress any order of men with a view to raise the character of a particular party. Let such unworthy views be far removed from us. But is it not a melancholy truth? (Sorry should we be, there is so much ground for seeing it.) Is it not a melancholy truth, I say, that too many preachers of our time have not the Lord Jesus, either for their matter or end? Is not He the stone rejected by the builders, though He be the head of the corner (Luke 20:17; Acts 4:11; 1 Peter 2:7)? Are there not many preachers who are perhaps better versed in classical authors than in the Holy Scriptures?

Polite Apostates from God's Grace, to Wit
How much reason to fear, lest a pretended rational religion has obtained among us, little different from Deism and having scarcely any relation to Christ Jesus the Lord? Some publish philosophical inquiries and moral disquisitions and call them sermons; into what times are we fallen! And even the more serious part of the ministry are too much strangers in many places to the evangelical method of winning souls to Christ. "For Moses of old time hath in every city"— I will not say in every synagogue but in many synagogues—"them that preach him…every sabbath" (Acts 15:21). As in the days of this apostle, the two great competitors with the doctrine of Jesus Christ were the philosophy of the Gentiles and the ceremonies of the Jews (1 Cor. 1:23); so in the days wherein we live, Jesus's two great rivals seem to be "the boasted light of nature"[9] and the imperfect works of the law.

SECOND,
and will it not require an extraordinary charity for us to think of many preachers in our day, that they have the glory of Christ and the salvation of souls for their great end, who will intrude themselves upon reclaiming[10] congregations, in flat contradiction to all the principles both of religion and generosity?[11] What can be more

---

9. Editor's note: This expression appears in Philip Skelton, *Deism Revealed* (London, 1751), 142, which may conceivably be McEwen's source.

10. Editor's note: A "reclaiming" congregation was a dissenting congregation that was reclaiming its right to call its own minister. See William Wilson, *A Defence of the Reformation-Principles of the Church of Scotland* (Glasgow, 1769), 446.

11. Editor's note: This section of McEwen's sermon is basically a defense of the secession from the established Church of Scotland in 1733. Here, he addresses ministerial unfaithfulness in terms of the willingness of men to be forced upon congregations which, were they free to choose their minister, would not have accepted such a presentation by the Heritor of the parish, who had a feudal jurisdiction over the church in the parish.

evident from the Word of God than that it is the province of the church members to elect and nominate her own officers (see Acts 6:6)? We read, indeed, of the centurion who built the Jews a synagogue (Luke 7:3–5), but not that he acted as a patron, to present a teacher unto it, though he might have pleaded power of doing it upon a better foundation than any modern patron. Yea, is it not an encroachment upon the very rights of mankind and the liberties of a free people? You may, indeed, choose your lawyer, or your physician, but not your minister; no, this belongs to the patron of the parish, no matter whether he be a heretic, or a profane person, or a bitter enemy of the church. If he has money enough to purchase this right of presenting, no other qualification is requisite in the least. Perhaps he has some friend to gratify, and therefore he authoritatively presents a person you never saw, nor ever heard of, or a person whom you would not willingly take for your pastor. But, if you mutter or reclaim,[12] then you must be held for a seditious or schismatic set of men that can be pleased with nothing. Alas! How shall a patron be a proper judge of the person who is to take the charge of my soul, when there are too many patrons that have no concern for their own souls?

Pardon me if I say that it is a custom shocking to common sense as well as diametrically opposite to the rules of the Word of God. And whether it has ever tended to promote religion, peace, and unity in the church, let experience declare and testify.

I know, indeed, there is a very strong exception to all that we have said on this subject, which is considered by very many as an irrefragable argument for compliance with the present method of settling vacant congregations. And it is this: "That the settling of congregations by presentations is according to law; and there is no other way of obtaining a settlement but by accepting a presentation." Indeed, this argument is so convincing that I would not so much as attempt to make any reply were I also convinced that religion is a thing merely political and that we need not pay any regard to

---

12. Editor's note: I.e., dissent.

The Great Matter and End of Gospel Preaching 323

the rules of the Word except insofar as they comport with a present civil administration.[13] But the argument happens unluckily quite to enervate itself by proving more than is necessary. For it would also prove that the pleading of the Jews, in another case, was strong and valid: "We have a law, and by our law he ought to die, because he made himself the Son of God" (John 19:7). And here a large field might be opened for just invectives against those persons, who with their utmost efforts promote this anti-Christian usurpation and yet are always declaring against divisive courses, though nothing can be more evident than that they themselves are taking all possible methods to rend and divide the poor church. Yet they will not take with the charge in the least, but raise a hideous noise of schism and division against such as adhere to those principles, which are presently professed and authorized by the fundamental laws of this land.

But let us rather talk of this ungrateful subject in the style of lamentation. "O God, thou hast cast us off, thou hast scattered us, thou hast been displeased; O turn thyself to us again" (Ps. 60:1). How deplorable is it that this enormous grievance, so heavily complained of by the greatest part of serious ministers and people in this national church, and even inconsistent with the very fundamental articles of the union of the two nations,[14] should not only be patiently

---

13. It is not hereby intended in the least to distill disloyal principles into the minds of any or to foment disaffection to the present civil government. Everybody knows that the persons who complain of patronages, as a grievance, hard as firm friends to His Majesty, and the Protestant Succession, as any subjects whatsoever. Yea, it is very well known that the yoke of patronage was released about the neck of this church, at a time when the state ministry inclined to Jacobitism, in the latter end of Queen Anne's reign, in resentment to the zeal for the Hanoverian family, which was showed at that time by the Church of Scotland: of this his late Majesty King George I was so sensible, that when application was made for a redress of this grievance, and Act was passed in the year 1719 making the presentee's acceptance necessary to the validity of the presentative. And if it had not been for those men, who acted such a mean part as to snatch at presentations wherever they could obtain them, without the least regard to the inclinations of the people, this church would have been, by that favorable Act, restored to their former privilege.

14. In the Act passed by the Scottish Parliament, 16 January 1707, ratified by the English Parliament, March 7 ensuing, it is enacted "that the true Protestant

submitted unto by the prevailing party in our judicatories but considered by them rather as a privilege than a burden. Do we not seem to be in love with our fetters? How easy were it for our judicatories quite to enervate the Patronage Act,[15] if they had a mind so to do, by prohibiting the accepting of presentations, which no law presently in being forbids to be done? How have our "hands made the snares wherewith we are caught"? Are there not abundant reasons to think that God is saying to us, "I will go and return to my place, till they acknowledge their offence, and seek my face" (Hos. 5:15)?

THIRD,

lastly, you that are gospel hearers and fellow Christians may also be informed, from the doctrine we have taught, what should be your aim in your attendance upon divine ordinances. As it should be our great design to preach Christ, so it is yours to learn Christ. Though the minister should preach Christ ever so much, unless you learn Christ, you do what lies in your power to make him labor in vain and spend his strength for nothing. Alas for the unprofitable, negligent, and wanton hearing of the Word that prevails at this day and time! Christ Jesus the Lord is the great subject of our sermons; and a noble theme He is, indeed, to expatiate upon. In His name and by His authority we preach to you the gospel of your salvation, and woe! woe unto us, if we have not His glory for our ultimate end, if it is only your applause we are seeking after. Yet are there not

---

religion, as presently professed within this kingdom, with the worship, discipline, and government of this church, should continue without alteration in all succeeding generations." Now, it is evident that the settling of kirks by presentations, contrary to the will of the people, was a very material alteration in the government of the church.

15. Editor's note: The Patronage Act of 1712 in the British Parliament was, to use its longer title, An Act to Restore the Patrons to Their Ancient Rights of Presenting Ministers to the Churches Vacant in That Part of Great Britain Called Scotland. This cast a long shadow across the Scottish church and was the material cause of the Secession of 1733, from which came the various Seceder churches and the Relief church in the eighteenth century, and the Disruption of 1843, from which the Free Church of Scotland emerged.

The Great Matter and End of Gospel Preaching

many hearers who come to hear the minister preach, not as though he were to preach Christ that as though he were to preach himself? It is not that they may be acquainted with the Christ, whom the minister preaches, but that they may be acquainted with the minister that preaches Him, that they may know what he will say on such a subject and how he will acquit himself upon such an occasion.

Forget the Man and Consider the Message
But, my brethren, if we are what we profess to be, it is neither your applause we are courting nor do we dread your censure in the faithful discharge of that ministry we have received of the Lord to fulfill it; and if you do not learn Christ Jesus, and the truth as it is in Him, though you should commend us ever so much, it will be but a poor compensation for our labors. We beseech you, therefore, to forget us altogether and to consider principally the message we bring; for truly it is "worthy of all acceptation" (1 Tim. 1:15), "for we preach… Christ Jesus the Lord" as the only all-sufficient Savior, every way adapted to your need, whatsoever you are.

- Art thou a foolish sinner? We preach Christ Jesus the Lord, as made of God, unto you, wisdom (1 Cor. 1:30).

- Art thou a guilty sinner? We preach Christ Jesus the Lord, as made of God, unto you, righteousness (1 Cor. 1:30).

- Art thou an unholy and polluted sinner? We preach Christ Jesus the Lord, as made of God, unto you, sanctification (1 Cor. 1:30).

- Art thou a miserable and captive sinner? We preach Christ Jesus the Lord, as made of God, complete redemption (1 Cor. 1:30).

- Art thou a hardhearted sinner? We preach Christ Jesus the Lord, a Prince and Savior, exalted to give unto you repentance (Acts 5:31).

- Art thou a diseased sinner? We preach Christ Jesus the Lord, as the balm in Gilead and the physician there (Jer. 8:22).

- Art thou a dead and lifeless sinner? We preach Christ Jesus the Lord as "the resurrection, and the life" (John 11:25).

Preaching Christ the Great Ordinance for Your Salvation
Sinners of every nation of the world, of every station of life, of every sex and age, sinners of every size and temper, we "preach Christ Jesus the Lord" as God's great ordinance for your salvation. And we testify and declare that if any of you shall perish, it shall not be for want of a Savior.

- And if you will not hear but will despise this Christ Jesus the Lord, whom we preach, saying, "How shall this man save us?" then be it at your peril; for, "How shall [ye] escape, if [you] neglect so great salvation?" (Heb. 2:3).

- And whether you embrace the Savior or not, know that the election shall obtain: as many as are ordained to eternal life shall believe (Acts 13:48) and purify their heart in "obeying the truth through the Spirit" (1 Peter 1:22).

"Ye see your calling, brethren, how that not many wise men after the flesh, not many mighty, not many noble, are called: but God hath chosen the foolish things of the world to confound the wise; and God hath chosen the weak things of the world to confound the things which are mighty; and base things of the world, and things which are despised, hath God chosen, yea, and things which are not, to bring to nought things that are: that no flesh should glory in his presence" (1 Cor. 1:26–29). For we preach Christ Jesus the Lord—to the Jews a stumbling block and to the Greeks foolishness, but to them that are called, both Jews and Greeks, "Christ the power of God, and the wisdom of God" (1 Cor. 1:23–24).

THE CHARGE TO THE MINISTER

Dear Brother,

The work and office to which you are now separated and called, to serve God in the gospel of His Son as a minister and a witness, is indeed very great and important. According to the judgment of an apostle, "Who is sufficient for these things?" (2 Cor. 2:16), "but [y]our sufficiency is of God," and your reward is with Him (2 Cor. 3:5). I shall suggest but a very few things unto you relative to your deportment in that character werewith you are now clothed. And "I beseech you to suffer the word of exhortation," which I desire also to take to myself.

Preach Christ, Not Yourself

First of all, I would say unto you, let it be your resolution, with the apostle, to "preach not [yourself], but Christ Jesus the Lord" (2 Cor. 4:5). Make the peculiar doctrines of Christ your great theme. Let the blessed Jesus live upon your lips and reign in all your ministrations. Though profane wits should scoff and call you babbler, still let your sermons savor of Christ in every place. This lovely name will add unto them an ornament of grace. This, dear brother, will make your lips like "lilies, dropping sweet smelling myrrh" (Song 5:13). O what a noble theme have we to enlarge upon! A theme not unworthy of angels and archangels. Even these glorious beings desire to pry into the profound mysteries of revelation (1 Peter 1:12). Christ is the great subject of the Scriptures; why should He not to be the great subject of our sermons? The Scriptures are the ring; Christ is the diamond. The Scriptures are the circle; Christ is the center. The Scriptures are the field; Christ is the treasure hidden in that field. The Scriptures are the box; Christ is the spikenard.[16] The Scriptures are as

---

16. Editor's note: Spikenard is a perfumed ointment highly valued in the ancient world, and still available today, although less costly. It is mentioned in the Old Testament (Song 1:12; 4:13–14). In the New Testament, Mary anoints the Lord's feet with a quantity that would have cost a year's wages for a day laborer (John 12:3–5; also Mark 14:3–5).

the building; Christ is the foundation. The Scriptures are the body; Christ is the soul. What is the Old Testament but Christ concealed? What is the New Testament but Christ revealed? Make the glory of Christ your great end. Seek not your own glory but the glory of Him that sent you. You have Christ for your example. If any viper of pride should fashion upon our hand, let us speedily shake it off by repentance and deep abasement. O how vain is the breath of popular applause! How soon will the momentary buzz of renown expire and cease when our rest together shall be in the dust!

Maintain Fellowship with Christ
And that you may "preach Christ Jesus the Lord" with the greater success, seek to maintain fellowship with Him and to taste, yourself, the sweetness of the divine truths concerning Him you are to declare unto your hearers. When His name shall be as ointment poured forth unto your own soul, with what raptures of delight will you spread it abroad unto others! O! Did we have the thorough persuasion, the suitable impression of the truths we deliver, how would heavenly eloquence flow from our tongue! "For out of the abundance of the heart the mouth speaketh" (Matt. 12:34). Would we follow the direction which this maxim of our Lord would hint unto us, I have often thought it would be a better way to attain the perfection of eloquence than by a strict attendance to the precepts of the greatest masters of elocution.

Preach by Your Life
But I must not forget, likewise, to put you in mind that you are to preach by your life as well as by your doctrine. It is not sufficient that you give God your tongue; for He says, "My son, give me thine heart" (Prov. 23:26). Let your life be a commentary on what you preach. Endeavor not only to avoid all just censure as much as possible, but let your conversation be adorned with "whatsoever things are pure, whatsoever things are lovely, whatsoever things are of good report" (Phil. 4:8). "Let your light so shine before men, that they may see your good works, and glorify your Father which is in heaven" (Matt.

5:16); and those of the contrary part "may be ashamed" when they "speak evil of you…falsely" for His name's sake (1 Peter 3:16). Be thou an example to the believers in word and conversation, in charity and spirit, in faith and purity. "I give thee charge in the sight of God…that thou keep this commandment without spot, unrebukable, until the appearing of our Lord Jesus Christ" (1 Tim. 6:13–14), "and when the chief Shepherd shall appear, ye shall receive a crown of glory that fadeth not away" (1 Peter 5:4).

THE ADVICE TO THE CONGREGATION

I will now say a few things to you, my brethren of this congregation, touching the duties you all owe unto your pastor, who is, I hope, the Lord's anointed unto you. You have this day seen with your eyes his solemn separation to the work of the ministry, and I trust it is the answer of many prayers lodged at the throne of grace in behalf of this event. "Receive him therefore in the Lord with all gladness" (Phil. 2:29). And if you would really profit under the ordinances dispensed by him, I offer you the following advices: "yet not I, but the Lord" (1 Cor. 7:10).

Love Your Minister

First of all, see that you love, esteem, and reverence your minister. It is natural for us to hearken to the instructions of those we love and value, while on the other hand we are prejudiced against the best instructions of a person who is the object of our contempt or hatred. Be assured of it, your edification is at an end when you cease to reverence and love him. It has pleased the Spirit of God to adorn the ministers of the Word with very distinguishing and honorable epithets. They are the stewards of the mysteries of God, the lights of the world, the salt of the earth, the angels, the fathers, the overseers, the rulers of the church, the ambassadors of God and of Christ. Let a man, therefore, so account of them and "esteem them very highly in love for their work's sake" (1 Thess. 5:13). I do not say that all persons of whatsoever character are to be esteemed and reverenced if they have the name of ministers; for, if they be unjust stewards, extinguished lights, unsavory salt, fallen angels, unnatural fathers, negligent bishops, tyrannical rulers, and treacherous ambassadors, God's soul "loathe[s] them, and their soul also abhor[s] [him]" (Zech. 11:8); nor do His people owe them reverence. But insofar as your minister acts up to those sacred characters—which I hope he will, through grace, be enabled to do—you owe unto him not only civil honor but a religious respect, and "he…that despiseth, despiseth not man, but God" (1 Thess. 4:8).

Submit to Your Minister
In the next place, submit yourselves unto your minister and "obey them that have the rule over you, and submit yourselves: for they watch for your souls, as they that must give account, that they may do it with joy, and not with grief: for that is unprofitable for you" (Heb. 13:17). Be not as them that lay snares for "him that reproveth in the gate" and "make a man an offender for a word" (Isa. 29:21). When you repair to the place of the holy, let it be your resolution to "hear what God the Lord will speak" (Ps. 85:8). Do not merely propose to use and divert yourselves, but submit your consciences to the power of the Word. Though the authority of church officers, as the ambassadors of Christ (2 Cor. 5:20), is sneered at by some in these times, it is certain there can be no profitable hearing without a due regard unto it. When, like the hearers of Paul, you receive your minister "as an angel of God" and "even as Christ Jesus" (Gal. 4:13–14), it will be impossible for you not to pay a suitable deference unto the message he brings, though it should encroach upon your lusts or reprove particular parts of your conduct.

Care for Your Minister
As touching worldly maintenance, my brethren, you have no need I should say much unto you; for yourselves know that it is a maxim of our Lord that "the labourer is worthy of his hire" (Luke 10:7; 1 Tim. 5:18) and that it is the rule of His apostle that as they who served

at the altar "are partakers with the altar" (1 Cor. 9:13), so they who preach the gospel should live by the gospel. Brethren, if you should suffer your minister to entangle himself with the carking cares of this life, it were not only an injury done to him but to your own selves. For how should he give himself wholly to these things, which are the proper business of his calling, if the cares of this life should be suffered, through your negligence, to divert and perplex his mind? It is true indeed, ministers of the gospel must not be "greedy dogs which can never have enough" (Isa. 56:11). What a pity it is if any give "occasion to the enemies of the LORD to blaspheme" (2 Sam. 12:14) by betraying a mercenary spirit or covetous turn of mind. Nevertheless, the minister of Jesus Christ can produce (if he were to insist upon it) not only a civil but a religious right unto his worldly maintenance. Nor can it admit of the smallest doubt that where there is a real esteem of the gospel, or any profiting by it, he who is "taught in the word" will "communicate unto him that teacheth in all good things" (Gal. 6:6). But there is no occasion for me to insist upon this.

Profit by Your Minister

Let me further exhort you, my brethren, that ye rather seek to profit by your minister, then to be familiar with him. Do not mistake me; I do not at all mean but you may and ought to be familiar with your minister, and he with you—the humblest of you not excepted. But there are some who place a great deal more than they should in being familiar with ministers, never regarding whether their souls are prospering by the means of grace or not; and it is usual for such persons to make them unnecessary visits, to the great wasting of their time. Time is the most precious of treasures, and it is much to be regretted that we should suffer such a large portion of it to lie idle and without any improvement. But ministers' time is still more precious than any other person's whose work is not so important. And therefore, Christian prudence doubtless will direct you make your visits short when you have not some particular thing to talk about.

Pray for Your Minister

Prayer for your minister is another duty I would earnestly recommend unto you. Brethren, pray for him, "that utterance may be given unto [him], that [he] may open [his] mouth boldly, to make known the mystery of the gospel… as [he] ought to speak" (Eph. 6:19–20). His work is difficult, and there is no doubt but he will meet with various trials and discouragements in the faithful discharge of his office. On this account he is entitled to your prayers for him, always when you pray for yourselves. Besides, if he act suitable to his profession and character—as there is ground to hope will be the case—he will pray for you, and you ought in return to pray for him. The better it fares with your minister's soul, your own edification will be the more furthered. When, therefore, you pray for him, you are upon the matter praying for yourselves and agenting your own cause. There are "many unruly and vain talkers" (Titus 1:10) who make no other improvement of the ordinances on which they attend but to criticize or applaud the speaker. As to praying for the minister "with all prayer and supplication" (Eph. 6:18), they are utterly unacquainted with it. Alas! They cannot pray for themselves; how can they pray for another! But, my brethren, let it not be so among you. Pray without ceasing (1 Thess. 5:17). When you pour out your spirits to God in prayer, it is likely that God will pour out His Spirit to you in hearing. See that for the performance of every duty ye make constant believing improvement of Christ Jesus the Lord, whom we preach. "The Lord make you to increase and abound in love one toward another" (1 Thess. 3:12).

And, finally, my brethren, "I commend you to God, and to the word of his grace, which is able to build you up, and to give you an inheritance among all them which are sanctified" (Acts 20:32). AMEN.